IN PAIN

IN PAIN

*A Bioethicist's Personal Struggle
with Opioids*

Travis Rieder

HARPER

An Imprint of HarperCollins*Publishers*

IN PAIN. Copyright © 2019 by Travis Rieder. All rights reserved. Printed in the United States of America. No part of this book may be used or reproduced in any manner whatsoever without written permission except in the case of brief quotations embodied in critical articles and reviews. For information, address HarperCollins Publishers, 195 Broadway, New York, NY 10007.

HarperCollins books may be purchased for educational, business, or sales promotional use. For information, please email the Special Markets Department at SPsales @harpercollins.com.

FIRST EDITION

Designed by Nancy Singer

Library of Congress Cataloging-in-Publication Data has been applied for.

ISBN 978-0-06-285464-3   33614081457508

19 20 21 22 23   LSC   10 9 8 7 6 5 4 3 2 1

For Sadiye and Sinem, who gave more than I could have asked.
I love you.

Remember, effective relief takes just two.

—*Advertisement for OxyContin, 2002*

Life is pain, Highness. Anyone who tells you differently is selling something.

—The Princess Bride

CONTENTS

AUTHOR'S NOTE   XI

PART I

CHAPTER 1
A Salvage Situation   3

CHAPTER 2
Pain and Drugs   25

CHAPTER 3
The Swinging Pendulum   45

CHAPTER 4
The Opioid Dilemma   67

PART II

CHAPTER 5
Abandoned   85

CHAPTER 6
Dependence and Addiction   113

CHAPTER 7
What Doctors Owe Patients   139

PART III

CHAPTER 8

Recovery   161

CHAPTER 9

Pain, Drugs, and Doing the Right Thing   181

CHAPTER 10

America's *Three* Opioid Epidemics   213

EPILOGUE

Making a Difference   241

ACKNOWLEDGMENTS   259

NOTES   265

INDEX   285

AUTHOR'S NOTE

I spent eight years in graduate school training to be an academic philosopher. Spending inordinate amounts of time thinking deeply and writing about stuff like "the nature of practical reasons" can make one feel at a remove from what the rest of the world cares about on a daily basis.

As I neared the end of my studies, I began to worry about this rather solipsistic aspect of academic life. I enjoyed the intellectual challenge (and I loved my time in graduate school), but it was also occasionally a bit unfulfilling. It felt a bit like playing sudoku. And while sudoku is fun, it doesn't always seem like a good use of my time or the educational resources that have been spent on me.

One way to alleviate this worry about my very abstract education was to start thinking more about how philosophy can engage directly with the world. So I began to hang around the Kennedy Institute of Ethics at Georgetown and work on more practical problems; after finishing my PhD, I moved to Johns Hopkins University for a postdoc in bioethics. It was there that I really found my home, using what I'd learned about philosophy in the service of addressing urgent problems in medicine and public health. I spent my time on real-world challenges, and I began to write for magazines in addition to the academic journals that often don't reach a wide audience.

This was the background that I carried with me when I was

rushed to the hospital in 2015 after a motorcycle accident. I had become the kind of person who wanted to know when and why things go wrong in medicine, and becoming a patient reveals a lot of that. I came to understand more about pain than I ever wanted to, and, as a result, more about pain medicine. Specifically, I gained a lot of familiarity with a central tool of the trade: opioids. And then, in the most horrifying moments of my life, I learned just how bad our healthcare system is at managing opioids.

Suddenly, the situation in America (and to varying extents in other countries) started to look less surprising. In the wake of my brush with the healthcare system, I became desperate to learn more about how we treat pain and what this has to do with the opioid epidemic.

This book is the result of that exploration. It wasn't easy to write, and it isn't easy to share. Anchored in my own experiences, it's a profoundly personal project. But I've come to believe that I learned some important lessons about the ways in which our healthcare system is desperately broken and how this affected my own care, as well as that of millions of others. And I don't want to just play sudoku with these ideas; I want to help fix what's broken.

Because I've interwoven my own narrative with the broader story of what, in my opinion, has gone wrong in pain medicine, a couple of remarks are in order. First, I didn't know I was writing a book—not for a long time, actually—and so I didn't treat my own experiences as a journalist would. I didn't carry an audio recorder or jot down everything people said to me. So, although I stand by what's written here as an accurate representation of events, I don't expect that I perfectly remember every word said during every conversation. Quotations are used to indicate the general meaning of a conversation, not exact phrasing. When possible, I have shared drafts with other people involved to confirm my memory. My partner, Sadiye (who you will get to know quite well in these pages), has also served as my fact-checker of sorts, helping me to reconstruct those times that I was heavily medicated and confirming my account of events.

Second, I decided early on that I wouldn't name my doctors or the hospitals where I was treated, and so the names in the text are pseudonyms. The reason for this is simple: it doesn't matter who they are. It doesn't matter because those doctors and those hospitals aren't unique. I'm choosing not to name them because the problems I identify exist everywhere in the country, at small clinics and world-class hospitals alike. In short: my doctors are any doctors, and my hospitals are everywhere.

Thank you for opening this book. I'm glad you're here. I hope against hope that what I do in these pages is at least a little helpful—to medicine, policy, and to people who are suffering. If you're reading because the topics of pain, opioids, or addiction have touched your life in some way, then I want to say: I'm so profoundly sorry. I've heard from many people like you, and I've tried to impart the power of your stories onto these pages. And if you haven't been touched by these topics, but are willing to think about them anyway, then I want to say *thank you*.

It will take all of us to solve the challenges I raise here. You have my sincere gratitude for opening your ears and mind to them.

Gratefully,
Travis N. Rieder
Columbia, MD

IN PAIN

PART I

A Salvage Situation

May 23, 2015, started out as such a good day.

Awoken by the sweet jabbering of my daughter, I quietly slipped out from under the covers, snuck out of the bedroom, and pulled the door closed behind me. The giggles were coming from just one room over, and I smiled as I entered to find Baby Girl standing in her crib, holding her favorite blanket, waiting patiently for her rescue. Stretching her arms up as I approached, she inquired, "Baba?"

"Good morning, sweet girl," I whispered as I crossed the room. "Now let's be quiet so we don't wake mommy, okay?" I hoisted her out of the bed and pulled her tightly into my chest with a shush, before sneaking her quickly downstairs, leaving my partner, Sadiye, to get just a little bit of extra sleep. Those are the rules in our house: if you're planning to leave for the day, you get morning duty. And I had a date with the beautiful, winding roads of the Shenandoah Valley. Just me, my riding buddy Nathan, and our motorcycles on a sunny, Memorial Day weekend.

One-and-a-half-year-old Sinem was in a good mood, and for two blissful hours I enjoyed one of those perfect mornings of early fatherhood, where the work of parenting is easy and you just get to soak up the good stuff. We made breakfast together, played on the floor, and watched cartoons. I had been lucky enough to stay home for the first eight months of Sinem's life, and now that I was almost a year into my new career as a junior faculty member at Johns Hopkins, I really missed this. "Soak it up," I would tell myself, looking at her face and realizing how much she'd already changed. Although her incredibly fine brown hair remained short and fuzzy like an infant's, that was the only sign of the baby she so recently was; she was tall and lean, and her looks of curiosity and happiness seemed to reflect more depth of personality than I would have thought possible at this age. If I blinked, I was sure I'd be dropping her off at high school.

Later in the morning, Sadiye woke up and took over kid duty, and I pulled on my leathers, body armor, and full-face helmet. "Have a wonderful time, sweetie," she said, walking me to the door. I smiled and bounded down the few steps from our townhouse to the parking lot where my bike waited, and turned around to see Sadiye with Sinem on her left hip, both of them waving goodbye. Although Sinem was thin like her mom, she had gotten more of my complexion, and her fair skin contrasted with Sadiye's more olive tone and thick, dark hair. I blew them both kisses through my helmet, threw my leg over the seat, and fired up my Triumph Daytona. Relaxed and excited for the day's adventure, I pulled out of the driveway and settled in for the thirty-minute ride to meet Nathan.

As it turned out, my morning with Baby Girl would be the only good part of that day. I hadn't even gone three blocks when I saw an ominous-looking white van ahead to my left. My rider's sense of alarm went off because the driver, although seemingly looking right at me, appeared to be nudging into the intersection. I had no stop sign and was simply going straight, and it looked like he was going to turn left out of a housing development onto my street. Although I had the right-of-way, I didn't trust him; I closed the throttle to decelerate and looked to my right to see whether I might have an escape route.

I hadn't even fully taken in my options or begun shifting my body weight for evasive maneuvers when I felt the impact. In just those few seconds, I had covered the distance to the intersection, and the van hit me squarely on my left side.

Although it happened in an instant, I seem to have recorded minutes' worth of memories.

I remember seeing the van's bumper contact the front wheel and the bike's fairing, and the feeling of the bike rippling underneath me. I remember the fleeting thought that maybe I was just getting bumped a little, and while that was certainly not good, maybe I could stay on the bike. Somehow, in that mere instant, I feel like I had an entire debate with myself about whether this was going to be an unfortunate incident that made me late to my ride or if I was about to really hit the ground. I'd crashed before, and I knew what it felt like to go down; I also trusted my gear to protect me from the asphalt. I wasn't panicked. At least, not at first.

But then everything felt different: there was what I can only describe as pressure on the whole left side of the bike and my left leg, as the full force of the collision transferred from van to motorcycle. One moment, I was in control of my body and my bike, and the next moment I wasn't. I was in the air. For an improbably long time. I clearly remember landing on my back and the bike landing on top of my left leg. My head snapped back as I hit the ground, my helmet cracking against the asphalt with a sickening sound. But even after that, I wasn't worried. "No pain yet," I remember thinking. "The helmet seems to have done its job."

But then the pain did come—just not from my head. The bike was sliding on my left foot, and something was wrong. My foot really hurt—in that very alarming, this-is-not-okay, danger-alerting sense of "hurt." As I slid to a stop, the bike flipped off of me and I felt an explosive pain on the bottom of my foot.

I had barely stopped moving before I was reaching down to take off my boot. The pressure on my foot was more painful than anything I had ever experienced, and I had to get it off. Armored boots aren't the easiest things to put on or remove quickly, but I was motivated—

while one shaky hand fumbled to open my helmet visor so that I could breathe, the other was undoing Velcro flaps and unzipping. At about the same time that I had the boot completely open and was pulling it off, I heard a voice from across the street. A witness to the accident was jumping out of his car to come to me, yelling. I think he was saying, "Leave the boot on!"

But it was too late. I slipped the boot off with a gasp and was relieved by the release of pressure, but only for a second. Because almost immediately after the pain from the pressure had eased, it was as if the contact between my foot and the air caused a vacuum, sucking a new, more intense pain into my foot. I had traded the pain that my boot was keeping in for the pain that my boot had been keeping out, and it was not a good trade.

I thrusted my head back and gritted my teeth, breathing in sharply while muffling a cry. I closed my eyes and took a moment to gather myself before opening them again and looking down to see what my boot had been hiding. My thick, wool riding sock was red with blood, and what should have looked like a foot from the top looked like a fat, shapeless mass. The sock had somehow torn on the bottom of my foot, which I thought was weird; it was as if something had exploded outward from inside my foot. And indeed something had. As I folded my leg to get a closer look, I saw that sharp, broken fragments of bone were sticking out through the large hole they had torn in the bottom of my foot. The hole was deep, but there was very little blood in the wound itself; instead there was raw meat, bone, and white tendon.

I gingerly set my foot back down and started shaking as the first witness arrived at my side. The street sign above me read ISLAND COURT. I was three blocks from home.

It had started out as such a good day.

Someone called an ambulance. A helpful witness—who had some medical training—stayed by my side while we waited. He kept me calm, assuring me that the accident hadn't been my fault. I was relieved, but also still in shock. I wondered out loud whether I would make my Memorial Day plans to cook out at a friend's house the next day. My new friend smiled sadly at me. "I'm sorry," he said, "but I don't think you'll be doing anything very soon."

I groaned. "It's bad, huh?" I looked back down at my mangled foot and tried to flex my ankle to get a better look at the bottom. Although I could only see part of it through the torn, bloody sock, it looked like something from a zombie movie.

"Yeah, it's pretty bad," he said. "Look, you're going to be okay. But you're going to need some surgery. This isn't just a broken foot."

Surgery? I hoped against all reasonable belief that this guy didn't know what he was talking about. After all, I had a new job, a family. I didn't have time for surgery. I laid my head back down and tried not to think about my exploding foot. I also tried not to think about the phone call I needed to make. I needed to let Sadiye know what had happened, but I didn't want her to see me like this. Gritting my teeth, I pulled my cell phone out from my jacket and dialed her number.

"Hey, sweetie," I said, my voice shaky despite my best efforts to sound casual. "Now, don't worry—I'm fine. But I need to let you know that I've been in an accident."

"Okay . . ." she responded slowly.

"I got hit by a van just down the street. Now, I'm going to be okay, but my foot is broken, so an ambulance is coming."

"Oh my god," she whispered. I could hear tears and panic sneaking into her voice. "Let me get Baby Girl ready, and I'll be right there."

I tried to convince her not to come, but in retrospect, that's proof that I wasn't thinking straight. There was no way she would stay home.

When Sadiye got there, I could see that it took all of her strength not to freak out. I knew it looked bad, but in my mind, it only *looked* bad. I had a broken foot, but I would live. The helmet did its job, and nothing else felt badly hurt. As Sadiye ran up to me, I opened my mouth to say something, and I'm not even sure I knew what I would tell her. What came out, all in a rush, was something like, "I'm so sorry I did this, I can't believe I kept riding on the street, I'm done with motorcycles, I'm just done, this was so stupid, I'm so sorry . . ."

Now, motorcycles had been a huge part of my life for almost a decade—a fact that had not always made Sadiye very happy. She worried about me riding, and I know that she would have been thrilled at my decision to stop riding at any other time. But this was not any other time, and so she did something that must have taken every ounce of willpower. She breathed deeply, took control of herself, and said, "Well, you're in a lot of pain right now, so we'll just talk about that later."

"Okay," I said. "We'll talk about it later. But I'm telling you now that I'm done with motorcycles. I can't believe I risked this. I can't believe I let this happen to us." The overwhelming feeling of the moment was guilt and shame, and the only thing I could do right then was assure her that I would never let something like this happen again. She smiled at me and said, "Okay."

By this point, police officers had shown up, and they began to ask Sadiye for information. The pain was becoming unbearable. I started asking when the ambulance would get there. "Soon," I was told. I think they were right.

I remember my leathers and my armor being cut off of me, and I remember it being so cold. I heard bits and pieces of reports being made by the paramedics, and one of the things I heard them say was "potential degloving of the left foot." I knew what "degloving" meant, and hearing that was the first time I was really scared (if you don't know what that term means, just imagine that your skin is a glove, and the injury is exactly what it sounds like). I think I asked a lot of questions, but I don't remember most of them. I do remember asking if it was cold out, or if there was something wrong with me. I remember Sadiye saying, "Yes, it's cold, baby. You're okay." I was, after all, lying on the street in my boxer shorts.

I started to wish that I would pass out. The pain was all-encompassing. I didn't know that pain could be like that. I mean, it was just my foot. How could it hurt like this? Getting me strapped to the gurney and getting my head immobilized was taking a long time, and I finally asked whether there were IV pain meds on the ambulance. One of the guys said to me, "Oh yes. We'll get you taken care of." And he kept his word. When they finally loaded me onto the ambulance, the paramedic said to the guys riding in back with me, "Travis here would not turn down some morphine."

"You got it," said another paramedic. As he worked to get the IV line hooked up, the driver called back that Memorial Hospital was prepped and ready for me.

"Why Memorial?" I asked. I was confused, and I struggled to express my confusion. "Is there some kind of contract between particular ambulances and hospitals or something?" It was a strange thing to ask, but we would pass a half-dozen hospitals between the accident site and Memorial, and I was beginning to get a sense of urgency about seeing a doctor and getting some answers.

"Oh no," said the paramedic. "Memorial is the trauma center. Trust me, that's where you want to be."

That was more scary information.

The paramedics closed the doors, the sirens came on, and we took off. Someone told me that the morphine was coming, and then things got very strange. There was heat in my arm at the site of the IV, and then in my chest, and my face. After that, an incredibly strange, unpleasant sensation crept across the top of my head and began moving down the back of my neck. As the morphine completely took hold, I felt as though my brainstem was melting, sliding down my spine. I started to open my mouth to say something to the paramedics; but then suddenly: the pain was gone. As was thought, attention, or any other feeling. For the moment, the world was reduced to motion, noise, and chaos.

My memories get selective after that.

I remember that being wheeled out of the ambulance and into the hospital is just like it is on TV: a flash of fluorescent light bulbs whizzed past my field of vision, since I was immobilized on the stretcher. I remember that I was in and out of consciousness throughout most of that day, and that every time I woke up, it was because the pain had gotten unbearable and I needed more morphine, or fentanyl, or Dilaudid (the brand name for hydromorphone—all names that I would get more and more familiar with in the coming days).

Later that day, I remember a nurse coming in to see me. It was early evening, and I still hadn't gotten to surgery—it was Memorial Day weekend, after all. Sadiye told me that there had been a bunch of bicycle accidents and that some of them involved head trauma. Despite having a gaping hole in my foot, my injury was nowhere near the most pressing on this particular day. I was starting to worry that if the surgery was put off any later, I might have to stay in the hospital overnight, which I'd never done. So I asked the nurse, "Do you think I'll be able to leave tonight?" And I remember her expression—it was like the expression of the helpful witness at the crash site when I asked about making it to the next day's barbecue, and like one that I would see on many people's faces over the next few days. She said softly and sweetly, "Oh, honey. I don't think you'll leave tonight. In fact, I think you probably won't leave tomorrow." She paused. "You might be here for just a little bit."

And still I didn't understand the full extent of my injury.

What happened next was the first of three hospitalizations, during which I had the first three of six—to date—surgeries. It was also the beginning of my coming to terms with the truth: that I had sustained a serious trauma, and that this was different from the other kinds of accidents, broken bones, and injuries that I had incurred throughout my life.

Now, to be sure: by traumatic standards, mine wasn't that bad. Many people, all over the world, find themselves in situations much worse than the one in which I found myself. But traumatic injury is a different sort of thing to have happen to oneself, and I hadn't realized this in my rather fortunate life up to this point. Even seeing war vets come back from Iraq and Afghanistan with debilitating injuries, or understanding intellectually how serious it could be to be in, say, a car accident, I hadn't appreciated that these are not merely serious injuries; they are a different kind of thing.

A trauma.

The very earliest seedling of this understanding had begun while lying on the road, talking to the witness, and it continued for days (or likely weeks), but I can pinpoint the turning point in my understanding quite easily.

In the first couple of days after the accident, when I was conscious, I was in fairly good spirits. I'm not a dark person, and while this was a bad injury, I'd been injured before. This was going to suck, for sure, but I would heal and things would be fine. I joked with nurses, and I told my friends and family not to get worked up. But in retrospect, I could identify an uneasiness I had from early on when talking to my family. They all seemed so sad and so serious. Whether in person in the hospital, or video-chatting on the phone, I could see it in everyone's faces. I tried to liven up the situation—I mean, I was alive! I would be fine!—but they were so worried.

On day three, I found out why. Dr. Patel, the orthopedic trauma surgeon, had come in to give me and my family an update. In the first surgery, he had inserted several metal pins that stuck out of my foot in various directions. He would come in regularly and check different parts of my foot for feeling, and check on those pins. On this day, he was telling me what the goals were for this next set of procedures, and I must have asked him something about recovery time, or number of surgeries. At this point he looked up at me and said something confusing and frightening.

"Look, this is a serious situation. I'm sure your wife told you . . ." He let his sentence trail off and looked at Sadiye. She looked surprised and angry at being put on the spot, and then shook her head and said something like, "I really didn't think it was best coming from me." Her eyes directed fury at Dr. Patel, and her voice cracked as she answered. I was confused and getting more worried every second. I looked at the doctor apprehensively.

"Travis, you need to realize that you will likely lose this foot, or at least part of it."

My chest froze up. I couldn't breathe. Pressure was building throughout my body, my stomach twisted, and I rocked forward in agony. I looked at him, and then at Sadiye, and then back at him. I was in complete shock.

"Travis," he continued, "the purpose of these surgeries is to do what we can to save as much of your foot as possible." He paused and took a breath. "This is a salvage situation."

The words echoed around my brain: *a salvage situation.*

I stayed frozen. Sadiye had known. Our parents had known. But they couldn't bring themselves to tell me because they knew I'd have questions that they couldn't answer. I would eventually come to understand their reasoning, but at this moment, I simply couldn't process what was happening. I started shaking on my hospital bed, while involuntary sounds escaped from my mouth.

And at that moment, for the first time since the accident, I cried.

I suddenly understood what everyone else already knew: I was going to be an amputee. I was going to need assistance. Would I ever walk again? I had been an active guy: I liked to work out, to run, to compete in races and obstacle courses, and to hike and explore. I liked to physically push myself. How many of those things was I going to lose?

Oh God. And what about my daughter? Would I ever carry her around again, or wrestle with her on the floor? These questions and more assaulted me all at once and left me in total ruin.

I had finally started to appreciate my situation. I was thirty-three years old, and my life would never again be the same.

Although Dr. Patel's revelation helped me begin to understand the seriousness of the situation, I now know that it still hadn't really set in. There are lots of reasons for this. Drugs are a big one, and shock is another. I cried for a while that day, and then my dad (who had come down from Indiana the day before to be with me) and Sadiye held my hands while I met my first physical therapist. She told me that she thought I'd keep my foot, and she thought I'd walk again. I was young and otherwise healthy, and she didn't believe Dr. Patel's prediction. I decided at that moment that I didn't either, and I chose to believe, instead, that this was a bump in the road. I would heal, and this would be a nasty memory of a bad time.

Largely—to a truly shocking degree, in fact—I was right about this. But I still had no real idea of what it meant to have an injury that your body can't fully come back from. It never could have occurred to me in those early days that physical therapy would last years, and that I would be in some amount of pain for the rest of my life. This wasn't information that I could really internalize in a few days' time.

So instead, I focused on more immediate goals. I needed to be a good patient, to give my doctors the best chance of saving my foot. I needed to learn what I could do to get home to my daughter the fastest. I needed to keep my pain under control so that I could sleep, but I also needed to keep my oxygen levels up, as they could drop dangerously from the pain medication. These sorts of considerations became our—me and my family's—all-encompassing focus. So we asked questions of the doctors and nurses, and I tried my best to do what they told me to do.

The morning of my second surgery, Dr. Patel came by the room again to discuss the upcoming procedures and do his normal tests. I hadn't had feeling in most of the top half of my foot since the accident, but this morning, as he traced his finger along various parts of my foot, I snapped my head up in surprise: "I felt that!"

Dr. Patel looked taken aback and immediately began pressing and poking on surrounding areas, some of which I could also sense. And for the first time since the accident four days prior, Dr. Patel smiled.

"Well, it's certainly not a done deal," he said cautiously, "but you might just get to keep the foot—and maybe even all the toes. Your body is trying very hard to keep this tissue alive."

Although he would issue many caveats, and continually tell me not to get my expectations up, I knew at that moment that he wasn't going to take my foot. Pessimistic Dr. Patel would tell me before each of the surgeries that, although I was doing better than anyone could have predicted, this was still a salvage situation; even if he could keep the foot alive, clean up the obliterated bones, rebuild some of them, and remove the shards of others—even if he could do all of this, there was still the issue of the large hole in the bottom of my foot where the bones had exploded outward. The process for closing that wound would be handled by plastic surgeons, and how much of my foot—and its function—I could retain would depend on what they could do for that wound.

But I wasn't hearing these warnings as warnings; I was hearing a stepwise instruction book. First, I would get my foot put together. Then, I would get the wound closed. Finally, I would heal from the injury. Then, I would be back to being myself.

The strange sense of knowing the facts of the case but not really understanding what they mean is difficult to explain. Even as this first week in the hospital wore on, I don't remember exactly when it was that I finally conceded that our family's summer might be really altered. Sadiye and I had spent the last year planning a vacation—a honeymoon that we had put off for more than a decade—in celebration of our eleventh wedding anniversary. Plane tickets and hotels were booked, and itineraries were set. We were to fly out of Washington, DC, on June 6, departing for Northern Cyprus, where Sadiye's family lives. We planned to spend a week there, and then leave Sinem with her grandparents while Sadiye and I took our long-awaited, eight-day, fantastically romantic vacation in Italy. I think it was the second day in the hospital that Sadiye started telling me that we'd probably have to cancel the trip, which I refused to believe.

"So I'll be on crutches," I'd say. "I guess we probably will do less hiking. But there's no reason we can't go and eat and drink, right?"

Remember that sad, sweet smile that I said everyone would give me? Well, she'd give me one of those and say, "Okay, baby. We'll just wait to see how it goes. But it's really okay. If we have to cancel, we'll do it some other time. It's not a big deal."

Of course, that trip was rendered impossible the minute my foot was crushed between a van and my motorcycle. The recovery timeline from this accident wasn't going to be weeks, with some limited mobility. It would be years, with months of total incapacitation. When I finally got home from the hospital, leaving the house for doctor's visits would be major outings, requiring monumental effort. But none of this was something I could understand at the time.

After the first three surgeries, I was sent home to rest while my foot "granulated"—which is to say, while it prepared to accept a skin graft. In order to speed up the process, the hole in my foot was packed with a sponge and attached to a "wound VAC," which is a device that applies negative pressure to the wound and stimulates healing. Although I was grateful to be allocated a portable VAC and allowed to go home, the sponge needed to be changed every other day, and so a nurse would come to the house and pull the sticky material out of my foot before repacking the hole with a fresh sponge. These "VAC changes" were the stuff of nightmares, with blood-soaked sponge clinging to the raw tissue as it was pulled out. Each time felt like the nurse was pulling off my skin (which, in a way, she was, since the VAC was doing the job that skin normally does), and I was advised early on to load up on painkillers an hour or so before she arrived.

Even before the next surgery, the regimen of opioid painkillers that I had been sent home with was no longer keeping up with the pain of a continually retraumatized foot, and I was prescribed a stronger dose.

The goal of the fourth surgery was to harvest a layer of skin from my forearm and graft it onto the open wound. Looking back at the pictures, it's hard to believe that my doctors thought that a mere layer of skin would effectively cover such a large, deep hole. But they did, and I went to a separate hospital to have the plastic surgery team attempt the graft. Unfortunately, even if such coverage was at some point possible, more tissue had died while I was home, and after the surgeon cut away this necrotic tissue, there was no denying that the wound was now much too large to cover with a skin graft. Upon waking up, I was informed that the surgery had not been successful and that the team would need a new plan for covering the wound.

Again I was sent home, and again I wrestled with new, fresh, more intense pain from the now-expanded hole in my foot. In addition, the surgery had irritated the wound, which began to bleed significantly, requiring another trip to the hospital in which two young podiatrists cauterized the open wound without anesthetic. For nearly forty-five minutes, they burned the inside of my foot both with chemicals and with heat, trying to seal whatever veins and capillaries were soaking my bandages with blood.

My days revolved around trying desperately to stay ahead of the pain, watching the clock tick by so that I took my next dose of opioids the minute I was allowed to, and taking extra doses any time I needed a VAC change or if the doctors were going to do something to the wound. When it became clear that the medication was simply no longer able to keep the pain under control, the plastic surgeon increased the dose again.

Fortunately, the medical team came up with an ambitious solution to my foot's problem: my young surgeon's mentor from residency worked at a world-class limb-salvage center in the region, and she had agreed to take my case. Together with several other specialty teams, my surgeons would carve out a portion of my left thigh, harvesting muscle, fat, and skin to fill in and cover the wound in my foot; they would then clip an artery to deliver blood supply to the new tissue, and a nerve that would hopefully eventually allow sensation in that portion of my foot. The procedure is known as a "free flap," or a "full tissue transfer," and my new doctor, I was told, did them all the time.

In the very early hours of June 15—just over three weeks after the accident—Sadiye loaded me into the car and drove me to our third hospital for the free flap surgery. We were told to expect the surgery to last eight and a half hours, as each tissue would need to be transferred and the artery and nerve would need to be microsurgically connected to my foot's existing structure. It was a delicate process, and there was no guarantee of success; but my team was exceptionally good, and we were optimistic.

After each of the surgeons had paraded by my pre-op bed to introduce themselves, the anesthesiologist came by to give me the initial sedative. I said goodbye to Sadiye, and they began to wheel me away. The last thing I remember thinking is that when I woke up, I would finally have a whole foot again.

Before I could even open my eyes, the pain and panic overwhelmed me. I don't remember thinking about where I was, or what had happened; all I could think about was the pain. But I was having trouble communicating it.

"It hurts . . ." I moaned, trying to get someone's attention. I could tell that my gurney was being moved, and I could hear people talking around me. "It *hurts!*" I cried, more insistently, trying to move my arms and head.

As I slowly opened my gummy eyes, the blurry image of a hospital hallway came into view. A middle-aged nurse in blue scrubs turned her attention from whatever conversation she had been having and tried to calm me. "You're okay, Travis. You're just coming out of anesthesia. You've been under for a long time, so it might be confusing. Now where does it hurt?"

"My arm. Oh Jesus, the inside of my elbow. What's wrong with me?" I was in excruciating pain that I didn't understand, but I also felt sick and unable to speak clearly.

"Your arm is fine," the nurse reassured me. "The surgery was on your foot, remember?"

Although my foot was in pain, I had become accustomed to that, and my half-working brain found the new pain terrifying. "You don't understand," I told the nurse, working to enunciate each of the words. "Something is wrong with my arm."

Having studied and taught disturbing medical ethics cases, I knew a bit of the literature on medical error, which is the name given to avoidable negative outcomes that result from some mistake in the hospital setting. A landmark study by the Institute of Medicine (now the National Academy of Medicine) had shaken the medical establishment a decade and a half earlier by estimating that as many as ninety-eight thousand people die each year from avoidable medical error. And many more are grievously harmed in ways that don't result in their death; some such outcomes are so terrible that they are called "never events"—the kind of thing that should never, ever be allowed to occur but somehow still happens. One never event that has haunted me ever since I learned about its existence is something called "wrong site surgery," in which the surgical team operates in the wrong place, sometimes even amputating a healthy limb. All my anesthetized brain could think was that one of my doctors had mistakenly done something to my arm, perhaps cutting it open by mistake.

When I was able to look down and focus my eyes, however, I could see that the inside of my right elbow was free from any obvious damage. So I tried to bend my arm, which led to an involuntary yelp and another panicked plea to the nurse to figure out what had happened. She promised me that she would find a doctor.

As my gurney came to a stop in the postoperative room, a little bit of the fog lifted from my brain and my panic turned to a more steady concern. What in the world had happened in that operating room? I had lots of questions: Had the surgery been a success? What time was it, how long had it taken? And *where the hell did this new pain came from?*

As I began to take stock, I realized that I had other sites of new pain as well: my left thigh, from which the surgical team had harvested the tissue, slowly became the source of the most dominating pain, edging out both my foot and the strange searing in my arm. I couldn't see either of the surgical sites—the thigh from which the tissue had been taken or the foot to which it had been attached—but as the general anesthesia wore off, the extent of the surgery began to become clear. The pain of shattered bones played second fiddle to the boiling pain of carved tissue, which extended from my toes up past my ankle, and then from my knee all the way to my hip. The process of coming out of anesthesia was basically the process of discovering how awful it was to be conscious.

Thankfully, before too long, someone came by to load up my IV with fentanyl, which would make all of those pains fade away (along with consciousness, typically). I did, however, start to get answers to my questions, both before the IV dose and during later spells of awareness. The surgery had been a success and had taken nearly nine hours. That, combined with my time in post-op, meant that it was late in the day before they let Sadiye back to see me. And no one knew what happened to my arm. Each nurse and doctor gave the same response: a quizzical look and a statement of the obvious—that the surgery hadn't involved my arm at all.

As the pain in my elbow slowly faded in seriousness next to the severe pain of my two surgical sites, one of the surgical nurses who came by offered a hypothesis: My arm had been left dangling off the operating table, palm up. Since the surgery had been so long, it had slowly hyperextended. "It happens," she said. The pain would subside.

It happens? I would have been furious if I'd had the energy for it.

She was right, though, and the pain did subside, although it certainly remained noticeable. But as I was moved into the intensive care unit (ICU), where I would stay while the medical team kept an eagle-eyed look on my very delicate, newly transplanted tissue, my hyperextended elbow was the least of my immediate concerns. When it occasionally made me wince while moving, Sadiye and I would make frustrated comments about how the surgical team had let it happen. I mean, surely this wasn't the first time they'd had to worry about how someone was positioned for a long surgery, right? But the team had also just pulled off a miracle, saving my foot using a piece of my thigh, so I supposed I should cut them some slack.

I would think to myself: if a sore elbow is the worst thing that happens after all of this, I should be grateful.

By the morning after the free flap surgery, my pain was spiraling out of control. Overnight, the regularly interspersed doses of oral oxycodone and IV hydromorphone were just barely taking some of the edge off the bone and tissue pain in my foot, and the new surgical site on my thigh only ramped up in intensity. This new, worsening pain was different and sharper—sometimes fiery, sometimes electric—and I could sense that I was losing the battle with keeping any semblance of control. No matter how recently I'd gotten the drugs, all I could think about was needing something more. The only relief I got was when the powerful IV drugs would knock me into a short, restless nap for thirty minutes or an hour. But then I would wake up to pain even worse than before. I started to panic.

When I first reported my uncontrolled pain in the ICU, that report was made to physician interns, residents, and nurses. This is often the case, since these clinicians are the ones who have the most contact with patients; however, it can also result in things moving slowly, as interns and residents are doctors-in-training, under the supervision of an "attending" physician, and nurses do not have prescriptive authority. So I became frustrated as my pain began to snowball and I received no attention. Although I don't remember for sure, I likely began to lose my patience with the kind doctors, who checked on me regularly but wouldn't prescribe anything to get my pain under control. I imagine I stopped being quite as kind and compliant a patient as I tend to be.

After some time like this, I noticed a large flock of white coats pausing outside each room's door, and eventually coming to mine. Since I work with clinicians, and have spent time in hospitals for my own clinical ethics work, I knew that this group of doctors was on "rounds"—with the attending physician leading the residents, each of whom has taken responsibility for some number of patients and makes recommendations to the attending regarding those patients' care. She, in turn, would then make the ultimate decision concerning how to treat each patient. This is a core component of the clinical training for young physicians. I found it strange that they stood outside my door, far enough away that I couldn't participate, as I kept hearing my last name being mentioned. At my own university hospital, rounds are typically performed in the room, with patients (and their families) invited to participate. I was confused and frustrated that I wasn't part of the process.

After what seemed like quite a long discussion in the hall, the group of doctors entered the room and asked me the by-now-routine questions, while checking my vital signs. I anxiously waited for the attending to ask about my pain so that I could blurt out, "It's really bad; I haven't had it under control since I came out of anesthesia; something's really wrong. Isn't there something else you can give me?"

Although it barely registered at the time, my foggy, underfunctioning brain must have noticed that there was something strange about the attending's response, because I remember it perfectly. She looked at her residents and her clipboard, and then looked down at me and said, somewhat curtly, "Yes, Mr. Rieder, your repeated requests for more pain medication have been noted. My team and I will discuss its appropriateness." And then they swept out of the room.

Its appropriateness? I didn't quite understand what had just happened, but I knew enough to feel insulted and somehow ashamed, as if I had done something wrong. Why did this doctor, whom I had never met before, talk to me as if I were a suspect? As if I were merely trying to get high? Did she not notice the two major surgical sites on my body, or the pins sticking out of my foot? Maybe she hadn't seen in my chart that I had just had my fifth surgery in as many weeks?

"Are they really not going to do anything about my pain?" I wondered, desperation sneaking up on me as I contemplated my undermedicated future. Sadiye was at work for the day, and being without my advocate made me feel especially vulnerable.

So I rang the bell on my bed to call for one of the ICU nurses. When she came in, I asked her if she could get ahold of my plastic surgeon's residents—not one of the ICU residents (the group who had just been on rounds) but one of the young physicians training under my limb-salvage surgeon.

Finally, that got the ball rolling, as one of the residents stopped by just a little while later. Although I don't remember his name, I remember his face well, as he always spent a little extra time with me. He was an enthusiastic and warm young man—almost certainly younger than I was—who had made a point of telling me how good my surgeon was, and that young doctors fought for a residency spot with her. When he first checked on me the night before, he had asked about my academic work, and he was the only physician at any of the hospitals to refer to me as "Dr. Rieder" rather than "Mr. Rieder." I was relieved as soon as I saw it was him who came by, and I begged him to figure out something for my pain. He assured me that his attending would have a plan.

And he kept his word. A little while later he stopped by just to tell me that he had spoken with his attending on the phone. She, in turn, had requested a pain management "consult," in which the hospital's in-house pain specialists would come talk to me and try to help get my pain under control.

I could have hugged him.

Like everything else in the hospital, the process took some time, as the pain team's residents came first to ask a long series of detailed questions about my pain. They then reported back to the attending pain physician, who didn't make it to my room until much later in the day. When he finally did come by, though, he was well briefed and ready to fix me up.

After confirming his notes from the residents, the doctor gave me his theory: "It sounds to me like you've gotten 'behind the pain,'" he said, "which makes catching up more of a challenge. So we're going to make some changes to your opioid regimen. We'll increase the dose of both your long-acting oxycodone and your short acting oxycodone, and that should go some way toward providing relief. But to help catch up, I'm going to order three doses of IV acetaminophen over the next two days, to help you make it through between doses of hydromorphone. Okay?"

I certainly had no opinion on the matter, so I just nodded.

"Now, the fiery pain in your thigh—that's probably neuropathic pain, from where they clipped out that nerve. The problem here is that opioids don't work particularly well for neuropathic pain, so we're going to add a regimen of gabapentin, which is particularly good for that." Oh thank God, I thought.

I thanked the new doctor profusely, and he gave orders to the other clinicians in the room to set up my new pain management strategy. In my current state, I certainly didn't think to ask any follow-up questions, or about whether the doctor knew how long I would be on these medications. And he didn't offer any of that information. I was in pain, and he had something to address that. He told me what we'd do, and I enthusiastically and gratefully accepted his help.

The outcome of that meeting was, as far as I could tell, nothing short of a miracle. The gabapentin almost immediately dulled the electric nerve pain, the increased doses of opioids took the edge off the bone and soft tissue pain, and the interspersed IV acetaminophen provided a truly shocking degree of relief, getting me through to the next heavy hit of hydromorphone. I remember thinking that the IV acetaminophen—the same drug that you can take orally under the brand name Tylenol—worked nearly as good as morphine for short-term tissue and bone pain.

I was amazed, and I thanked the pain doctors every time they came to check on me. The work that this specialist team did was incredible, and although much of the rest of this book will be spent discussing the challenges of pain management, I was and still am grateful to live in a time and place where my severe pain was able to be medically managed.

CHAPTER 2

Pain and Drugs

Pain is strange. Mundane, yes, and something that we all live with, sure—but it's also deeply philosophically puzzling. And although that might seem surprising at first (How could such a familiar experience be genuinely puzzling?), it takes only a few moments of reflection to recognize just how strange the reality of pain is.

The first thing to note about pain is that it seems, for all the world, to be located in some place—to be in our bodies. If you stub your toe, it's your toe that hurts; and if you whack your funny bone, your elbow vibrates with that awful, sharp, electric pain.

Indeed, pain even seems to exist within specific tissue of one's body. Over the course of many months, I became quite good at isolating the deep bone pain in my shattered metatarsals versus the sharp surface pain of soft tissue from stitches or VAC changes. The damage to our bodies causes pain, and it seems true when we say things like, "My broken foot hurts."

If this description, which seems straightforwardly and obviously true, were in fact the whole story, then a couple of other things would be true: first, only our actual tissue could hurt; and second, other people would (in theory) be in a pretty good position to know whether or not we hurt. This is because the pain would always be "out there, in the world," as a direct result of some damage. So I would only be able to have foot pain if I had a foot (where the pain could be located), and a doctor, for instance, could have a pretty good idea of whether I was in pain by examining the foot for damage. An undamaged foot couldn't be in pain (and a nonexistent foot definitely couldn't be in pain).

It turns out that both of these implications are wrong. And that makes pain much stranger than it initially appears.

Pain actually happens *in the brain*, and the brain—being quite good at what it does—largely uses the pain experience to alert us to damage in particular parts of our bodies. So a mangled foot typically tells the brain to signal severe pain to the owner of the foot, and typically the brain won't signal severe pain in one's foot if it's not mangled. But here, like in all aspects of life, the body's systems can misfire in interesting ways, leading to a disconnect between actual, observable damage and one's subjective experience of pain. This leads not only to the problematic case of pain that a doctor can't identify ("Huh, as far as I can tell, there's nothing wrong with this foot.") but also to the far stranger case of "phantom pain," or the amputee's perception of pain in a nonexistent limb. How does one experience pain in a foot she doesn't have? Well, because pain doesn't occur in the foot, but in the brain.

All of this initial observation is in service of a fairly obvious but crucial point in understanding the challenge of pain medicine: namely, that pain is an *essentially subjective* phenomenon, meaning that only the person experiencing a pain truly knows what that experience is like. I can never know what your pain is like, and your doctor can never know what your pain is like. Never truly know, that is. Like with all things, we can communicate, describe, and discuss our pain, but someone who has never experienced childbirth simply cannot know what the pain of childbirth is like, and someone who has never experienced traumatic or surgical pain can never know what those are like either.

This point is so important in understanding the nature of pain that it gets built into the definition promulgated by the International Association for the Study of Pain (IASP). According to that group, pain is an "unpleasant sensory and emotional experience associated with actual or potential tissue damage, or described in terms of such damage." They then add a lengthy note to the definition, which includes the following claims: "Pain is always subjective . . . Many people report pain in the absence of tissue damage or any likely pathophysiological cause; usually this happens for psychological reasons. There is usually no way to distinguish their experience from that due to tissue damage if we take the subjective report. If they regard their experience as pain, and if they report it in the same ways as pain caused by tissue damage, it should be accepted as pain."

So pain, according to the IASP, *tends* to be associated with tissue damage, but is, most importantly, an *unpleasant experience* that is accessible only to the person in pain.

You might not be impressed by this point, as all of one's mental states are essentially subjective. You can't know what my experience of the color blue is like, and I can't know for sure what you see when we look at the same chair. This point is a favorite of philosophers for blowing the minds of eighteen-year-old college freshmen: We think that we all perceive fairly similar worlds because we are able to navigate them together. But there is no way to know for sure that what I experience as blue is the same as what you experience as blue. We both call the color created by light reflecting off certain objects "blue," but we each have our own, private experience of that color.

The difference between seeing something as blue and being in pain, though, is that the physical features of the world that cause us to perceive colors are located out in the world, accessible to everyone. You see something and I see something and we talk about it, coming to the conclusion that we see approximately the same thing. Although my experience of the things in the world is subjective, those things are *intersubjectively available*, which is just a fancy way of saying that other people can confirm my experience. Our very ability to act and cooperate depends on the fact that others can confirm one's experience of the world. The progression of science is precisely the gathering of evidence that is available to be checked and rechecked by anyone.

But pain is not like that. Not only is my experience of pain subjective, but it only *tends* to be associated with physical features out in the world, accessible to anyone. What is essential to pain is not that it is caused by tissue damage, but that it is an unpleasant experience. And so if I'm having that experience, even in the absence of any verifiable tissue damage, I'm in pain. Neither you nor my doctor can check that I'm reporting my pain "correctly," because that's just not the kind of thing pain is.

As a result, I seemingly can't be wrong about my own pain. Although I can be fooled by an optical illusion (a stick in the water that appears bent), or mishear something said to me ("Did Grandma just say she launched the granola into space? Oh, she wants to be in control of her own space!"), there is no standard concerning my pain other than how I experience it. And so if I perceive myself to be in pain, then I am—that's even if the pain is "in my leg" but my leg has been amputated. If I said, "My leg is purple," despite anyone else being able to see that my leg had normal coloration, then it would make sense to correct me. Even if I sincerely believed that my leg was purple, the fact that others could check on my observation means that I could be wrong in my sincere belief. But since my pain isn't available for "checking" by others, there is no meaningful sense in which I can be wrong in my perception about how much pain I'm in. Of course, I could insincerely report—lie—to others about my pain; but I can't be *wrong*. This is why the IASP encourages physicians to take patient reports of pain as pain, even if there doesn't seem to be an obvious physical cause.

These reflections all might sound a bit philosophical and abstract in the bad sense—in the sense that could reasonably lead one to ask, "Why should I care about all of this?" But the subjectivity of pain is not a mere philosophical puzzle. Humans go through life desperately trying to avoid pain, or to recover from pain, and the institution most directly responsible for addressing our pain is that of medicine. Doctors have as an explicit goal to relieve suffering, and our physical pains cause much of the suffering that drives the practice of medicine. So we go to doctors and ask them to relieve our pain, making our pain an object of medical concern.

But since the doctors can't directly access our pain, we task them with addressing a symptom that they can't objectively measure or confirm. This is where the philosophical problem of pain runs headlong into the real world of medical practice.

The very basic tension that lies behind so many of the ethical challenges facing pain medicine today is the fact that physicians are scientifically trained to find a biological cause of ill health and to use objective tools for evaluating medical problems. But since pain is essentially subjective, it will at least sometimes elude biological explanation, and no advancement in technology will solve this problem for us. X-rays, MRIs, and other impressive equipment make the job of a physician easier in some cases: if I come in complaining of moderate to severe pain in my arm, and it's swollen, and the X-ray reveals multiple fractures, then the physician is left with a confident story about my pain. My body is behaving like we think it should, alerting me to actual tissue damage that medicine is now able to isolate, and the X-ray ordered by the physician provides something concrete that she can share with colleagues and on which to base her clinical judgment. But it doesn't always happen that way, and patients who suffer with severe chronic pain are more than familiar with the frustration of their doctors, who look for the source of pain but can't always find it.

Pain is a special object of medical concern, then, but is not directly accessible by clinicians. They can take my temperature and blood pressure, check my oxygen levels and pulse, but they cannot simply access my pain level. Pain, in other words, is a *symptom*, like nausea or dizziness; it is not an objective measure, like temperature. And that is the basic problem of pain medicine.

So what do we do? Well, we talk about our pain. That doesn't feel very specific, but it's what we've got. If we didn't care about pain all that much, we wouldn't worry about this inaccessibility; but in the twenty-first century, in America in particular, the medical community is *very* concerned with treating pain, and so this problem stands in desperate need of a solution. Indeed, the Institute of Medicine (now National Academy of Medicine) released a report in 2011 detailing the overwhelming cost of pain in America and concluding that relieving pain should be a national priority. If we are to take such a charge seriously, physicians need some way to access the pain of patients, even if that access is indirect.

Anyone who has been to a doctor for pain treatment in the last couple of decades can probably guess what the medical community's solution to this problem is. It's the "pain scale," which is a tool for helping patients assign numerical values to their pain. In the simple cases, clinicians simply ask patients to rate their pain using a 0–10 scale; since not all patients have the same capacity to speak English or to conceptualize a numerical scale, however, these numbers are also sometimes accompanied by a spectrum of cartoon faces, with one end of the spectrum showing a smiley face and the other showing a severely pained grimace. The pain scale, then, basically asks patients to assign numbers to the concepts of "no pain," varying degrees of "some pain," and "the worst pain." If the only access you have to a patient's pain is self-report, and you want to be able to quantify and follow up on that report so as to appropriately treat the pain, then you need the patient to have some way to measure and report her pain. The pain scale is thus the simple solution to the phenomenally complex problem of pain.

On the one hand, the pain scale really shouldn't be all that helpful. My assigning some value to my own pain tells the doctor very little about how she, or anyone else, would evaluate my pain. But on the other hand, self-report is all we have, and the pain scale gives us a way to start to contextualize our own pain experience. Having gained more practice with the pain scale than anyone should ever want, I was surprised at how useful it eventually came to be.

The first time anyone asked my pain level was in the ambulance from the site of the accident. I remember the EMT's question—identical to what I would be asked a dozen times a day during each of my hospital stays—"How would you rate your pain on a scale of zero to ten, with zero being no pain at all and ten being the worst pain you can imagine?"

Despite my shock, I found the question absurd, for exactly the sorts of reasons already outlined: I could assign any number I wanted, and the EMT would have no way of knowing what it meant (yes, professional philosophers are very strange humans). So I fumbled around for a minute, trying to come up with any sort of justification for assigning one number rather than another. Realizing that my friendly medical professional was going to withhold the morphine until I gave him an answer, I eventually replied, "I don't know. It's really bad, but I've got a pretty good imagination. Maybe a seven or an eight?" I was totally unconfident in my answer, but the EMT accepted it without hesitation and prepared the morphine dose. Even in my totally broken state, I wondered to myself how in the world he thought I had given him any meaningful information.

At some point after I got to the hospital, the morphine was wearing off and incredible pain—much worse than I'd had originally—began creeping back. I moaned and begged for more drugs, telling whoever would listen that I couldn't take it. When a nurse asked me what my pain level was, I reasoned quickly to myself: it was clearly worse than before, but surely it wasn't the worst I could imagine. It was all-consuming pain, like being on fire—the kind of pain that doesn't let you think of anything else—but it also seemed possible that its intensity could be dialed up. So I responded, "At least an eight . . ." and then, gritting my teeth through a particularly bad moment, "Oh God, maybe a nine."

Again, the nurse didn't question for even a moment; she was already working on my IV. "This is fentanyl," she said. "It's one hundred times stronger than morphine, so it should do the trick." *One hundred times stronger than morphine.* I wondered how I'd survive it. And then came the disorienting, disturbing, unpleasant feeling of my brain melting again, which is the last thing I remember from that encounter.

Whenever I woke up on that first day prior to surgery, it was always because the pain was creeping back, and it was always scary. There would be panic at the thought that I might not flag down a nurse quickly enough to keep the pain from spiking again, but Sadiye would always be there and would always find someone. As the day wore on, I found myself making judgments of my pain level in a relatively consistent way: Getting under a 5 meant that my pain was manageable. I never reported a pain level below a 3, no matter how medicated, because if I was conscious, the pain was serious enough to be disruptive (after all, I had bones sticking out of my foot). Above a 5, the pain began to be all I could think about, and the fear and panic would start to creep in. Above a 7, I wouldn't be able to stay still or keep from moaning. So I quickly developed an intuitive rule that, at 5 or below, I wouldn't ask for more meds. Taking the meds, after all, had a cost—they did the brain-melty thing, and then I would typically lose consciousness. And while that may not sound bad given the alternative, I wanted to be with Sadiye and to know what was going on. My world was chaotic enough without constantly having to reorient myself.

Over the course of that first day, then, the numbers began to take on real meaning (which would continue to be refined in the days following): 1 to 2 was relatively minor pain, which I wouldn't feel again, while fully conscious, for weeks. 3 to 5 was definitely uncomfortable, and would spike and throb in ways that distracted and occupied me. That was not a nice way to live, and it was comparable to what I would have identified in my pre-trauma life as serious pain. 6 to 8 was bad: if there wasn't medication available, it would be all-consuming, and the spikes in the higher range would make me wish for unconsciousness. And the 9 that I hit on that first day was the worst pain I'd ever experienced, and it had been devastating.

Although I was convinced that it could be worse, I wasn't sure what it would mean to be worse; I mean, how would I be able to tell if I hit a 10? In the throes of agony, wouldn't I always be able to stop and imagine it being just a little more intense?

By the time that first emergency surgery ended, it was relatively late in the day. The only thing I remember about waking up was that I immediately asked for Sadiye, and the nurse brought her to the big, open post-op room where my bed was. I was coming out of general anesthesia, which is very disorienting. I don't remember any details from that evening except that we seemed to be in that space for a long time. At some point, Sadiye had to go home; after all, we had a baby girl to look after, and it was only through the kindness and good graces of very many friends that we made it through those first weeks at all.

By the time I got to my hospital room, it was night, and the only person I would see regularly would be the night-shift nurse. I remember that many of the nurses at this hospital were wonderful, beautiful people, and they played a big role in helping me to keep both my physical and mental health during that first week. But the nurse that first night—whose name I can't even remember—took on a kind of "savior" status for me. He was a young man, and he would take good care of me for several of the days that I was there; but that first night was different from the others.

Since I had just come out of surgery a few hours earlier, and it was the middle of the night, the only pain regimen I had available was the fairly generic one that the surgeon had written before going home. According to his instructions, I was allowed to take a relatively small dose of oxycodone orally every four hours, and then IV hydromorphone as needed for breakthrough pain, no more than every four hours (interspersed with the oxycodone). Both of these drugs are powerful synthetic opioids: oxycodone is the main ingredient in Percodan, Percocet, and OxyContin, while hydromorphone is best known under the brand name Dilaudid.

The staggered schedule of the oral and IV pain meds left me with two hours to get through between each dose. And although I was able to hold it together for the first few hours after getting to my room, I began to worry almost immediately. It was about ten p.m. when I took the oxycodone dose, and by midnight I was wide awake, watching the clock, waiting to request the IV hydromorphone.

At midnight, the hydromorphone did its thing and knocked me out; but I was awake well before two a.m., in terrible pain. I called the nurse and told him I didn't think I could wait until two, but he calmed and comforted me, asking me if I could at least try. So I did. It was one of the worst moments of my life, but I made it until 1:45 a.m., when the nurse went ahead and gave me the oxycodone.

I relaxed and waited for the drug to help send me to sleep, but it didn't happen. Within a few minutes, the oxycodone had taken the edge off, but it didn't really reduce my pain level that much— not back below a 5, where I would start to feel like I could manage for a while. Instead, it merely became a dull, thudding, throbbing 6, with peaks to 7. I called the nurse, and he tried to help me relax again, but it wasn't working. I looked at the clock: it wasn't even 2:15 a.m. yet, and I was already thinking about my four o'clock dose of hydromorphone.

I began to panic, and as my anxiety level rose, the pain got sharper. And as the pain got sharper, the panic began to boil over. I forgot about the big red button at the side of my bed for calling the nurse and just yelled down the hall, moaning and twisting my torso in my bed. When he got to my room, he asked that familiar question, "What level is your pain?" And I told him an 8. But as bad as that was, what really scared me was the clock: I had well over an hour of this left to endure. I panicked more. The nurse said he would try to get ahold of the surgeon.

While he was off making calls, the pain snowballed. I felt like my foot had caught on fire, and there was no longer any pulsing to the pain—no peaks of intensity or valleys of reprieve. All I could do was lie there and live in my suffering.

And then, unimaginably, it got worse. I wish I could explain how, but I can't. And that's one of the many strange features of pain: when you're not in it, you can't fully appreciate its terribleness. I remember thinking that I felt like my skin was boiling, or that acid was being poured right onto my nerves. I was sure that, even though my foot was entirely covered, somehow someone was dragging nails directly across my gaping wound, pausing to dig and twist. I began to make noises—I'm not entirely sure what kind of noises—but I couldn't keep quiet or still. The thing about being in that kind of pain is that you can't let the world stay the same. Something has to change, and so you do all that you can, which may only be moaning and rocking in pathetic little motions.

My dear, sweet nurse came back in, looking worried. "What's your pain level, Travis?" he asked softly.

"Ten," I gasped. And I suddenly understood how you could know that you'd hit a 10 on the pain scale. Because what you know, at that moment, is that things cannot possibly get worse. You are in hell, and if things did get worse, then either you would lose consciousness or you would have to find a way to knock yourself out. Smashing your head against the wall starts to seem like a reasonable plan.

My nurse, looking nervously at the clock, and then worriedly back at me, began preparing another dose of hydromorphone. It was at least an hour before my dose was due, but he gave it to me, and this time the loss of sensation and thought was incredibly welcome. The fiery, boiling, acidic pain certainly didn't disappear, but it cooled below the point of terror, and my panic slowly subsided. It sounds dramatic, I know, and I suppose it's probably not literally true, but what I tell people about that nurse is that he saved my life.

As my initial skepticism of the pain scale gradually turned into facility at using it, I began to understand some of its value. The numbers took on real meaning for me, and experiencing truly awful pain helped to contextualize other pains. Sure, the chronic pain that I now live with is unpleasant—and maybe once upon a time, I would have rated it as fairly bad—but it's barely a blip on the radar for me, having gone through what I did. When I see my orthopedic surgeon or my pain doc and am asked to rate my pain, I feel guilty even mentioning it. "It's maybe a one or two most times," I say. Annoying, but not disruptive.

Hitting a 10 on the pain scale was horrifying, but it also gave meaning to the rest of the scale. I knew already what it was like to have no pain (a 0), but until I experienced a pain that I couldn't imagine getting worse, I didn't have another bookend to my scale. It was always a random-feeling guess when I assigned a 6 or 7. After that first day in the hospital, though, I felt like I understood what the scale basically looked like, with comfort on one end, torture on the other, and lots of muddy middle ground in between. As I progressed through months of treatment, this ability to differentiate my pain levels was important, since I needed to know whether my pain was getting worse or better, and how close it was to being unmanageable.

That's the best case I can make for the pain scale. And it sounds pretty good. It allowed me to take my private, subjective experience of pain and objectify it somewhat (putting it in a context) to make it available to others (again, somewhat: I can give those numbers to my doctor so that we have a shared measurement to discuss). That's not nothing.

It doesn't *solve* the philosophical problem of pain, though. Because here's the thing: my use of the pain scale is every bit as subjective as my pain. Sure, I can make my own judgments more and less consistent, but no amount of reflecting on the pain scale will tell the physician how bad my pain is *objectively*.

Consider the following distressing possibility: Perhaps the 10 I hit on the pain scale would be more like a 5 for someone else. Now, I have a hard time believing that. As I noted in my description, I only conceded to assigning a score of 10 when it felt like any worse pain would be incompatible with consciousness. In line with the instructions for the pain scale, I simply couldn't imagine it being worse. And that seems important.

But maybe I'm just pathetic and weak. Maybe a stronger person could have dealt with the pain better. I can't quite bring myself to believe it, but I can't *know* that it's not true.

And when we get further away from the very margin of the pain scale, it gets harder. What if I had never had the first, undermedicated night in the hospital? I used my all-consuming terror of that experience to contextualize the rest of my judgments; but if that hadn't happened, maybe a bunch of pain that suddenly seemed manageable by comparison would have seemed absolutely horrific.

The case for the pain scale gets even worse, because there are yet more complications. Recall the observation that we can't really remember what it's like to be in pain. Sitting here at my desk, I can remember the mental descriptions I made of certain pain, and I can remember judging that it was some level of bad. But for the life of me, I can't remember the *feeling*. If you've given birth or passed a kidney stone or had major surgery, sit for a moment and try to remember what the pain from that experience was actually like—not how you described it, but how it *felt*. If you're anything like me, you can't do it. And to be honest: thank God, right? If we were able to put ourselves into torturous pain simply by casting our minds back to another time, I would never want to think about any element of this experience again. But since I can't really remember specific pains, that makes comparison much harder.

As my pain ebbed and flowed over the course of a single day, the judgments were easier: I'm wincing and groaning more, flinching, and unable to concentrate; it wasn't like that this morning, so there must have been an increase in my pain level. And going from worse pain to better is accompanied by a profound sense of relief, and that relief can help to make judgments of decreasing pain. But what about the pain that I experienced sixty days into my recovery, after five surgeries, followed by three weeks of freedom from interventions? Or the pain I experienced after my sixth surgery, which wouldn't take place until December of that year? How reliably would my judgments of postsurgical pain in early January 2016 compare to my judgments of postsurgical pain from June 2015?

Finally, we can add one more element of pain that makes judgment and comparison hard, which is that we can become *accustomed* to pain. Part of what makes it embarrassing to rate my chronic pain as serious enough to warrant attention is simply because it is fairly minor pain compared to what I've been through. But another element is that I've now had it for years, and I've simply grown used to living with it. Even when the arthritic pain of obliterated joints flares up in the fall and winter, I sometimes have to be told that I'm limping. "Oh yeah," I might say after reflecting and realizing that my pain is worse. "The cold and rain are a little hard on the foot."

To be clear, there are serious limits to how beneficial this sort of plasticity can be. Someone suffering from fibromyalgia, severe chronic pain due to spinal injury, cancer pain, sickle cell anemia, or a million other causes likely does not simply "get used to" being in desperate pain. But it is possible that these people, if they have wrestled with pain for a long time, deal with it better than many of us would if we suddenly experienced their level of pain. So the experience of severe pain can help us to contextualize other pains in our lives, but the experience of living with pain can also change how we experience it.

To sum up, then: pain is deeply puzzling and difficult to deal with;

we demand that doctors help us deal with it anyway; and our best tool for helping us communicate about pain is still deeply flawed. It's not flawed in the sense that it should be better, but in the sense that we simply cannot make it work. We cannot turn an essentially private, subjective experience into an objective phenomenon. Pain medicine is thus tasked with a profoundly difficult job.

This very basic problem at the core of pain management undoubtedly raises lots of challenges both for practitioners and for pain patients. It makes pain management difficult and time-consuming, and it requires that physicians listen carefully and communicate well with patients who may struggle to convey information about their pain.

But there is another, very particular challenge raised by the subjectivity of pain, and it's one that every physician has wrestled with: the most powerful class of pain medications we have is also a profoundly addictive, recreational drug. And this class is, of course, opioids.

Opioids are desired by many patients, and they are important and effective for many patients. Sometimes patients who can be genuinely helped by them are also patients who want them. And sometimes patients who want them lie about "needing" them. The whole lesson of the subjectivity of pain is that a physician can never know for sure which kind of patient is standing in front of her.

The pharmaceutical industry has developed many valuable classes of painkillers. The most common, over-the-counter medications for treating pain are acetaminophen (Tylenol), nonsteroidal anti-inflammatory drugs, or NSAIDs (such as ibuprofen, the main ingredient in both Advil and Motrin), and acetylsalicylic acid (ASA—much more commonly known as Aspirin). Although many patients scoff at the idea that these are serious pain medications, that may be a result of either never using them for fairly serious pain or expecting too much. I, too, scoffed at the power of Aspirin, Tylenol, and Motrin for much of my life; after all, I had been injured many times, and they never seemed to eliminate my pain.

All of these medications, however, have their place, and can make serious headway against serious pain. While it's true that they often will not eliminate pain entirely, the idea that they are supposed to is likely a myth of marketing. Painkillers—both over-the-counter and prescription—are often able to make pain more manageable, and a completely transparent medical, pharmaceutical, and advertising system would make this goal clear, so that patients could set appropriate goals for their treatment (we'll come back to this idea much later). So in fact, although I used Aspirin mostly as a blood thinner to reduce the risk of clots after surgery, both acetaminophen and NSAIDs played a major role in my post-trauma life. Indeed, for years after the accident, a prescription NSAID called celecoxib was able to keep my chronic pain under control.

In terms of raw analgesic (that is, pain-relieving) power, though, opioids are in a different league than these more modest pain relievers. They are capable of treating truly severe pain, as in the case of traumatic, surgical, cancer-related, and end-of-life pain.

What makes something an opioid is its molecular relationship either to the opium poppy plant or to the human body's "opioid system." The poppy plant itself produces a sticky, milky liquid that can be dried into a fine powder: that powder is opium. Opium has been used as an analgesic, as well as for recreational and spiritual reasons, for more than five thousand years. While opium is an impressive natural painkiller, it's relatively mild, as what we now think of as the active narcotic compounds make up a relatively small percentage of the liquid and powder volume.

As we advanced our chemical knowledge and methods, we then developed the ability to derive more powerful drugs from opium. The most straightforward way to do this was simply to isolate the active components—what are called "alkaloids"—which include morphine, codeine, and thebaine. These alkaloids can then be further processed, however (for example, following a fairly simple recipe can turn extracted morphine into heroin). All of these drugs are "opiates," which just means that they are derived (in some way) from the opium poppy.

What makes opiates so powerful, however, is not the plant that they come from but, rather, the role they play in the brain. Opiates owe both their pain-relieving and their euphoric effects to their chemical function in the human body: both morphine and heroin fit into certain chemical receptors which, when activated, send signals to the brain that block pain sensation and induce a general sense of calm. What's important about the chemistry, though, is that a molecule need not have been created naturally as part of a plant in order to do this (indeed, the reason we have these brain receptors is because the body has its own molecules that produce these effects: endorphins, which are so named because they are like "endogenous morphine"). And so the continuing development of chemistry led pharmaceutical companies to create synthetic compounds that mimic the effects of endorphins, as well as that of opiates like morphine, codeine, and heroin. These synthetic compounds were then called "opioids" to distinguish them from the natural "opiate" compounds and included many of the common pain medications of today, such as oxycodone, hydrocodone, fentanyl, and methadone.

Today, the term "opioid" is used to cover the entire category of drugs that operate on the brain's opioid system. This includes naturally occurring compounds like opium, derivatives of those natural compounds, and synthetic compounds that were created specifically to activate the opioid receptors. What holds this category together, then, is not the source but the molecular structure of the compound and the resulting effect it has on the human brain.

And now we're getting to why opioids cause us problems. Perhaps the human body could have existed such that the system which most reliably blocks pain signals to the brain had no other effects. If that had been the case, and if opioids were able to cause the release of those signals, then the drugs would not be problematic in the way they are in our actual world. But in the actual world, our bodies developed in a much more complex way.

Endorphins, which are part of the body's natural opioid system, are released in response to pain. Part of one's natural ability to function after a major injury, in fact, is due to the body's powerful endorphin response. But we also release endorphins when running (responsible for the so-called runner's high), when eating pleasurable food, and when having sex. In these latter instances, a common way of understanding the effect of endorphin release is "euphoria," or a sense of happiness, calm, and well-being.

The opioid system, then, has multiple functions. Importantly for our purposes, it both blocks bad signals (pain) and produces good ones (euphoria). And that makes drugs that act on this system particularly desirable, as both pain relief and euphoria are valuable states worth pursuing. If you could get a feeling similar to what you get from sex but from a pill, would you want it? Maybe not everyone would, but it's not hard to see why some people might. In fact, it's not even very hard to see why some people might develop a habit out of taking such pills, but we'll return to the science of "habit" later.

The complexity of opioids is not exhausted by these first two prongs though—the opioid system does more than just block pain and induce pleasure. Importantly, and tragically, it also sedates various bodily systems. Part of sedation is simply becoming sleepy, as I experienced whenever a dose of morphine, fentanyl, or hydromorphone would knock me out. But there is a much more dangerous aspect of sedation, as the opioid system also slows the respiratory system. As more and more of the drug enters a user's body, she takes fewer and fewer breaths, reducing the amount of oxygen that gets to the brain. And eventually, if the dose is high enough, she simply doesn't breathe again. The respiratory system shuts down, oxygen stops flowing to the brain, and the brain dies.

The cause of death in such a case is opioid poisoning. Or more colloquially: overdose.

We now have all of the ingredients needed to understand how the philosophical puzzle of pain leads to a desperate problem for pain management. Opioids are powerful pain medications, and doctors want to relieve suffering. So they want to prescribe these medications that can make suffering go away. But, there's a problem: these drugs can also make you feel good, even if you aren't in physical pain. At least, for some people (people experience the effects differently—I wouldn't personally describe the feeling of being on opioids as "good," but I do get the attraction). They're desirable enough that people will try to get them. But they're also phenomenally dangerous, able to kill with a single dose. As a result, they're illegal without a prescription. And so doctors are a source of a powerful, desirable, but deadly drug.

Now let's add back in the fact that pain isn't objectively measurable. So how do we assess pain? Well, we talk. The patient describes the pain to the doctor, trying to contextualize it in terms of how bad it feels. But both the patient and the doctor know that a certain level of pain can yield an opioid scrip. And opioids are desirable.

The result is that every physician who ever treats pain has a story—probably many, many stories—of the patient who comes in with a complaint that's a bit too precise. A complaint about specific pain that doesn't respond well to over-the-counter treatments. Sometimes even a pain that doesn't respond well to the weaker opioid painkillers, like low-dose hydrocodone. Funny enough, it turns out that this patient has exactly the kind of complaint that might generate a prescription for oxycodone. In some of these stories, the doctor uncomfortably says that she won't prescribe an opioid, either for a first-time patient or for a pain like this, and the patient turns aggressive. Sometimes violent, sometimes threatening. This happens especially in the emergency department, where one-off patients are most likely to be seen. Every doctor has one or many of these stories that taught them what it means for a patient to be "drug-seeking."

Of course, not every patient who comes in complaining of pain is drug-seeking. And the physician knows that. But the experience of drug-seeking behavior makes vivid an important lesson: a doctor's prescription pad is one source of a desirable drug, and there is no way for the physician to know for sure whether a patient is in pain, or whether the pain is as serious as the patient says. Because, of course, pain is an essentially subjective experience.

In short, what doctors learn is that some patients have an incentive to lie about their pain, and there's no way to ensure that they're telling the truth. But the same drugs that relieve pain and induce pleasure can kill you, and if the doctor were to hand out prescriptions without care, she would almost certainly be responsible for some number of deaths.

This is the deep challenge of modern pain medicine, and this is the precarious position into which we have put every physician who treats pain. Opioid-based pain medicine is ripe for tension and conflict.

CHAPTER 3

The Swinging Pendulum

In retrospect, one of the most confusing aspects of my own experience with pain medicine was the way in which I had my pain aggressively, and often effectively, treated, while also occasionally being undermedicated or even treated as a drug-seeker. On the first night in the hospital, this is understandable, even if unfortunate: the prescribing doctor was following the sensible advice of today's guidelines, to "start low and go slow" with prescription opioids; but when the pain became excruciating, my lovely nurse couldn't bear to see me suffer and gave me another dose of hydromorphone. Much later, the contrast was even more stark: at the same hospital stay—indeed on the same day, after the free flap surgery—I was looked at with suspicion by one doctor and medicated into comfortable oblivion by another. The question I found myself returning to again and again as I tried to make sense of my experience was: what is the source of this tension?

The seeming incoherence of modern pain medicine that I witnessed is, it turns out, entirely common. And although it's confusing and frustrating to experience, it's also completely understandable when we look at our current situation as the consequence of a long, historical battle between conflicting attitudes about pain and opioids. Pain medicine is at an inflection point, during which we're deciding what to think about opioid painkillers. But this is far from the first time we've been here. And reflecting on our past inflection points can teach us much about the dangers of the current moment.

In the nineteenth century, America—like much of the rest of the world—fully understood both the value and the danger of the poppy plant. The manufacture of morphine early in the century had proven crucial for treating severe pain, but the risk of addiction was well known and worrying. The number of Civil War soldiers who battled addiction after prolonged morphine exposure for traumatic and surgical pain had led to a growing concern among the public. Chinese "opium dens," too, were introducing civilians to both the euphoric and the addictive potential of the milky innards of the poppy plant. Too many people who were exposed to recreational opium or medicinal morphine ended up "hooked," and so the opioids of the day gained a reputation for being dangerous. According to historian David Courtwright, *this* was America's first opioid epidemic. An underground world of recreational opium and indiscriminate use of the even more potent morphine (paired midcentury with the newly invented hypodermic needle, capable of delivering a large dose of morphine directly into the user's bloodstream) proved a devastating combination.

But of course, morphine was used for a good reason: in terms of pain relief, it was in a class by itself. The analgesic, or pain-relieving, effects of opioids were unparalleled, and so abandoning them altogether didn't seem like an option. Thus was born the search for the Holy Grail of pharmaceutical manufacturing: a nonaddictive opioid. Any company that could develop a painkiller with the analgesic effects of morphine but without its addictive (and sometimes fatal) side effects would both provide a great benefit to medicine and make an unbelievable amount of money.

Just before the turn of the century, a small chemical firm in Germany (previously specializing in the development of coal tar dyes) thought it had made just such a discovery. A young chemist named Felix Hoffmann had recently joined the company's expanding drug research program, and he had accidentally synthesized the compound diacetylmorphine while trying to create codeine. Although diacetylmorphine had been discovered more than twenty years before by a British scientist, no one had trademarked or commercialized the product until Hoffmann pushed the research forward. Early tests—both on animals and humans—were promising, and he began calling the drug "heroisch," after the "heroic" feeling that it gave he and his coworkers when they sampled their own product. The name stuck, and in 1898, diacetylmorphine was trademarked under the name "Heroin." Hoffmann's employer—the relatively small chemical manufacturer that, until recently, had focused on coal tar dyes— was called Friedrich Bayer and Company. Or, as it is simply known today: Bayer. The company that would eventually turn into a global pharmaceutical giant under its flagship product, Aspirin, was responsible for unleashing Heroin onto the world.

The interest in opioids was immense, and for multiple reasons. Not only were they the most powerful pain medications known, but they were also an impressive cough suppressant. At a time of uncontrolled tuberculosis and widespread influenza, this property was crucial.

At the release of Heroin, Heinrich Dreser—the head of Bayer's pharmacological group—relentlessly promoted the drug: it was many times more powerful than codeine or morphine, but nonaddictive, he claimed. So it could safely be taken for pain or to relieve cough or even just as a sedative for those having trouble sleeping. In fact, it could even be used to treat addiction to morphine. Bayer marketed directly to physicians, and Dreser wrote for medical journals in support of his wonder drug. In addition, pills, cough drops, and elixirs were sold directly to the public in pharmacies. Heroin, like morphine, was used to alleviate headaches and menstrual cramps and given to fussy children during teething. For anyone who developed respiratory problems, whether due to tuberculosis or a simple cold or flu, Heroin could soothe the cough and allow for a decent night's sleep.

Upon the release of Heroin, public opinion of opioid therapy received a marked boost; although the risk of addiction had begun to undermine confidence in morphine, this was a concerted, largely successful effort to promote the idea among both the medical community and the public that opioids were important and safe. Unfortunately, the swing in opinion occurred in response to a drug that was industrially manufactured, and so could be widely distributed. Also unfortunate: the central claim of Bayer, that Heroin was non-addictive, was false. And the result of this widespread embrace of a devastatingly addictive drug is precisely what you would expect it to be: a continued and expanded epidemic of addiction, overdose, and death.

As early as 1899—one year after the release of Heroin—stories of tolerance, dependence, and addiction began to bubble up among those who used it. But a change in perspective takes time, and Heroin was, in fact, very good at doing what it was designed to do: alleviate pain, cough, and inability to sleep. So despite a low rumble of anecdotes and reports concerning "habit," most medical reviews of the drug remained positive for years. Indeed, in 1906, the American Medical Association approved the use of Heroin and recommended that it be used in place of morphine (despite noted reservations about habit formation).

And so the epidemic grew, despite documented concerns about addiction. By 1908, President Teddy Roosevelt had had enough, and he appointed Hamilton Wright—a physician from the Midwest—to become America's first opium commissioner. Wright, like Roosevelt himself, had a fairly uncomplicated view of opioids, claiming that Americans had "become the greatest drug fiends in the world."

As Wright worked to find ways to stop the spread of Heroin, Bayer saw the writing on the wall and—comforted by the sale of

Aspirin, which was by then taking off—discontinued Heroin manufacturing in 1913. Just one year later, the Harrison Narcotics Tax
Act was passed, which both heavily taxed and strictly regulated several drugs, including heroin (since Bayer ceased manufacturing the
brand-name drug Heroin, I will use the lowercase "heroin" to refer
to the generic diacetylmorphine drugs that continue to be called by
that name). After that, heroin was available only by prescription,
and it could not be prescribed to patients suffering from addiction.
While the medication was technically still available, the arrest of
physicians for violating the Harrison Act had a significant chilling
effect on prescribing, driving heroin sales underground and creating
a black market. Ten years later, in 1924, the Heroin Act officially
outlawed the importation, possession, or manufacture of heroin.

While the swing toward open embrace of powerful opioids like
morphine and heroin lasted only a few decades, the resulting swing
back slammed the pendulum into prohibition, lodging public opinion solidly into fear of opioids and a certain amount of disgust toward
their users. By eliminating medical use of opioids, and driving its use
underground, society turned addiction and opioid use into something
to be spurned and reviled. Addiction became a criminal problem
rather than a medical one, its victims worthy of scorn rather than
sympathy. Opioid users of the early twentieth century eventually had
to dedicate much of their life to supporting their "junk" habit, and
so eventually were given the essentializing epithet "junkie." Some
sources even claim that the term "junkie" came about as a result of
the desperate career heroin users found themselves pursuing—that
of gathering and selling scrap metal, another form of junk.

The junkie joined Hamilton Wright's "drug fiend" or the newly
popular "dope fiend" as a favorite dehumanization of anyone suffering
from addiction. And since the drug trade was driven underground,
the drug user was a criminal. Opioid use was no longer the prov-
ince of the middle and upper classes (as it had been when doctors
were the primary access point to the drugs); instead, it was common

among gamblers, prostitutes, and other members of the criminal underworld. The junkie and the dope fiend became important charac-
ters in American history, simultaneously serving as justification for
a prohibition that would eventually turn into a full-blown "War on
Drugs," while also attributing addiction to individuals' moral failing,
thereby creating some psychic space between "us" and "them." The
weak, sad creatures of the opioid underworld were both the reason
for strict narcotic laws and sufficiently unlike the rest of us to comfort us as we treated them like criminals rather than victims. For
nearly half a century, the pendulum refused to budge, and America
remained wary of opioid use, even in medicine, as each new opioid
developed appeared to carry the same risks as heroin.

Of course, this is an uncomfortable position because the practice of medicine requires analgesia. Trauma visits terrible pain on
patients; surgery itself, despite being therapeutic, causes terrible
pain; and as modern medicine continued to increase the average
American's life span, the chances of their living long enough to
suffer from desperately painful conditions like cancer continued
to increase. In short, opioids continued to be our most powerful
pain medication, and the advancement of medicine meant an ever-
increasing population of patients with genuine, severe pain. As a
result, after several decades of a thoroughgoing prohibitionist attitude toward opioid painkillers, the tide began to turn—ever so
slowly at first—in the latter half of the twentieth century.

In 1974, a young neurologist named Kathleen Foley began her career
at Memorial Sloan Kettering Cancer Center in New York, where
she would soon find herself overwhelmed by the enormity of cancer
patients' suffering. Despite having the means to alleviate pain with
opioid painkillers, fifty years of prohibition and stigma had taken its
toll on the medical profession and the public alike. Not only was
treatable pain left untreated by physicians, but patients—even at the
very end of their lives—often didn't want to take opioids. In a 2001

interview with the *New York Times*, Foley noted that "it's very common for patients to say, 'I don't want to be in pain, but I don't want my family to think I'm an addict.'"

Foley's experience with cancer patients led her to play an important role in the sea change that was coming. In 1981, she founded the country's very first pain service in a cancer center, which she directed for almost twenty years. From this position, she began pushing the medical community to take patients' pain more seriously and to abandon the fear and stigma surrounding opioid therapy. It was an idea whose time had finally come; in the wake of the country's civil rights movement, underrepresented groups began to gain confidence and a willingness to advocate for themselves. The language of "patient rights" began taking hold, and this sort of activism made it difficult for the community to ignore needless suffering. In Foley's own words, echoing what became something of a slogan in the pain advocacy community: inadequate pain care constitutes "torture by omission."

The 1970s and '80s thus saw a slow ramping up of serious pain care and the birth of a full-blown advocacy movement on behalf of pain patients. The first targets were, like Foley's patients, cancer victims, many of whom would experience excruciating pain for months or years, or even right up until their cancer killed them. This was the most sympathetic community, and it was nearly impossible to deny the logic of the pain advocacy movement: these patients were suffering greatly, and many of them would suffer for the rest of their lives. Worries about addiction seemed perversely puritanical in the context of a terminal disease; what, after all, is the benefit of avoiding addiction risk when one is dying?

The eventual yielding to the pain movement's demands in the context of cancer led to a kind of tripartite division of pain: there was cancer and end-of-life pain; chronic, noncancer pain; and acute pain (from injury, trauma, surgery, etc.). As opioid therapy became more accepted for cancer and end-of-life treatment, a natural question emerged: what about other kinds of pain? If failure to treat pain constitutes torture by omission, and we have the ability to treat pain with powerful medications, does it matter that not all chronic and acute pain is cancer related? What about pain from back injury? Or nerve damage? Or chronic pain from bone trauma? What about fairly moderate pain as the result of routine surgical and dental procedures?

The pendulum had finally dislodged from outright prohibition against opioids, and the question now being raised was how far back it would swing. And while the empathy and destigmatization of the early pain advocacy work is easy to praise in retrospect, what happened next gets harder to evaluate. After all, the country was still scared of opioids—they hadn't magically stopped being addictive—and so more widespread use would need to address that fear. Some of those well-meaning physicians, many of whom were just trying to relieve their patients' pain, began to chip away at that fear by questioning how serious the worries about addiction really were.

An early volley against the consensus view of opioids as addictive came in what should have been a quickly forgotten letter to the editor in the *New England Journal of Medicine*. In 1980, Drs. Jane Porter and Hershel Jick suggested that, contrary to popular opinion, addiction was actually rare in patients treated with opioid medication. This was not a study, but a short letter describing addiction outcomes from hospitalized patients in one database in Boston. The appropriate conclusion of the letter was that, in a highly controlled setting, when opioids were used sparingly for inpatient treatment of largely acute pain, addiction occurred in less than 1 percent of patients. It was an interesting observation that very few people should have remembered.

According to journalist Sam Quinones, the letter doesn't appear to have drawn much attention until 1986, when it was cited in another paper. And this new paper was by Kathleen Foley and her young, idealistic colleague Russell Portenoy. Portenoy had come to

Sloan Kettering just a couple of years before to train under Foley and, like her, he believed firmly in the value of pain medicine and the mission of destigmatizing opioids for the benefit of the suffering.

The 1986 paper was published in the journal *Pain* and, like the Porter and Jick letter, probably should not have been all that influential. In the paper, Foley and Portenoy reviewed thirty-eight cancer patients on chronic opioid therapy and noted that only two of the thirty-eight developed an addiction, and that both of those patients had a history of substance abuse. Their conclusion, drawing on their own data and the letter by Porter and Jick, was that addiction is a much less serious worry than it had been made out to be. Given the great potential for pain relief offered by opioids, and the relatively small risk, the obvious implication (which both Foley and Portenoy sincerely believed) was that we should be using these medications much more freely than was being done.

The Foley and Portenoy paper, and the Porter and Jick letter that they cited, entered the medical community knowledge base, slowly becoming the tip of the spear for the pain advocacy movement. Patients are suffering, advocates could say, and we have the means to stop that suffering. And what about addiction? The risk is small, as these papers in world-class medical journals show, and those who do succumb to addiction are likely to be those who have problems outside of the presence of opioids. At the time of this writing, the five-sentence letter to the editor by Porter and Jick has been cited more than a thousand times; Portenoy and Foley's paper has been slightly less influential, with a mere eight hundred citations.

And so the pendulum of opinion began picking up steam.

Although historical counterfactuals are always hard to evaluate, it seems unlikely that the pain advocacy movement by itself would have led the U.S. medical system to where it is today. We probably would have continued to debate the science of addiction and the appropriateness of certain levels of aggressiveness in treating different forms of pain. Maybe that would have meant that the fate of American pain medicine would have been controlled by experts and the peer-reviewed literature, as we tried to earnestly determine the right thing to do.

But that's not what happened. Instead, just as medicine was (appropriately) abandoning its knee-jerk and stigmatizing attitudes against opioids and (more questionably) embracing opioid therapy as widely appropriate, a new player came on the stage. Just as had been the case a hundred years before, the new player came from the pharmaceutical industry. And just as it had done a hundred years before, this new player came with a message of hope, for it had discovered precisely the medication that would solve our problems. It had achieved the Holy Grail of pain medicine: a less-addictive opioid. The company, like Bayer before it released Heroin, was not on many people's radar. But it would be before long. Its name was Purdue Pharma, and its new wonder drug was called OxyContin.

OxyContin was not Purdue's first foray into pain medicine. In the 1980s, as it was becoming more appropriate to treat cancer pain with opioids, Purdue had patented MS Contin, which was an extended-release formulation of morphine ("Contin" here, and with Oxy-Contin, is short for "continuous" release). The idea was that cancer patients need around-the-clock pain relief, and being woken up by the petering out of short-term pain relievers was less than ideal. So MS Contin replaced immediate-release morphine with a version that slowly dissolved, releasing its opioid payload over many hours. The drug was a success, though not a blockbuster, and funded Purdue for many years. But in the early 1990s, the company was looking at the expiration of its flagship patent, so it began looking for a replacement therapy—something to restart the patent clock and fund the company through another round of drug discovery. Taking the continuous-release technology and applying it to the opioid oxycodone, rather than morphine, did just the trick, and in 1996 Purdue announced the release of OxyContin.

OxyContin was not so different from MS Contin; although oxycodone is more powerful than morphine (one milligram of oxycodone is equivalent to about one and a half milligrams of morphine), the drugs were both extended-release opioid painkillers, and so there was no reason to assume that OxyContin would be more revolutionary than MS Contin was. However, as Purdue was preparing to release OxyContin, nearly a decade after it had released MS Contin, the landscape of American pain medicine was changing profoundly. What Purdue was able to do, then, was to exploit this changing environment (and, indeed, ultimately to contribute to it) in a way that would propel their new drug to almost unimaginable sales.

The key to OxyContin's success was a rather technical detail concerning its labeling. Drug manufacturers in the United States are regulated by the Food and Drug Administration (FDA), and the label for each drug is extensively negotiated between the company and the FDA, who must approve every word describing the medication, its effectiveness, risks, side effects, etc. In the case of OxyContin, Purdue's label included the following peculiar claim: "Delayed absorption as provided by OxyContin tablets, is believed to reduce the abuse liability of a drug." The reasoning in support of such an idea appears to have been something like the following: addiction is a result of the brain being trained to pursue a certain habit; and habits are reinforced as a result of how immediate and intense the reward from some activity is, and how regularly one engages in the activity. OxyContin, it was suggested, produces fewer and less intense "highs" by slowly releasing the opioid payload over time. This feature prevents the need to redose regularly, while also reducing the rapid, sharp upswings in drug levels making it to one's brain. In short, taking an extended-release pill is less intensely and less immediately rewarding, and it can be done less often. Rather than repeated spikes of pain relief and euphoria throughout the day, OxyContin could be taken only twice a day, leading to a long, slow, steady relief of one's pain. Fewer peaks, fewer valleys, and so less addictive potential.

The problem? Purdue offered no empirical evidence to support this claim. No data, no studies, no reason at all to think it was true. And in fact, two important features of the medication would quickly undermine their case: first, the pain-relieving effects rarely lasted twelve hours, so patients would actually need to take the medication much sooner, or else supplement with immediate-release opioids; and second, those looking for more serious pain relief, or a more intense high, could easily circumvent the extended-release technology by crushing the pills and snorting the powder or even mixing with liquid and injecting it. Doing so would deliver the entire opioid payload all at once, rather than spread out over twelve hours. And since the medication was designed to be released over half a day, Purdue manufactured massive doses, such as the 80mg tablet, or the unprecedented 160mg megapill.

Despite the lack of evidence offered by Purdue, the FDA—in a completely mysterious move—approved the labeling of OxyContin as having less abuse liability due to its extended-release technology. And so in 1996, into an ethos of pain advocacy and a growing demand for aggressive opioid therapy, Purdue introduced its "less-addictive" solution to the problem of undertreated pain. Almost exactly one hundred years after Bayer sold the world Heroin as the Holy Grail of pain medicine, Purdue tried the same move with OxyContin. And it worked.

The stars had begun to align for a truly revolutionary attitude toward treating pain, and Purdue tapped into the swelling tide. As more and more physicians followed palliative care leaders like Foley and Portenoy in calling for aggressive pain care, not only for cancer patients but for those suffering from a wide variety of ailments, Purdue gave them the medication needed, and a story that made it easy to embrace. All they had to do was get that story out into the hands of the medical community. All they had to do, that is, was market.

And it just so happened that Purdue Pharma was owned by a family who had made untold millions of dollars in marketing and promotion over the years—the Sackler family.

The result of this perfect storm of forces was an unprecedented pharmaceutical marketing campaign in which Purdue—guided by the experience and savvy of the Sacklers—hired tens of thousands of drug reps to pound the pavement. The reps had good news to spread, and an audience ripe to hear it: Undertreating pain amounts to torturing one's patients, but there now exists a powerful medication for alleviating that pain. And it's safe—the FDA has confirmed that it's less addictive than other opioids—so it shouldn't be restricted only to severe cancer pain. All sorts of pain can be life limiting, whether due to cancer, injury, or other chronic conditions. So OxyContin can and should be used for moderate to severe pain of all kinds. And as studies and reports have shown, the risk of addiction when opioids are used correctly is "less than one percent." Indeed, another component of OxyContin's label focused on low rate of addiction, stating,

> Iatrogenic [a result of medical care] "addiction" to opioids legitimately used in the management of pain is very rare. "Drug seeking" behavior is very common to addicts. Physical tolerance and physical dependence in pain patients are not signs of psychological dependence. Preoccupation with achieving adequate pain relief can be appropriate behavior in a patient with poor pain control. Most chronic pain patients limit their intake of opioids to achieve a balance between the benefits of the drug and dose-limiting side effects.

In other words, opioids aren't that dangerous in general when used "legitimately," and OxyContin is even less dangerous than other similar drugs. Prescribing doctors can rest easy.

In the years following the release of OxyContin, Purdue would

sponsor extravagant "pain management" conferences in exotic locations, with all expenses paid for physicians to go hear the good
word. The company paid speakers to endorse opioid therapy and
recruited an army of a sales force to distribute their message. These
employees were well trained to pitch OxyContin, taught to recite
the medication's misleading label and to claim that OxyContin is
"virtually nonaddictive"; they were also told to explicitly cite the
1 percent figure from the Porter and Jick letter, contributing to
its legacy. The sales tactics were so successful that by 2001, Purdue paid out annual bonuses (based on sales) averaging more than
$70,000 and ranging up to $240,000. Companywide, bonuses to-
taled $40 million that year—a large sum, but only a fraction of the
$200 million total marketing expenditures.

Purdue also donated money to professional organizations, including the American Pain Society (APS), which was already endorsing
the broader cultural swing toward permissiveness with regards to opioids. In 1995, the president of APS, Dr. James Campbell, coined the
phrase "pain as the fifth vital sign," which would eventually be em-
braced across the country as an ideal in pain management. The basic
claim was that pain is not merely a symptom—it is a vital sign akin
to heart rate, respiration, temperature, and blood pressure and should
be similarly monitored. In the same way that physicians are expected
to "take vitals" and react accordingly, medicating any problematic
fluctuation, so too should they regularly assess a patient's pain and
respond accordingly to fluctuations. And while most references to
pain as the fifth vital sign don't explicitly say that doctors ought to
medicate all increases in pain, asking patients about their pain and
thereby hearing about it leads to an impetus to *do something about it*.
So long as we have safe, effective pain medications, that seems like
an appropriate response to learning about your patient's pain.

Of course, recalling the lesson of the previous chapter, we can
immediately identify some issues with this model, since pain, unlike the traditional four vital signs, is inherently subjective. Indeed,

the challenge of pain medicine is precisely that pain is a *symptom* rather than a sign. That is, measurement cannot be taken with an objective tool of medicine, such as a thermometer or sphygmoma-nometer (blood pressure monitor). And this brings us back to the development of the pain scale—the idea that patients should regu-larly rate their pain on a scale of 0–10, with 0 being no pain at all and 10 being the worst pain imaginable. It is the physician's job to ask every patient about her pain, which she can rate on a numerical scale; now, having received quantitative data from the patient, the physician has an obligation to address problematic scores. You have pain? Fortunately, now there's a pill for that.

Pain as the fifth vital sign was a phenomenally successful move-ment, which Purdue was happy to both benefit from and help dissem-inate in its training. As the success of the broader pain movement coupled with the incredible resources of Purdue's marketing plan, a rapid shift took place in America over the last few years of the twen-tieth century. In 1998, the U.S. Department of Veterans Affairs (VA) hospital system, which is the largest hospital system in the country, explicitly adopted the language of pain as the fifth vital sign and re-quired physicians to check patients' pain and react accordingly; it even published a "Pain as the 5th Vital Sign Toolkit," which explained how to implement the "Pain as the 5th Vital Sign Mandate." Then in 2001, the Joint Commission on Accreditation of Healthcare Orga-nizations (JCAHO), now simply known as the Joint Commission—which accredits more than twenty thousand healthcare organizations and programs in America—also adopted the view that pain should be regularly evaluated and treated. Although it didn't officially en-dorse the language of the "fifth vital sign," the relationship between its requirements and the broader movement were clear, and between the VA hospitals and the hospitals accredited by JCAHO, treating pain as a vital sign became standard practice across the United States (along with those ubiquitous 0–10 questions). By the early 2000s, the pain revolution was in high gear, and the pendulum had clearly swung fully in the direction of opioid embrace. OxyContin, which had played a starring role in this transition, was making Purdue more than a billion dollars a year.

In 2007, after years of battling lawsuits, Purdue would finally admit wrongdoing in court, pleading guilty to "misbranding," a charge associated with misleading doctors and the public about OxyContin's addictive properties. The company was fined $600 million, and three of its top executives were fined an additional $34.5 million. By then, however, OxyContin was firmly ensconced in the medical community's pain regimen; indeed, some eight years after the settlement, "OxyContin" would be one of the names written on my own prescription bottles.

The extent to which the fallout from our carefree embrace of opioids in recent history mirrors a similar embrace a century before is striking. While the need for a less-addictive opioid drove sales of Heroin at the turn of the twentieth century, the same need—combined this time with a self-aware, passionate pain advocacy movement and an unprecedented marketing campaign—drove sales of OxyContin at the turn of the twenty-first. However, the damage from this new epidemic was not focused largely in urban areas, as it had been the last time. Instead, the addictive potential of OxyContin was seen first in the rural areas of Appalachia and in the small towns of New England. The devastation wrought in places like West Virginia, Kentucky, and Ohio led to a nickname for OxyContin that made explicit the comparison with its molecular cousin: OxyContin became known as "hillbilly heroin," and it sold for about a dollar per milligram on the street. In short, just as had been the case a century before, the result of widespread, uncareful prescribing of opioids, combined with a message that they are safer than they in fact are, led to a rapidly growing epidemic of addiction, overdose, and death.

Between the years of 1999 and 2010, opioid prescribing quadrupled, leveling off only after American clinicians were writing more than a quarter-billion prescriptions per year. The saturation of the American market was so extreme that, during the peak years of opioid prescribing, clinicians wrote enough prescriptions for every American adult to have a bottle of pills. Now certainly, OxyContin was not the only prescription opioid to play a role during this time period, nor was Purdue the only company to eventually be charged with wrongdoing for the way in which it promoted its drugs. INSYS Therapeutics settled for over $4 million in 2017 after it was accused of engaging in unfair and deceptive marketing practices, and then agreed to pay at least $150 million in 2018 to settle a Department of Justice probe into whether it paid kickbacks to doctors who prescribe their medication; and the McKesson Corporation settled for $150 million in 2017 for failing to report suspicious orders of controlled substances to the DEA. The number of companies named in lawsuits continues to climb. However, the role of OxyContin is hard to ignore: According to data from the International Narcotics Control Board, the average American went from consuming less than twelve milligrams of oxycodone per year in 1995—the year before OxyContin was released—to consuming nearly *240 milligrams* of oxycodone in 2012. In less than two decades, the average American's use of oxycodone increased *twentyfold*. During that same period, OxyContin sales steadily climbed, passing $1 billion in 2000, and eventually peaking at more than *$3 billion* in 2012. It's not surprising that, in a *New England Journal of Medicine* survey of high-profile and class action settlements against opioid companies, fully *half* of the twelve lawsuits name Purdue.

Over the course of the first decade of the twenty-first century, as the epidemic was winding up most aggressively, overdose deaths from prescription opioids also quadrupled, perfectly following the trend in prescribing. In short order, death from drug overdose—driven by the sharp increase in opioid overdose deaths—became the nation's leading cause of accidental death, displacing automotive accidents. By the time opioid prescribing peaked, Americans—who make up less than 5 percent of the global population—were consuming 80 percent of the total global opioid supply, and more people were dying every year from drug overdose than ever died in a single year during the HIV/AIDS epidemic. The terminology of an opioid "crisis" or "epidemic" suddenly seemed very fitting, and it began to be used by leading thinkers and politicians.

If history is any guide, we should expect that the level of destruction wrought by the opioid epidemic would terrify the American public, politicians, and the medical community, leading to a backlash against the prescription drugs that played such a prominent role. And indeed, that is exactly what has happened. Just as doctors who trained in the heyday of the pain advocacy movement had been told repeatedly to stop torturing their patients and were required by the Joint Commission to constantly evaluate and treat pain during clinical interactions, doctors trained against the backdrop of an epidemic are being told to stop killing their patients. Opioids are deadly drugs, and the medical community has a lot of blood on its hands, they are told. As Thomas Frieden—former director of the Centers for Disease Control and Prevention (CDC)—puts it: "The prescription overdose epidemic is doctor-driven. It can be reversed in part by doctors' actions."

In 1914, it had taken a new law, taxing, and restricting narcotic use, to slow the flow of legal heroin into the United States. A hundred years later, the organizational response largely took the form of prescribing guidelines and recommendations from various bodies. In 2016, the CDC took the unprecedented action of releasing its own guidelines for prescribing opioids, urging doctors not to see opioids as first-line therapy for noncancer chronic pain patients and to use opioids only sparingly, in low doses, for short amounts of time for treatment of acute pain. Although the advice was perfectly sensible and grounded in the best evidence available, pain advocates, chronic pain patients, and many physicians immediately began to worry that it and similar guidelines would have a significant chilling effect on the prescribing and management of opioids for all sorts of reasons, as doctors would become wary of these dangerous drugs that they were being advised not to use. And since not every doctor can be an expert on when opioid use is appropriate, it is easier to interpret the guidelines and recommendations as a virtual prohibition. If I'm a physician and I don't prescribe opioids, the thinking went, then I won't be responsible for anyone dying of overdose.

We apparently had not learned the appropriate lesson from history. The Harrison Narcotics Tax Act of 1914 and then the Heroin Act of 1924 had driven the opioid trade underground and created a black market. When pain patients, or those who were already addicted to opioids, couldn't get access to the drugs they needed, they found someone who would help out, even if that person was a criminal. And so we might expect a decrease in opioid prescribing to correlate with an increase in black market opioid use. And indeed, there is some indication that precisely this has occurred. At approximately the same time that prescription opioid use began to decrease, heroin use began to increase.

Making matters worse, today, heroin is much cheaper than illicit prescription opioids, so those willing to go to the black market to get their drugs are incentivized to switch to heroin. In a recent study, 75 percent of heroin users who began using opioids in the 2000s claim to have started with prescription opioids. But this switch to heroin is not merely swapping one dangerous drug for another; while prescription opioids are standardized, allowing consumers to know what they're getting, heroin is cut with all sorts of other products, some of which are phenomenally dangerous. Heroin is now regularly contaminated with illicit fentanyl, which, recall, is fifty to one hundred times more powerful than morphine, and it is increasingly even laced with carfentanil, which is used as a tranquilizer for elephants and is 10,000 *times* more powerful than morphine. Indeed, carfentanil is so potent that an amount the size of a grain of salt can be deadly.

As opioid-prescribing rates have leveled off and slowly begun to decrease since about 2012, then, the result has not been all that we hoped it would be. Far too many people are still dying from prescription opioid overdose, but even more are dying from heroin and illicit fentanyl. We have multiple generations of doctors, trained according to vastly different models of pain care, but we've told all of them to stop killing their patients with these dangerous drugs. As one might expect, this has been taken up in lots of different ways. Experts in pain medicine may feel comfortable reducing reliance on opioids while still aggressively treating pain. Stanford University pain specialist Sean Mackey, for instance, has very complex views on the appropriate use of opioids, regularly commenting that he has more than two hundred medications that he can use to treat pain, the vast majority of which are not opioids. Someone as expert as he is has a huge number of options to consider when treating severe pain, and a wealth of experience from which to draw when he does decide to prescribe opioids.

Most physicians, however, do not have Dr. Mackey's expertise. General practitioners, who cumulatively prescribe the largest percentage of opioids, tend to have none of the training required for the kind of sophisticated and nuanced care that a skilled pain physician can offer. This may lead them (as it undoubtedly has in the past two decades) to simply prescribe opioids, which they were told were effective and safe. Or, in light of the mounting pressures from the medical community, the government, and the public, they may see prohibition as the only reasonable option, hanging signs in their office advising patients that they do not prescribe opioid painkillers. Indeed, there are now even opioid-free emergency rooms. After all, if you don't know how to prescribe a medication and it's killing people, virtual prohibition may not seem like an unreasonable position.

And of course, there are probably many positions in between these extremes, where physicians uncomfortably prescribe opioids because it's what they know how to do, but they are also aware of how dangerous it is. I have spoken with many such physicians in re-cent years, and their position is a self-consciously nervous one: they know that opioids are dangerous, and they also know that they can be highly effective; they don't know, however, whether an opioid is called for in many particular cases, and so they end up making decisions *ad hoc*, in a way that is clearly not guided by evidence or experience.

The pendulum has begun to swing back toward prohibition, but it's not yet clear how far it will go this time. Pain patients who have been turned away from physicians may already feel like we've entered a period of prohibition. And yet, prescribing remains significantly higher than it was prior to the mid-1990s, and many thousands of people are still dying from prescription opioid overdose each year. We don't yet know what story history will tell about this moment.

Against the backdrop of this historical narrative, my experience of pain management is suddenly quite understandable. My entrance into the medical system in 2015 landed me smack in the middle of a culture change. I found myself surrounded by doctors who saw my traumatic and postsurgical pain as in desperate need of medication, and many of them had been trained during the "decade of pain," in which they had constantly been admonished to stop allowing their patients to suffer. The very existence of my pain management team, who was profoundly successful in getting my spiraling pain under control, is due to the swing toward aggressive pain treatment.

But I also found myself surrounded by doctors scared of the medication that could relieve my suffering. They were constantly told—in the newspapers, in continuing medical education courses, by the government, by their colleagues—that prescribing lots of opi-oids risks getting blood on their hands. When public figures take the stage to discuss the opioid epidemic, the message they hear is "You're killing your patients." Many doctors have told me that they live in fear of getting a call from the police saying that someone has been found dead from a suspected overdose and that their name is on the prescription bottle.

In addition, any doctor who *ever* treats pain has plenty of experience dealing with "drug-seeking" behavior: because we have a large population of patients wrestling with opioid use disorder, and a prescription pad is one place that such patients can get their fix, many physicians deal regularly with patients demanding drugs (sometimes violently) to feed their addiction. These are precisely the sorts of experiences that could easily lead a physician to withhold medication out of caution but also to express suspicion of patients who ask for opioid medication too aggressively.

And there I was, lying in a hospital bed in the wake of five major surgeries, begging for pain medication. I represented one of the medical community's most distressing dilemmas: a patient in obvious severe pain but begging for medication that is killing tens of thousands of people a year. The fact that different doctors, in different moments, treated me in radically different ways is completely unsurprising. Because no amount of public hand-wringing or blunt policy tools is going to make it clear what to do with patients like me. We're a problem, and there's no obvious solution.

CHAPTER 4

The Opioid Dilemma

Opioid prescribing happens all over the country, in all different kinds of clinical encounters, for all sorts of reasons. Many people think that pain doctors, anesthesiologists, and surgeons must prescribe the most opioids, and indeed, they do it a lot; but the physicians who cumulatively prescribe the most opioid painkillers are general practitioners, who see patients day in and day out for pain. And although this is changing, during the liberalization of opioid prescribing, dentists and oral surgeons also prescribed a surprisingly high percentage of all opioids, often sending patients home with a bottle of Vicodin or Percocet after relatively minor procedures.

One of the most difficult prescribing environments, however, occurs in the emergency room. In the ER of any major hospital, physicians are faced with the decision of whether to prescribe opioid painkillers on virtually every shift. Not only does the urgency of the situation make powerful pain medication a crucially important tool, but the fact that patients can come in to see a random doctor, rather than one's family doctor (or if one doesn't have a family doctor), makes the ER a natural spot for those "shopping" for opioids.

In a normal shift, then, ER docs are likely to see fairly easy cases in terms of whether to prescribe: there is likely to be a trauma victim, for instance, who clearly needs morphine or fentanyl for truly severe pain. Many such patients will look approximately like I did, or worse, with bones protruding through skin after an accident of some kind, or perhaps with gunshot or knife wounds. Most physicians are comfortable prescribing opioid painkillers in such instances.

Then there are harder (or at the very least, less comfortable) cases: the patient who shows every sign of opioid use disorder, and whose behavior seems to indicate that she or he is looking for a prescription to feed a habit rather than to treat (non-addiction-related) pain. Most physicians feel uncomfortable prescribing opioids in such cases, although they may prescribe them anyway—out of fear, the desire to get rid of the patient, or perhaps even a recognition of their limitations as clinicians; after all, they can't know for sure that the patient isn't in severe pain.

And then, of course, there are all sorts of cases in the middle. Patients come in with fairly run-of-the-mill injuries or moderate pain and can become upset if they are told to go home and take ibuprofen. Aren't doctors supposed to make them feel better? Or patients who undoubtedly have pain from an injury or chronic condition but also raise some red flags—they may be very young, have a history of substance abuse, suffer from a variety of mental health disorders, or have any number of other circumstances that increase their risk of addiction.

Now, as we know from the last chapter, depending on when these doctors trained, they may have been taught either that it is their duty to relieve patients' suffering with the powerful tools of modern medicine or that it is their duty to protect patients from the deadly risk of those same powerful tools. So on any given shift in the ER, there may be doctors who have completely different philosophies regarding opioid painkillers and who would handle the exact same patient in drastically different ways.

The central, ethical difficulty facing physicians in such a case is that neither "side" is straightforwardly correct. Return to our history lesson from last chapter: Does complete embrace of opioid painkillers work as a medical philosophy? Obviously not, as we are witnessing right now in America. But is radical rejection of all opioid analgesia the correct answer, then? Well, no, that doesn't look right either. After all, fear of heroin in the twentieth century led to many decades of unnecessary suffering. The important lesson to take away from America's history with opioids is that appropriate use is somewhere between unreflective embrace and unreflective fear of these drugs.

I refer to the challenge of living in this difficult, gray area between those two extremes as the Opioid Dilemma. What physicians recognize is that they have a duty to relieve suffering, which makes it very difficult for them to simply leave pain untreated or undertreated, especially when they have a powerful painkiller in their toolbox. But they also swore the Hippocratic oath, which commands them to "first, do no harm," and so they also are appropriately concerned not to prescribe a medication that might harm their patients in the long run.

In other words, the Opioid Dilemma is the very real, very difficult requirement that physicians take pain seriously and treat it responsibly, while simultaneously being responsive to the power and danger of a central pain-relieving tool—one that is contributing to an epidemic of addiction, overdose, and death.

So, how do physicians avoid undertreating pain while simultaneously avoiding overuse of opioids?

If medicine swings too far toward fear of opioids, we risk undertreating severe pain, and if doctors continue to be too comfortable prescribing opioids, we risk continuing to flood the country with dangerous medications. And if we fail to get clear on how to address this problem, we may well bounce erratically back and forth, without any real direction, undertreating pain and overusing opioids *simultaneously*. Indeed, this seems to be precisely what happened in my own experience, as multiple doctors prescribed ever-increasing doses of opioid painkillers right alongside other doctors who treated me with suspicion or undertreated my pain, likely out of fear of the medication.

The Opioid Dilemma simply names the reality of every physician who treats pain and who must decide for each patient if she is erring in one direction or the other. This is a hard problem. Unfortunately, the dilemma is even harder than it looks. This is because doctors—like all of us—make systematic errors in judgment. That is, they, and we, are *biased*. In the context of pain management, that means that not only do physicians tend to both undertreat pain and overuse opioids but their use of opioids follows predictable (and problematic) patterns.

When I was treated with suspicion by the attending ICU doc after my free flap surgery, I was hurt, ashamed, and, eventually, *livid*. I felt wronged by the physician, and it would be a long time before I could articulate the kind of wrong that I had experienced. But now I think I understand: the doctor had disrespected me in a very specific way, by not taking my words—my testimony—seriously. I told her that I was in pain, and by treating that claim as if it were the kind of thing that she should check on—because I was unreliable and might be trying to get drugs—I was denigrated in a way that I hadn't remembered ever experiencing before.

But here's the thing: the very fact that I could be surprised—no, *shocked*—at this doctor's ability to disregard my testimony reveals my privilege. Because as those in less powerful social positions know well, the experience of not being heard or taken seriously is a part of many peoples' daily lives. There is even a term for it in the academic literature: "epistemic injustice" is the experience of not having one's testimony taken seriously due to being part of a particular group. When a woman's suggestion is overlooked in a meeting, until the same suggestion comes out of a man's mouth, this is an instance of epistemic injustice. Or if a black man's opinion of the economy is ignored because of his hair and dress, this is epistemic injustice.

Whether intentionally and consciously or not, when someone fails to take the claims of another person seriously because she's a woman or a person of color or a member of any other marginalized group, this silencing is an insidious form of disrespect.

As a white man, I had gone through my life with the invisible (to me) privilege of largely having my claims taken seriously and my position at the table acknowledged. When I became a pain patient, I—perhaps for the first time in my life—became part of a group that is stigmatized and marginalized. Because pain is subjective, it's always been suspicious; after all, if there's any reason at all to "fake" pain, then patients have a reason to deceive doctors. And in the era of opioid plenty, there is a ready-made reason to feign pain: to get those good drugs. And so I, now a pain patient, was part of a group whose testimony is taken to be unreliable.

But of course, suspicion is not distributed evenly. Sure, pain may be a stigmatized condition, but some of us bear one such stigma, while others bear many. With all of my privilege due to race, gender, profession (recall that the one resident who referred to me as "Dr. Rieder" rather than "Mr. Rieder" is the one who got the ball rolling on my pain management consult), and likely much more, I managed to go through my entire hospitalization encountering suspicion only very rarely. That is, unfortunately, not everyone's experience.

To see how suspicion might be unevenly distributed, try to put yourself into the shoes of an emergency room physician (if you have no medical training, don't worry—I'll highlight relevant features of the story). Now consider the following case.

On a slow weeknight in your large university hospital, you enter an exam room to meet your next patient, Darius, who is grimacing and trying to massage his lower back. Darius is a young man, although he looks older than his thirty-one years. His baggy clothes are crumpled, his hair is disheveled, and he looks exhausted. He tells you that he's been struggling with severe back pain for years and that this is his fourth time in the ER this year—his chart confirms the visits. Each time, he was given powerful opioids, although in differing amounts.

Although he seems a fairly quiet and gentle personality at first, he quickly begins to lose his patience. After you ask whether he's tried ibuprofen and ice, Darius snaps, "You seriously gonna recommend Advil and ice for this? I'm *dyin'* here. My pain's an eleven out of ten, and you want me to put ice on it?" He goes on to say that the only thing that seems to work for his pain is OxyContin.

And there it is: the ask. Just write a scrip for this incredibly powerful opioid, and he'll be on his way.

For experienced physicians, several aspects of Darius's story raise red flags. First, the repeat ER visits, often in the middle of the night, complaining of what we can call a "nondefinitive condition"—a pain that often has no visible diagnostic presentation. Unlike broken bones, complaints such as back pain, neck pain, or abdominal pain may well be present without any obvious (to the clinician) reason. These are the complaints that bring the subjectivity of pain to the fore. All that the doctor has to go on regarding the patient's pain is his word.

Second, Darius rates his pain as an 11 out of 10. This is a dramatic move. Remember my own struggle in rating my pain, even after traumatic injury: assigning a 10 (or more) to a pain signals certainty that the pain couldn't be worse, and it's a bit difficult to believe that most people will experience this level of pain very often.

And finally, Darius asks for a specific, powerful medication: OxyContin, Purdue's blockbuster extended-release oxycodone—the same medication that I was given after each of my major surgeries. An opioid that is half again as potent as morphine.

These factors added up would lead many physicians to suspect Darius of drug-seeking. He comes into the ER late at night, complaining that his nondefinitive pain is off the charts and demanding a very specific medication with high abuse potential (and high street value).

The thing is: Darius's behavior is also explainable by being in severe, unexplained pain. The ER is the only place to go when the pain becomes crippling late at night; saying that one's pain is off the charts is what you would expect someone with off-the-chart pain to do; and if OxyContin has given him relief before, after other remedies didn't, then asking for it aggressively is pretty understandable.

So what should the doctor do? What would *you* do? Well, before you get comfortable with an answer, let's run one more check on our intuitions about Darius. Let's suppose now, that rather than Darius, the patient's name was Connor. And rather than saying that his "baggy clothes were crumpled" and that he looked "exhausted," I told you that he had removed his suit jacket and loosened his tie and that he looked tired from a long day at work. Now, finally, replace Darius's rather colloquial speech with a more entitled-sounding frustration; imagine that Connor says, "You're really going to recommend ibuprofen when both you and I know that it's not effective for serious pain? Look, I've struggled with chronic pain for years, and I get these attacks regularly. My pain is an eleven out of ten right now, so sorry if I seem a little short with you." He goes on to say that, while he realizes doctors are scared of opioids right now, he's been put on everything over the years, and the only thing that seems to work well is OxyContin, because it lasts for several hours, giving him a break from the pain long enough to rest.

Does your reaction to Connor differ from your reaction to Darius? Maybe it doesn't. But for some people, even if it's uncomfortable to admit, it probably does. And the reason it's uncomfortable to admit is that my description of these patients plays off stereotypes and bias. When I describe a patient named Darius, most readers probably picture a black man; and a description of Connor likely conjures up an image of a white man. And while the black patient is dressed unprofessionally and speaks conversationally, the white patient is dressed for a white-collar job and speaks in a way that (especially white) people hear as educated.

In other words, if you're afraid that you might have treated these patients differently, then what you're worried about is that your racial bias would have affected the health care you provide. In particular: you're probably worried that you would have treated the black patient as less likely to be in severe pain and more likely to be drug-seeking. And, disturbingly, if you made that judgment, you would not be anywhere close to alone.

Over the last couple of decades, research has demonstrated that white and black patients are treated differently when they complain of pain. A 2012 analysis of published data showed just how serious the disparities are: not only are black patients 34 percent less likely than white patients to be prescribed opioids for those "nondefinitive" conditions, but they are also 14 percent less likely to be prescribed opioids for traumatic and surgical pain. In other words, the pain of black patients is treated less aggressively *across the board*, both in contexts where the physician may suspect them of lying and also in contexts where their pain is undeniable.

Another recent study tried to explain why these differences might exist, and the results were appalling. The study, published in the *Proceedings of the National Academies of Sciences* in 2016, showed that a shocking number of people—including medical students and resident physicians—hold false beliefs about biological differences between black and white people. The survey asked subjects to say whether they believed a series of claims, including the false claims that "blacks' nerve endings are less sensitive than whites'" and "blacks' skin is thicker than whites'." Although relatively few of the medical students and residents endorsed the first claim (although some did), many endorsed the latter; in fact, a full 25 percent of resident physicians reported believing that blacks' skin is thicker than whites'. Even more distressing, physicians and medical students who reported more false beliefs about biological differences between the races systematically rated black patients as experiencing less pain

than white patients and recommended less aggressive pain treatment. Basically, having false beliefs about the difference between
races led students and physicians to undertreat the pain of black
patients.

The disparity in opioid therapy even extends to children. In
a 2015 study of pain management for children with appendicitis,
black children with moderate pain were less likely than white children with the same level of pain to receive any pain treatment. And
among all of those with severe pain, white children were more than
twice as likely as black children to receive opioids.

Nor does the unequal treatment of pain only apply to black and
white patients. Hispanic patients are also systematically prescribed
fewer opioids than non-Hispanic whites, and there is significant data
to suggest that women are less likely to have their pain aggressively
treated. In a 2001 paper, Diane Hoffmann and Anita Tarzian showed
that women are less likely to have their reports of pain taken seriously and to be prescribed opioids even though women have more
incidence of severe chronic pain than men.

A critical point about my story, then, is that it is undoubtedly
skewed. My brush with undertreated pain and being treated as a
drug-seeker was maddening, but it was also minimal. Indeed, the defining lesson of my personal story is the degree to which pain can be
treated in a truly aggressive fashion. But replace me with a black man
or a Hispanic man or a woman, and my experience likely would have
been very different.

This realization helps to put the Opioid Dilemma in an even
more complex framing: not only do physicians struggle to avoid
the dual burdens of undertreatment of pain and overuse of opioids, but those burdens are not evenly distributed across the population. White men are best positioned to have their pain taken
seriously, which raises serious concerns about both the pain treatment of minority patients as well as the respect they are given by
clinicians. Having one's pain undertreated is bad enough due to the

outcome (still being in pain); to know that it's because of one's race or gender adds the insult of injustice to the already existing injury. Further, the recent increase in opioid use disorder among white communities is also now suddenly less surprising. In this case, the privilege of having one's testimony taken seriously has come with a cost: treating the pain of white patients in a disproportionally aggressive manner has led to a similarly disproportionate increase in white patients with opioid use disorder.

The idea that opioids can be both underused and overused in the treatment of pain relies on a common belief, which my own story would seem to endorse: that opioids are good medications. And when I recall their ability to cool my own post-traumatic pain back below the point of seething terror, I get it: at times, opioids can seem downright magical. One minute, life is barely worth living; one shot into the IV later, life is a hazy daydream.

Given this perception, it's important to be clear concerning the costs of opioids as well. And boy do they have costs: everything from what may seem (to those who have never experienced them) like fairly mild side effects, like constipation (spoiler alert: this is *much* worse than it sounds), to constant grogginess, memory loss, mild hallucinations, and, most dangerously, respiratory depression. In short, life on opioids can be really difficult, and if we are going to be thorough in our appraisal of when and whether these drugs ought to be used, then we need to include an honest look at the costs as well as the benefits.

I had been heavily medicated for much of the month following my accident, but nothing compared to the first five or so days after the free flap surgery. The increased doses of oral oxycodone and gabapentin, combined with the regular doses of IV hydromorphone to control breakthrough pain, kept me somewhere between groggy and unconscious almost constantly. Especially in the hour or so after an

IV hit, I became accustomed to existing in a kind of mild hallucinogenic state that I called the "gray world." This is similar to the experience of some heroin users, who report visual and auditory hallucinations while on the verge of falling asleep; even the language is similar, as some recreational heroin users talk about the "shadow world" or "shadow men" they see during an intense high. While hallucinating is not common during more routine opioid use, the chance of it occurring goes up significantly with higher doses, making it unsurprising that my experience was more similar to that of a heroin user than someone on small doses of prescription painkillers.

The first time that I described the gray world to Sadiye, we both found it funny. The way it worked is that my eyes would slowly close, but without my feeling as though I'd lost consciousness—I would believe that I was still seeing and hearing the world, exactly as it was around me but in a kind of grayscale. I knew this was happening, but I would tell Sadiye upon opening my eyes that I hadn't realized they had been closed, because I didn't always know that I was in the gray world when I was there. So one day, I "woke up," or "came to," or whatever the appropriate verb to use is, and I asked Sadiye—totally casually—whether she and the nurse had just been doing yoga in my room.

"What's that, sweetie?" she asked, trying not to laugh at me. As I saw her surprise and hidden smile, I started to come more fully out of my fog and realized the absurdity of what I'd just said.

"Hmm. Yeah, you two probably weren't, in fact, doing yoga, huh?" She looked at me and we both cracked up.

A week or so later, after I had been transferred to a regular hospital floor, I began checking email and receiving visitors. In my backlog of emails, I found a note from a reporter, asking for a phone interview about one of my research projects. Evidence of my impaired decision-making, I told her that I was in the hospital recovering from an accident, but that I could do a phone interview. She quickly agreed, and we set up a time. Only afterward did I stop to think that

I wasn't always very coherent, and that I probably shouldn't trust myself to speak well or think clearly. Having already committed to the reporter, I asked two of my colleagues and coauthors to come visit me at the hospital and to sit in the room while I took the call, so that they could alert me if I said anything stupid. Miraculously, the phone call went fine, but it was a strange experience to realize that I couldn't trust my own brain.

Unfortunately, the side effects of prescription painkillers aren't always humorous or innocuous. After all, opioids can be fatal when taken in high doses, which is why America's opioid problem is often characterized as an epidemic or crisis: it is not merely that many people are taking the drug, or even that they are becoming addicted, but rather that many people are overdosing and dying. The risk of overdose and death is a result of opioids' depressive effect on the respiratory system—in short, taking high doses of opioids slows one's breathing and reduces the amount of oxygen that gets into the blood-stream (and so, ultimately, to the brain). In fact, although I never overdosed, this general feature of opioid use was definitely present in my case as well. The combined dosage of all of my medications de-pressed my breathing to such an extent that my oxygen level would regularly dip below 80 percent. If it got low enough, nurses would wake me up and put me through breathing exercises until I got the number back up near 100 percent. In other words, medicating severe pain with opioids involves some amount of flirting with the exact mechanism that causes overdose deaths.

I found out later from Sadiye that this was quite a frightening time for her, because my breathing would become so irregular—especially after a dose of the IV medication. So she would sit by the side of my bed and watch me breathe, listening as the pauses be-tween breaths got longer. If my breathing got too irregular, she would watch the oxygen numbers, ready to jump up and yell for a nurse if they dipped too low.

Opioids not only depress breathing, they also depress digestion, which is the cause of another well-known cost of opioid therapy—constipation. This is one effect that my nurses and physicians were very concerned about. I found it almost funny at first, since everyone who entered my hospital room asked about my bowels, but I eventually learned that opioid-induced constipation, or OIC, is not funny. Only after experiencing it did I start to notice how many commercials are on television marketing medications that are supposed to alleviate OIC. And now I know why these drugs are so heavily marketed: OIC is really quite terrible, and with the amount of opioids being prescribed, these symptoms must be widespread throughout America. Having OIC is like having a brick in your gut—as time went on and it continued to worsen, I became completely uninterested in eating, bending, or moving much at all. Further, these symptoms are not merely uncomfortable; opioids can slow one's digestion to such a degree that the constipation actually leads to a bowel blockage, requiring emergency abdominal surgery.

Ten days after the free flap surgery, I finally left the hospital to go home and ferociously guard my new, fragile foot. And that's when the costs of opioid therapy really began to weigh on me. The novelty of my situation was wearing off, and there were no immediate goals to "get through"—I had made it through five surgeries, and the plan now was simply to heal; but of course, that would ultimately take years. So we settled into a new, exhausting, terrible routine: I watched the clock so that I could take my pain medications the moment I was allowed, keeping my brain floating constantly in a vat of drugs; and Sadiye would do everything, for everyone—going to work and handling virtually all the childcare, while also taking care of me. Thankfully, my mom moved into our basement for a couple of months to help out as best she could, though she was a bit mobility-limited herself, thanks to a pair of bad knees. So although she could keep me from being alone all day every day, the burden of managing our home really fell on Sadiye. I was in pain, miserable from the constipation, and constantly groggy, while Sadiye was absolutely exhausted.

Our wonderful friends would regularly bring food, and sometimes come help out with childcare. Or they would just come visit to see how we were doing. Some of these I remember: my mentor from graduate school, who had supervised my dissertation, came out to the house and sat with me for a couple of hours, which I found very touching. But, being so heavily medicated, much of this time has actually been completely erased from my memory. For the year following, Sadiye would tell me that we did things, talked about things, and even met people that I don't remember at all. It's a strange feeling to lose several months of your life.

Opioid painkillers, then, come with a cost—a real one. Everyone's experience is different, and some people tolerate the side effects better than others. In all, I found the experience of being on opioids fairly miserable. Better than being in excruciating pain, for sure, but miserable nonetheless. If they hadn't been so good at dulling my pain, it would be difficult to recommend them.

But had they, in fact, been good at controlling my pain? It seems like an absurd question, after I've detailed the horror of traumatic pain. But what's important to realize is that over the course of two months, I experienced different kinds of pain. First, in the aftermath of the accident and the surgeries, I had severe, acute "traumatic" and "postsurgical" pain; it is difficult to imagine going through this experience without opioids. After the initial surgeries, though, my pain continued but became less acute—I was transitioning into a "chronic pain" patient. Given the damage to my foot, I wouldn't ever be pain-free again, and it would be years before my pain reduced to low, background noise. So what was the plan for my medication?

As I would come to realize only much later, my physicians had no plan for my medication, and so I kept taking it out of fear of the pain. And as I became tolerant to the pain-relieving effects of the opioids, my surgeons would write more aggressive prescriptions, increasing my dosage to keep up with the pain. I don't remember exactly what my pain levels were like by July, but I do remember continuing to watch the clock, popping pills every four hours, trying desperately to stay "ahead of the pain."

This mechanism of tolerance, combined with the side effects and dangers of opioids, is precisely why the medical literature now tells us something that initially came as a surprise to many in the healthcare community: opioids simply aren't very good medications for many kinds of pain. Traumatic and postsurgical pain? Yes. Powerful opioids are important and effective. But as the patient builds tolerance to the analgesic effects of the opioid, she will need more and more of the drug, and the respiratory depression will become more dangerous (increasing one's risk of overdose) while the digestive depression will become more uncomfortable. In addition, the general sedative effects can be dangerous as well. This is especially true for the elderly, who are at increased risk of falling while on opioids, but also for many other opioid patients, who may try to get back to their lives by doing things like driving without realizing that they are still impaired.

Making matters even worse is that chronic opioid use can actually have a perverse backfire effect—that is, opioids can actually make one's pain *worse* with long-term use. "Opioid-induced hyperalgesia," as it's known, leads opioid therapy patients to become *more* sensitive to pain as a result of their therapy. And because these patients are becoming more sensitive to pain, they feel worse and believe that they need more opioids. Hyperalgesia can then drive further use of the very pills causing the increased pain.

In light of these considerations, leading scientific bodies such as the CDC, the National Academies of Sciences, Engineering, and Medicine, and many others have issued guidelines emphasizing that opioids should not be considered first-line treatment for chronic pain. There is virtually no good scientific data supporting chronic opioid therapy beyond two or three months, and a wealth of high-quality evidence warranting extreme caution. Opioids are dangerous, and for long-term use, they don't work very well. Combine this with the observation that they have costly side effects, and the medical community has exceedingly good reason to be careful with these drugs.

The Opioid Dilemma, then, is devastatingly difficult. Doctors are charged, by us—patients and society—with prescribing a medication that can be both underused and overused. When I was in agony, withholding opioid medication was clearly a wrong; but overprescribing it is also wrong, and it is contributing to a massive public health crisis. Further, these risks are not evenly distributed, because doctors, like all of us, have biases. And to top it all off, opioids aren't nearly as good at controlling pain in some circumstances as we thought they were.

The question of when to prescribe opioids is clearly complex and challenging. And unfortunately, it's not the only such question related to opioid therapy. As I soon found out, there is also the challenge of when to take patients *off* of opioid therapy.

PART II

CHAPTER 5

Abandoned

In the middle of July, Sadiye and I found ourselves back in the orthopedic surgeon's office for another one of our very many follow-up
appointments. I don't remember a lot of specifics about how the day
started, other than we were filled with our usual nervous excitement.
Like always, I would be getting new X-rays, and we hoped that Dr.
Patel would have some more information about what my life might
be like in the future. These updates were a break in what was becoming an interminably long, difficult slog of just hurting, healing, and
occasionally hoping that I would eventually get back to something
like a normal life.

The visit did not, however, go as planned. Once I got the new
X-rays taken and we were shuttled back into the examination room,
Dr. Patel entered brusquely and began to run through his usual list of
questions, while hastily marking answers. When he got to the pain
question, I told him that I think the pain might finally be backing
off, as I had stretched as long as six hours between painkiller doses a
few times.

Dr. Patel's attention paused, and he asked somewhat carefully,
"So how much medication are you taking, then?" I had to pause to
calculate, and Sadiye and I did some basic math.

"Well, I take the twenty-milligram OxyContin twice a day,

and the fifteen-milligram immediate-release oxycodone every four hours," I replied. "But, like I said, I've stretched that a few times." I was quite proud of myself. "Oh, and the gabapentin, of course. That's three hundred milligrams, four times a day—but I've been able to skip my midnight dose pretty consistently now."

Dr. Patel turned serious, and all of his mannerisms slowed. My pride at what I thought was progress—completely self-initiated—evaporated. He was definitely not proud of me.

"Travis," he said, in a voice that I can only interpret as admonishing, "that's a significant daily dose of pain medication. You really need to be getting off the pills now."

And suddenly, I felt like a suspect—like I had done something wrong. *Had I* done something wrong? I had taken all of my medications, precisely as prescribed, deviating only to reduce my dose as I felt able, and yet I now felt as though I should have known better. I clearly had mishandled my medication, and it was enough to turn Dr. Patel into a serious, paternalistic presence.

I was caught so off guard that I don't remember the details of the rest of the visit. I sat in a kind of shock while Sadiye asked how we were supposed to go about reducing my medication. Since Dr. Patel hadn't been managing my prescriptions since the initial hospitalization, he suggested we speak to my plastic surgeon, Dr. Roberts, about a plan. We had an appointment with Dr. Roberts the next day anyway, so we added this item to the agenda.

In contrast to the seriousness of Dr. Patel's reaction, Dr. Roberts seemed almost surprised when we raised the issue with him. When we told him that we were instructed, in a fairly serious way, to get off the meds, he responded, "Well, sure; if you think you're at a point where you can handle it, then it's definitely a good idea."

Sadiye interjected: "Dr. Patel seemed to indicate that he can't just quit the meds altogether—that he needs a plan to wean off of them. How should we do that?"

Dr. Roberts's response gave no indication that he thought it mattered very much. "Well, the majority of your opioid dose is from the immediate-release oxycodone, and that doesn't really cause too many problems with dependence." (I have absolutely no idea why he thought that would be true. For the record: it's not.) "So I'd say to divide your daily dose into four, and then drop one-quarter of your current dose each week. If the pain isn't too bad, you should be medication-free in a month."

Sadiye was suspicious. "We should wean the opioids and the gabapentin at the same time?" she asked.

"It should be fine," Dr. Roberts responded offhandedly. "Gabapentin doesn't really have withdrawal effects the way opioids do, so it shouldn't matter too much." (It's a little more understandable that he thought this was true, as many other doctors I've asked also believe it; the standard line is that since gabapentin isn't an opioid, it doesn't cause dependence. For the record, this is false as well.) Sadiye looked unconvinced, but Dr. Roberts seemed totally unconcerned. And of course, he was the doctor. He must know best, we thought.

So after the appointment, we began to plan out the month ahead. Since I had already dropped my midnight dose of gabapentin, that first week, I would just reduce my opioid intake by 25 percent. And then each week after that, I would make the same reduction in opioids, while also dropping one of the gabapentin doses. After four dose reductions, I'd be done. Easy enough.

That night, I dropped my first dose.

Most opioids have a short half-life, and so the effects of withdrawal can be felt surprisingly quickly after missing a dose. For me, the sickness started within a day of the first missed dose.

The early stages of withdrawal felt, for the most part, like a terrible case of the flu. It ramped up sort of slowly, with nausea, runny nose, and the sweats. Having felt pretty bad while on the medication also, feeling bad in this way wasn't *so* much worse, although it was definitely different. I still tried to make myself shuffle outside to the deck once a day, and for a little while at least, I tried to force myself to eat; but it was hard.

On the second or third night, I started having more trouble sleeping than normal, and my frequent (and much-needed) naps were getting shorter. I felt caffeinated, almost, too alert to sleep, and the longer days and nights added to the overall terribleness of the situation.

At about day six, though, I noticed an uptick in how I was feeling. I certainly didn't feel good, but it felt like I had gotten better rather than worse overnight, and that was a big deal. Although the long week of withdrawal symptoms had really started to wear on me, making me wonder if I could survive a whole month of this, the small improvement gave me some hope. Maybe my body is getting used to this, I thought. Maybe I'll make it after all.

But then it was time to make the next dose reduction, and my already depressing life got much worse. The flu-like symptoms dialed up in intensity to a level that I really didn't think was possible. I would sweat profusely while lying in the cold of the air-conditioning; and yet, if I managed to force myself outside, I would be covered in goosebumps while sitting in the hot summer sun. My internal thermostat had clearly gone haywire, and it was disturbing to feel as though I were malfunctioning so systemically.

The difficulty sleeping ramped up significantly, and I no longer felt merely alert—I was jittery, and often, if I lied down to really try to sleep, my limbs would start to feel like they needed to be moved; I found myself kicking, squirming, and shaking constantly. The result is that I would spend more and more time just lying on the couch, sweating, shivering, jittery, not sleeping but exhausted. When people ask me what these basic symptoms of withdrawal are like, I often say something like, "Imagine the worst case of the flu you've ever had, and then multiply it by a thousand. That's a start."

Week two also added a new, disturbing symptom, and this one

was very different from the others. I remember sitting on the couch with my mom sometime toward the end of that week, and she mentioned that she would have to leave soon to go back to Indiana. I knew this already, of course—it had been the plan all along. She had been there for much of the summer to help out, but her other grandkids were going to need her when they started back at school, and that was coming right up.

When she said it, though, something very strange happened. I looked at her, felt suddenly and immediately overwhelmed, and then burst into tears.

I was sad, of course, that my mom was leaving. And crying in fact made me even sadder. But the sadness didn't seem to be the *reason* I was crying. Rather, my tears felt like another symptom—uncontrollable and disturbing. I'm not a big crier by nature, but that time with my mom opened the floodgates, and it soon became part of my life. One of my most vivid memories of those first two weeks is of me sitting on the couch with my mom, crying with my head on her shoulder like I was still her little boy, asking her, "Mom, what is wrong with me?"

Toward the end of that week, Sadiye decided to call Dr. Roberts to see if he had any advice. It took a while to get him on the phone, and when she finally did, she began to go through the litany of symptoms. Although she described everything in some detail, he seemed to have really only heard the description of nausea and discomfort, as his first suggestion was to drink lots of fluids and increase my use of stool softeners to help clear out my guts.

Sadiye and I looked at each other exasperatedly while he answered, and I just shook my head. He clearly didn't get it. Sadiye finally cut him off, saying, "I'm not sure you understand. He's really in pretty bad shape. Is there nothing else you can do?"

To our total shock, Dr. Roberts replied, "Well, if it's that bad, he can just go back on his previous dose for a bit."

I perked up a bit as I heard this answer come through Sadiye's handset: dodging the sickness definitely was an attractive thought. But almost immediately, my interest was replaced with incredulity. "And then what?" I asked.

Sadiye relayed my question, and he responded: "Try again later."

Although I won't deny that escaping the withdrawal was tempting, I couldn't believe that my doctor's best advice was to reverse course, with no better plan for getting through it next time. After Sadiye hung up the phone, she looked at me and I simply said, "No way." She nodded in understanding.

In my heart, I knew I wouldn't be able to make myself go through this again. Those first two weeks had been terrible. For the first time in my life, I was truly miserable—abjectly and utterly miserable.

At least, that's what I believed at the time. I thought I knew misery. But that's because I didn't know what was coming next. Looking back, I now think of the first half of that month as "uncomfortable."

I awoke with a gasp, clutching my stomach and violently rocking forward. It was dark outside, and the living room was lit only by the muted television. I was covered in sweat—the damp couch, pillow, and blanket all cool from the air-conditioning—and the nausea that had woken me up was significantly worse than it had been for the last two weeks.

I was disoriented and working myself up into a panic. What time was it? Where was Sadiye? I didn't remember falling asleep, but I thought it had been light outside. And now I felt really sick. Did I need to get to the toilet? That had certainly been the first, frantic thought when I woke up. But now that I was sitting, my stomach seemed to be calming somewhat. I slowly, tentatively looked around and tried to get my wits about me. It was fully dark outside, with no light at all streaming through the window over the couch or lighting the kitchen on the far side of the living room. Yes, I must have fallen asleep. Maybe I'd gotten a decent nap and Sadiye was getting some badly needed rest. Thank God. Now if I could just keep that nausea at bay.

As if on cue, my entire core contracted again with a painful spasm, and I knew that time was up: I had to get to the bathroom. Much too quickly given my situation, I sat up on the couch and swung my legs onto the floor, lifting the damaged and bandaged foot with my hands. I frantically stood on my good foot and grabbed the "knee-scooter" that I always kept beside me, resting the knee of my bad leg on the seat and launching myself toward the basement staircase with the other. I careened recklessly across the hardwood floor until I got to the head of the stairs, where I jumped back onto my good foot and grabbed the single crutch that we kept there for getting down the stairs.

Now came the scary part: under the best, calmest of circumstances, getting down the stairs safely was nerve-racking, and Sadiye often asked me to just sit down and scoot. I did not, however, have the luxury of a slow descent right then, and there was no bathroom on the main floor (a fact that had gone from mildly irritating to really quite a problem in recent months). So the stairs it was. I put the crutch under my left armpit, grabbed the railing with my right hand, and began my one-legged hobble down the stairs. Crutch down the step first, reach down the bannister, hop down a step on my right foot. And repeat. When I miraculously reached the bottom of the stairs without incident, I dropped the crutch and grabbed the walker that was waiting for me. The basement bathroom was off the short hallway that connected the stairs to the main lower-level living area, and I ran-hopped the five or six steps to it.

I was frankly astonished that I had managed to make it in time, and I threw the walker to the side to make room to maneuver myself through the skinny bathroom door, dropped to the floor, and hugged the toilet. And after all that: my stomach wretched and heaved but nothing came up. The muscles of my core gave a solid effort, but when it became clear that it wasn't working, they slowly calmed. When I was sure it was safe to let go, I slid away from the toilet bowl to the cold bathroom floor, shaking from the effort, and tried to wipe the sweat and snot from my face.

Of course I couldn't throw up, I thought; how long had it been since I had eaten anything?

As I laid there gathering my strength, I tried to think through the day, looking for evidence of real food in my memories. Only when I rewound all the way to breakfast did I remember what today was: today was my third dose reduction. Early this morning, I had woken up and not taken any oxycodone, nor had I taken any for breakthrough pain in the afternoon. I also hadn't taken my afternoon gabapentin. That meant, I thought as I looked at my phone to note the time, that as of a little more than twelve hours ago, I had decreased my total medication consumption by 75 percent in just fifteen days.

"Can Can?" I called out weakly to Sadiye, using one of our Turkish pet names for one another (it's pronounced like "John John," a play on *canim*—literally, "my life," or "my soul"). It was a silly thing to do. If she had been awake, she would have heard me career down the stairs, as I certainly hadn't been taking care to be quiet. But if she was asleep, I definitely wasn't calling out loud enough to wake her up, two floors above me. And as soon as I performed that bit of logic, I realized that she was clearly asleep and that I mustn't wake her up. She needed rest so badly.

So, after staying there on the bathroom floor long enough to convince myself that I wasn't going to throw up, I backed against the toilet, reached up to grab the seat with both hands, and unsteadily pushed myself up with one foot. From there, I used the various edges of the bathroom as makeshift crutches so that I could hop out to my walker in the hallway. By the time I reached it, I realized I didn't have the energy to get back upstairs, and I didn't like to navigate them without Sadiye around anyway; I had already survived one unsupervised trip so far that night—best not to press my luck.

Our townhome had a walkout basement, which consisted primarily of a single large room with a fireplace and a sliding glass door that opened out to a patio, plus the hallway bathroom I'd just emerged from. We had set the space up as an additional bedroom for guests—this is where my mom had been staying, but she was gone now, having just left over the weekend. So the bed was vacant, and that's where I was heading. By the time I made it, I was sweating again from the effort, but I also was fiercely cold all of a sudden and sprouting goosebumps on my wet, clammy skin. I wrapped the green-and-maroon-checkered comforter around me from both sides like a burrito.

Once in bed, I slowly began to calm down from the night's sudden excitement, and my breathing eventually slowed to a reasonable pace. The nausea had receded enough that I didn't fear needing to run to the bathroom immediately, and I began to wonder if I might actually be able to rest. I closed my eyes carefully, as if to let sleep sneak up on my body without its knowledge. But my body was on much too high alert for such an amateurish attempt: the minute my eyes closed, the telltale feeling of restlessness built up in my legs, and my eyes snapped back open as the discomfort settled in.

I didn't sleep again that night.

With that third dose drop, the general feeling of restlessness that had been making sleep such a struggle would turn into what I came to think of as the "withdrawal feeling." That first night was only a harbinger of many similar days and nights to come. It was as if I had a fire in my core, and it would spread to my limbs, causing them to twitch and kick. If I tried consciously to lie still in order to sleep, my legs would constantly move, keeping me from getting any rest whatsoever. And if I tried with all my might to hold my legs in one place, it was like electricity built up inside my muscles, threatening explosion if I didn't release it. Eventually, no matter how hard I tried, I would flex or kick and eventually thrash about.

Trying to rest meant being tormented by my inability to sleep, and I finally stopped trying. The key to avoiding the worst of the misery was to do something else so that I wouldn't immediately feel my body build up the electric energy that would undermine my efforts. But I also was much too uncomfortable to really concentrate, meaning I couldn't work, write, compose emails, read, or even watch interesting films that required an attention span. The compromise that eventually dominated my life was unobjectionable but undemanding television. I filled my days and nights with HGTV, the Food Network, and *American Ninja Warrior* reruns, during which I would fantasize about having a fit, working body. When I was feeling especially ambitious, I would turn on a serial drama (although not one that was too cognitively demanding). If I was lucky, I'd find exactly the right mix to calm and distract my body without too fully engaging my brain, and I would slip off to sleep for sixty or ninety minutes at a time.

Those were the good times. That's when I was able to distract myself from the nausea, the fiery, rebounding pain, and the inward focus on my suffering. Whereas the crying spells had initially assaulted me as symptomatic, feeling like a neural misfire similar to the goosebumps that I got while lying in the August heat, those same attacks now took on a different meaning. The crying now brought with it darkness, and I would feel whatever peace I had managed to scrape together on that day slip away from me as the sadness descended. It came from anywhere or nowhere, and when it did there was no stopping it; I could be watching *House Hunters* one moment, fairly comfortably distracted, and then feel the characteristic swelling in my chest that portended bad things.

When the darkness swirled in, my mind went to scary places. I began to genuinely mourn what had happened to me, and also to believe that it meant the end of the happy life I had known before. As the days dragged on, I became convinced that I would never recover—not from the accident, not from the withdrawal. My mind and body had been shattered, and it was like believing in a fairy tale to think that anyone could recover from where I was. Surely there is a point beyond which one simply doesn't bounce back, and surely I had passed it. And with the arrival of these thoughts, I came to truly understand something that I had only abstractly known before: I now understood clinical depression, and the way in which each of us, despite our sense of being an ethereal, mental being, is lashed to a physical body that can malfunction. My brain was malfunctioning, and multiple times per day it would send me to the darkest place I've ever been.

Perhaps if my doctors had told me what to expect with opioid withdrawal, I could have intellectually prepared myself for what I had to do in order to resist. I could have reminded myself that I knew why this was happening and that I would get through it. But I had no preparation, and no help, so I let the darkness steer me. I thought that I had special insight into just how damaged I was, and the answer was: severely damaged. Too far gone to be salvaged. A good portion of each day, then, was spent sobbing and wondering what I would do if this was my new life. For a while at least, the darkness was intermittent; after crying for a bit, I would start to pull through it, and especially when Sadiye was there to talk to me, I could start to right the ship of my emotions. But as the days wore on, the darkness came more often and stayed longer, putting more and more pressure on Sadiye to be there to pull me out of a tailspin.

Our lives settled into a very tight, very hard, very stressful pattern. Sadiye would spend time with me in the morning (indeed, she often woke up in the middle of the night to come check on me, and to see if I was sleeping at all). Then she would leave for work, dropping Sinem off at day care, and I would try to make it through the morning without a depressive episode. I knew that if I could make it until close to noon, she would come back home during her lunch break, and I focused on that whenever the morning got hard. One of the local health clubs had a therapy pool, and we had discovered that floating in its warm waters could help ease my symptoms. Although getting to the pool, changing, showering afterward, and getting home was an almost impossible amount of work, it was worth it in order to feel like I might survive. And because she's clearly a saint, my superhero partner found it worth the effort in order to be doing something that really helped. So she would dart home; help get me out the door, down the stairs, and into the car; get me out of the car and into the gym; help me into the pool (which, designed for handicapped individuals, was fortunately easier than it might have been); tiredly watch me float for an hour or so; get me out of the water and into the shower; help me get dressed; and then take me back home to the couch again, before going straight back to work. Every day, she gave me something to look forward to, and often that would be enough to get me through the morning.

The afternoons were harder. They seemed to stretch on much longer, and I quickly got to the point where I rarely made it through an afternoon without breaking down in tears. I'd always know it was coming, and I tried to fight it. The game was distraction and a desperate hope for real rest. If I could keep my brain occupied—or, even better, if I could get in a nap—I could sometimes make it through the afternoon without a call to Sadiye to talk me down from whatever mental precipice I found myself on that day.

My beautiful, wonderful baby daughter gets left out of a lot of this story, and that's really part of the pain; I simply wasn't present, so I barely remember her being there at all. I know that Sadiye was somehow managing to handle childcare while also caring for me and running the house. And I vaguely remember Sinem occasionally crawling on me on the couch while Sadiye sat apprehensively on the ottoman just inches away, watching so that she could jump up and grab her if she got too close to my foot or the surgical site on my thigh. But most of what I remember is solitude and pain.

I do, however, remember one particular day, as it changed my view of what my one-and-a-half-year-old daughter was capable of. I had made it the whole day through late afternoon without crying, and without the depression crashing in. I had dared to hope that this might mean I was turning a corner and that maybe I was going to get some of my life back. And then, around four or five o'clock, I felt the telltale welling in my chest and the darkness circling. The feeling immediately caused panic, and then despair. Sadiye picked up on the first ring, and I blurted out through sobs, "I almost made it today. Oh God, I'm so sorry. I'm so sorry I had to call you. I started to think I could survive this. But I can't. This will never get better. I'm so broken, baby . . . I'm just so broken. How can a body possibly recover from this?"

She was already driving home. "You will survive this," she said. "Your hormones and your brain, they're betraying you. But it will get better. Now just hold on. I'm about to pick up Baby Girl, and then we'll be home to take care of you." I said okay and hung up.

When the car pulled up outside the front window, right behind my spot on the couch, I tried to stop crying, as I always did my best not to let Sinem see me like that. But it was no use. The harder I tried, the more explosive the sobs became, and I eventually just gave up.

Sinem tends to enter the house like a freight train, and this day was no exception. When the door opened, she burst into the living room, singing at the top of her lungs. Until she saw me. She stopped babbling midsound and midstep, and her face turned serious. As she slowly walked over to where I was lying on the couch, I just cried to her. "I'm so sorry, Baby Girl. Oh God, I'm so sorry. I hope you won't remember this."

She didn't seem upset, though. She seemed in control. I was lying on my side on the couch, and so I was about eye level with her. She walked until her face was inches from mine, examining me intently with the deep, dark brown eyes that she got from her mom, and she asked, "Baba crying?"

"Yes, Baba crying," I told her. "Baba hurts, but it will be okay." I didn't believe it, but I was trying my best to be strong for my daughter.

And then she did something that I didn't understand and will never forget. She put her tiny little hands on my cheeks and held my face firmly while she looked directly at me. And then she kissed my eyes, one at a time. I had never seen her do anything like that before, and I could hardly believe it. Maybe she had learned that at day care; maybe Miss Mary or one of her helpers had kissed her eyes after she fell down one time. Or maybe it was just an incredible, empathetic intuition by my little girl. Whatever the explanation, I grabbed her and hugged her as tightly as I ever have, and I told her that she had just helped Daddy get through one more night.

As the week wore on, I became progressively worse. My increasing insomnia meant that I had even more time to feel terrible, and the depression circled ever more closely during the long, lonely nights. Sadiye decided to call Dr. Roberts back and push him for something more helpful. I listened at Sadiye's side as her frustration with the doctor boiled over.

"I don't think you realize how bad it is," she said to him. "He's miserable, around the clock, and the longer it goes on the worse it gets." She listened for a minute as the doctor said something. "No. He's already told me—he absolutely won't go back on the meds unless you have a better plan for dealing with the symptoms next time. Why would he go through this again?"

After she listened for another minute, she seemed at least somewhat pacified. "No, we haven't tried them yet. We'll do that right now."

As she hung up the phone, I was already working myself up: "I won't go back on the pills. I already told him. What kind of advice is that? I won't do it."

"I know, baby," she responded, already on the internet looking for another number. "But he actually had a good idea this time. He said we should try the pain management team that saw you after the free flap surgery."

And with that, a light bulb came on. Of course, I thought to myself. My doctor clearly didn't know what he was doing, but this also wasn't his primary job; he's a plastic surgeon. But the pain docs are the ones whose job it is to deal with pain and pain medicine. Surely the miracle worker from the hospital, who had been able to brew the exact right blend of medications to control my pain— surely he would know how to deal with my symptoms. Since he hadn't been one of my primary physicians (in fact, I had only ever seen him twice), it hadn't originally occurred to us to reach out. But the recommendation suddenly seemed obviously right.

We were never even able to speak with anyone from the pain team at our hospital. After calling around and begging to be put in contact with the doctor who had overseen my care, we finally reached a nurse who put us on hold for a long time while she tracked someone down. She did not, however, return with a physician; she returned with a message.

"Hello, Mrs. Rieder?" The nurse was on speakerphone, since we'd been waiting on hold. "I'm sorry to have kept you waiting. Unfortunately, no one from the team is able to see your husband."

I was confused, and Sadiye was furious. "What do you mean 'no one's able to see him'? Like—ever?" Her normally calm voice rose as she unfurled the incredulity we both felt. "I'm sure they're busy, but we just need to talk with someone. He just needs someone to help with the withdrawal process . . . from the medication *they* prescribed. Can't you just put someone on the phone?" I sat quietly, hurt, abandoned, while she tried desperately to convince the nurse that this was not okay.

"I understand your frustration," the woman softly replied. "But our pain management team provides an inpatient service. Their job is to get pain under control during a patient's hospitalization. Although they prescribe opioids to manage pain, they do not oversee opioid tapering or manage withdrawal."

Sadiye and I were in shock. It was beginning to dawn on us that none of the physicians who had actually prescribed these medications were going to help me get free from them.

Furious, we called the plastic surgeon back one more time, expressing our feeling of total helplessness. Sadiye, being a research scientist, had started using her breaks at work to search the medical literature for articles on managing withdrawal, and she had come up with a list of suggestions. After telling him about the pain team's comment, Sadiye ran straight into her pitch.

"I've been looking through the literature," she began, "and I keep coming across the growing evidence in favor of using Suboxone in an outpatient setting for weaning patients off opioids. Could this help?" Suboxone is a combination of the opioid buprenorphine and the overdose-reversal drug naloxone, and it has been gaining popularity in the treatment of opioid use disorder. The article Sadiye found demonstrated its efficacy in moderating withdrawal effects during tapering. In fact, I probably wasn't a good candidate for the drug, as it's intended to serve as an opioid replacement for those who cannot wean off other opioids directly—typically, those who have been using opioids for much longer than I had. But that wasn't in the articles she found, and we didn't know any better.

When the doctor didn't reply right away, Sadiye plowed ahead: "There's also significant data supporting the use of clonidine to treat restlessness, trazodone to treat insomnia, and several other drugs to help deal with the side effects of withdrawal. Can you prescribe any of these? Maybe even just the clonidine? If he could just get some rest, maybe he would make it through . . ."

Dr. Roberts, clearly uncomfortable with this conversation, took a deep breath. Apologetically, he finally said, "Look, it's obvious that I'm out of my depth here." He paused. "I'm sorry. My initial advice was clearly bad, but I won't risk striking further out into a part of medicine that I don't know. My official recommendation is that Travis go back on his previous dose until you can find someone more competent to safely wean him off of the medications."

Sadiye hung up. I was almost at the end of week three, and I was in agony. I felt like this had been going on forever, and I just couldn't imagine going through it again. Reversing course with no guarantee that it would be different next time just wasn't an option. I told Sadiye that I would stick it out. I think my exact words to her were, "If I go back on these pills, I'll never be free of them. I just won't be able to go through it again."

We buckled ourselves in for the rest of the process.

After I dropped my last dose and entered week four, I thought I would die—either from the withdrawal itself or by my own hand. I didn't tell Sadiye that, but I think she knew. The nausea became overwhelming, the flu-like symptoms worsened, and the restlessness became the defining feature of my life, preventing even short naps. I was in total despair, and I became wholly convinced that I would never feel normal again.

And the belief that I was irreparably broken—that was the worst. Because life in the throes of withdrawal isn't worth continuing if you don't think you'll make it out. I had to wonder if this was to be my life, and then, inexorably, I wondered what I would do if it was. Although I never thought to myself the precise plan, "I will kill myself," I knew it was the logical conclusion of my train of thought. If I couldn't get better, I couldn't go on living. No one could. This was hell.

But then I would think about my family, and about my sweet daughter kissing my eyes, and I would get a few more minutes of strength. And Sadiye would leave work to take me to the therapy pool, where she would sit there and watch me float—content, because she was able to do something to ease my pain. And I would pull it together for a little while more. That was our life. An eternal recurrence of cycles of mere minutes, trying to find relief from the worst of the suffering for sixty seconds at a time.

A few days into that week, I stopped sleeping altogether. I couldn't even nap, and not even the pool provided much relief, so we stopped going. It was too much work for too little payoff. So my very little, rare contact with the world was eliminated, and our tight little routine became tighter. Sadiye continued to call every doctor that had been in charge of my care, as well as any general internists we could find, but none of them could or would help. The constant message: we don't manage opioid withdrawal; that's someone else's job.

The nausea continued to worsen. I became haunted by the memory of launching myself down the stairs in the middle of the night to get to the toilet, so one night I asked Sadiye to set me up in the basement before she went to bed. Although there was no mind-numbing TV down there, at least I would have access to the bathroom without fear of killing myself, and I would worry less about keeping her awake during my long, insomniac nights. After helping me down the stairs, she made sure I had plenty of water, my computer, the books that I tried intermittently to concentrate on, and all of the pillows and blankets I could need.

"My phone ringer is on, baby," she told me, just like she did every night. "So if you need me, just call. Do you want me to set an alarm to come down and check on you in a few hours?"

"No, no," I replied. "One of us has to be functional. Please, get some sleep. When you wake up, I'll be one more night closer to getting through this." She kissed me and said goodnight.

Within a few hours, my stomach, as if it knew that I now had access to the bathroom, revolted violently. The second I sat up in bed, tossing my laptop to the side, I knew this was not a drill. I swung my legs off the bed and hopped directly down to my walker, where it had been perfectly placed to be utilized in just such an emergency. I was only a handful of steps from the basement bathroom, and I thought I would make it without incident. But as I set the walker to the side of the bathroom door and carefully but quickly tried a controlled fall to the floor, I slammed my damaged toes into the hard floor tiles and yelped as I reached out for the toilet to steady my fall.

The sharp pain from my foot shot up my leg and into my guts, intensifying the nausea, and I immediately hugged the toilet in preparation.

Just as with last time, I hadn't eaten much, if anything at all, for days (who knows how long), and so there was nothing for my stomach to rebel against. But unlike the last time, my body now seemed absolutely committed to vomiting, regardless of the presence or absence of food. My stomach heaved so violently that I would cry out at the end of each spasm, and as this continued on, I felt as though the muscles in my core were tearing apart. My face was red-hot, and it pounded with the pressure of my body's contractions. I don't know how long this went on, but it felt like an eternity. And when I was finally convinced that I was done for the moment, I simply slid to the ground, sweating, shaking, hot, cold, and sobbing.

And that's where I stayed for the night. When I tried to gather myself for the walk back to the bed, a fresh wave of nausea threatened, and, terrified, I grabbed the toilet and waited for another trip through hell to begin. I learned quickly that when the moment seemed to have passed, it was better to just stay put. After the second round of violent heaving, I reached up and grabbed the purple bath towel that was hanging next to the shower and fashioned it into a makeshift pillow.

The whole night, I lay there, on the cold, beige ceramic tiles, shivering and sweating at the same time, thinking about my life and what I would do if I didn't recover. How much of this would Sinem remember? Was she going to grow up with a completely incapacitated dad? And however much I might be committed to being there for my family, what was the point at which my presence would be a net negative for them and they would be better off without me? I was already a hardship to Sadiye, and must have been a terrifying figure to my daughter.

As the morning slowly arrived, I waited desperately to hear evidence that Sadiye and Sinem were awake so that I could call this horrible night over. And finally, I did. There were banging sounds in the kitchen upstairs, and babbling sounds from my blissfully unaware daughter.

With every ounce of strength I had left, I slowly pulled myself up to a seated position and tried desperately to stand. But I was too weak.

"Canim?" I tried to call out to Sadiye, but my throat, massively dehydrated and scorched by stomach acid, made only cracked sounds. I tried a couple more times to call to her, but they were making plenty of noise one floor up, and it was clear that I wasn't getting to them.

My phone was by my bed, which was the opposite direction from the stairs, so I made the decision to go straight for the stairs. After I finally pulled myself to my feet, I spent a minute at the sink, washing my face and hair and drinking from the faucet, trying to make myself more presentable than I felt. Then I turned to my walker and made the few steps to the landing. Sadiye might have been able to hear me, but at this point, I filled with a kind of sad pride at having made it through the night and wanted to pull myself upstairs without help. So I backed myself up to the stairs and sat down, using my arms and my one good foot to scoot up in a seated position, one step at a time.

As I got close to the main floor landing, Sadiye heard me huffing and puffing, the stairs squeaking under me. Oblivious to my condition, she sang out to Sinem, "I hear Baba! You wanna go find him on the stairs?"

I heard Sinem's tiny steps running alongside Sadiye's more measured ones just as I ran out of steam, my shaking arms no longer able to raise me up another step. I wanted so badly to just pop up the last two steps as they turned the corner to find me, but it all came crashing down at once—the horribleness of the night I'd just been through, and the sheer exhaustion. As I looked up to see Sadiye turning the corner, my weak arms gave out completely, and I slumped back down on the previous step. The breath I had been holding as I strained to push myself up exploded out as a sob, and the pain, weakness, and fear all came pouring out.

Sadiye's expression changed immediately to fear and concern. She jumped down the top steps to sit behind me and put her arms under mine, like she was a lifeguard pulling me to shore. She practically carried me those last two steps as I burst out, "I'm sorry, I ran out of energy; I'm so sorry I just couldn't make it to you." I was such a weight on her, all I felt I could ever do was apologize. But I also desperately needed her, so the apology was partly for my continual, selfish reaching out.

"Why didn't you call me?" she admonished. "You didn't have to come by yourself!"

Sinem was just watching, confused, while her mom held her dad, rocking him as if he were also a toddler.

"I didn't sleep," I blurted out. "Not a minute. I was on the bathroom floor. Oh my God, I can't survive another night like that."

I probably wasn't making a lot of sense, but Sadiye understood enough to be alarmed. She stayed with me, holding me until I calmed down. "I won't go to work today, okay? I can stay with you today. Does that sound good?"

"Okay," I whispered. "Yeah, that sounds good." And that's when I realized that I was genuinely scared for myself. I was no longer just in pain, or just depressed. I was afraid. And I didn't want to be alone.

"When you're ready, I'll get you to the couch, and then go drop Baby Girl off, okay? Then I'll be right back."

At the mention of her name, Sinem sidled up beside us and sat down, snuggling into the comfort pile that her mom had started. I laughed and sobbed at the same time as I put my arm around her. "I'll bet this is all pretty confusing, huh, Baby Girl?" She just snuggled deeper into us.

After we recovered a bit on the floor, Sadiye took Sinem to day care and came back home, where I more calmly told her the story. Now she was scared, too, and we decided that we really needed to expand our calling efforts to try to find someone who could help me. So we picked up the phone and computer and started googling and calling again.

We called everyone: every doctor who had seen me in any capacity, as well as any general practitioner in the area. No one would see us. Most of the time, we didn't even get to speak to a doctor. In the cases where we did, we were told more than once that I should simply go back on the medication. When, frustrated, Sadiye tried to tell one doctor how badly off I was, he told her to take me to the emergency room. "For what?" she asked.

"So they can put him back on the meds until he stabilizes," he responded.

After a couple of hours, we found an independent pain management clinic and excitedly called them; since they weren't attached to a hospital, surely they couldn't take the cop-out that they were an "inpatient" team. But, incredibly, they said much the same thing that my own doctors had said—that if my prescription was out, they could see me and evaluate my need for more opioids, but they specialized in controlling pain, not withdrawing patients. Sadiye was typically the one who called doctors, but either I had called this clinic or I asked for the phone at some point. Because I remember pleading with them, and I'm sure the desperation was evident in my voice. "Isn't there anyone there who can help me?"

The receptionist's answer didn't mean anything to me at the time, but I now realize that she had made a judgment about me. She slowly and carefully replied that my problem sounded like something for addiction services, possibly a methadone clinic. I was no longer the purview of pain medicine, but of addiction medicine, and so was no longer her (or their) problem.

Just as Sadiye and I were starting to think we were out of places to call, a nurse from the hospital where I'd had my free flap surgery called back with a recommendation: on the other side of Washington, DC, was a rehabilitation clinic that, she thought, would help manage my withdrawal. She had discovered the clinic while doing research for another surgery patient who had become dependent on opioids, and she believed that he had been successfully weaned. We excitedly called the clinic and were thrilled when the receptionist told us that they do, in fact, help manage opioid withdrawal. Our excitement abruptly collapsed, however, when she told me that the first available appointment was on Friday of that week. It was Tuesday. I practically begged her to find something earlier. I told her that it was an emergency, and that I was desperate. She responded that, in that case, I should go to the emergency room. All she could do was put me down for the end of the week.

I was deflated. In two weeks of calling doctors, this was our first solid lead, but I couldn't imagine waiting out the week. Each minute was awful. Four more days may as well have been four more years. I thought I wouldn't survive that long. So I hung up.

Sadiye and I sat together, and I cried. Although I was doing that a lot these days, this time was different. This time I was defeated. I asked Sadiye to fill a prescription of the lowest-dose pills I had, and I told her that I couldn't do it anymore. I would at least try to start back with a lower dose so that next time would hopefully be easier, but I just couldn't detox any longer. So Sadiye called the rehab clinic back, booked us for Friday, and then went to pick up my prescription. At least next time, I would have help.

When she brought me the bottle, I just held it in my hands. My disgust with those little pills was visceral, and I couldn't believe that I was going to poison myself with them again. It was already evening, so I told Sadiye that I would at least try to go to sleep before taking anything, just in case I was close to coming out the other side. I wanted to be done so badly. I actually went to bed that night, for the first time in a long time. Sadiye helped me navigate the stairs up to our bedroom and then set the bottle of pills and a glass of water on my nightstand. I committed to trying my best to get some real sleep before giving in. It was early—probably around ten p.m.—and I told Sadiye that if I was still awake at two a.m., then I would take a pill.

Within an hour, I was asleep, and I slept through the night. When I woke up a little before six a.m., with the first rays of sunshine streaming in through the bedroom windows, the first thing I saw was Sadiye, lying beside me, watching me with a peaceful smile on her face. My memory of that moment is so vibrant, as if my life had just gone from black and white to Technicolor. The color swirls of the comforter popped, and even the light brown of the bed frame seemed to be glowing. Sadiye's eyes peered out from behind one rogue curl of her thick, dark Mediterranean hair.

"How do you feel?" she asked hopefully.

"I feel . . ." I searched my brain and body, tentatively moving, fearful that I would awaken a beast that for now felt dormant. "I think I feel good," I said in disbelief.

Now, "good" is a relative term, and I almost certainly did not feel what any normal person would call "good." But compared to where I had been, I may as well have been able to fly. I estimated later that morning, as we got ready to leave the house for a doctor's appointment, that my symptoms had abated by 80 percent. They weren't gone, and the sudden restless twitches in my muscles would cause ripples of panic, as I instantly thought I was sinking back into full-blown withdrawal. But I never did. These were simply the last remnants of the process, which in fact would stretch out over months, but not in a way that was anything more than annoying.

"I want to go out to eat," I told Sadiye, suddenly overjoyed at the prospect of food. She said that she thought we could arrange that.

Coincidently, that first day I came out of withdrawal we were heading to my next follow-up with Dr. Patel. At this point, it was still an
open question whether I would ever be able to walk again, and much
depended on the rather unpredictable ability of my foot to stitch
together new bones from the remnant shards of the old ones. There
was no real risk of losing the foot anymore; the tissue was alive and
the transplanted tissue from my thigh was perfectly healthy. But so
much of the function I would gain depended on what the bones did,
and that just wasn't predictable. So each new X-ray was exciting and
scary, and we went into the day's appointment with the usual angst,
but also some newfound hope.

When the surgeon came into the room to discuss my newest
X-rays, he said hello and nonchalantly sat down in his swivel chair
to quickly look at the images of my foot displayed on the computer.
In anticipation of his arrival, I had already hopped up onto the
examination table and peeled the oversize sock off my delicate left
foot so that he could take a look. With his back to us, he tapped on
the keyboard a few times, changing images of my deformed bones,
while Sadiye and I held our collective breath.

And then, completely casually—with no sense of weight or celebration—he spun around in his chair to face us and said, "Well, it
looks like it's time to get you in a boot and try those first steps."

We were stunned. Sadiye grabbed my shoulder between both
hands and turned to face me with a huge smile across her face.
"I'm . . . I'm going to walk?" I asked timidly, as if afraid to believe it.

"I don't see why not," the doc replied. In the fast-paced manner
of someone important, whose time is worth a lot of money, he had
already stood while responding, crossed the examination room to the
hand sanitizer on the wall next to the door, and given it a couple of
pumps. As I waited for his words to sink in, he was already rubbing
the quick-drying soap into his hands and crossing to where I sat,
reaching out to give my foot a quick inspection.

But before he could quite get his hands on me—to his total shock—I burst into tears. The goodness of the day so far, in comparison with the sheer awfulness of the past month, was just more than I could handle. Sadiye held me, and one more time, I shook with sobs—but this time of joy.

When the surgeon, for whom bedside manner was clearly not a strong suit, laughed at my response (to be fair, I'm sure this wasn't normal), Sadiye quickly and unapologetically admonished him: "Hey, you have no idea what he's been through." She gave him a stern, protective look. "This means so much."

The doctor, perhaps a little self-conscious now, muffled his laugh into a warmer smile. He reached out a little slower now and, gentler than normal, rested his hands on my foot and ankle. "Well, just make sure you stop crying before you walk through the waiting room, huh?"

After a quick examination convinced him that nothing concerning was going on—no signs of bone infection, no problems healing—it was time for the main event. A medical assistant brought in a massive black plastic boot that had a large rocker on the bottom and that went almost up to my knee. It came apart into two pieces in order to settle my fragile foot into it, and it had four thick Velcro straps to hold it together in the correct supportive position. When it was finally on, it felt more like body armor than footwear, and I swung my legs off the examination table.

Out of fear and habit, I slid down onto only my right foot, holding the boot an inch off the ground.

"It's okay," the assistant said. "Go ahead and give it a shot." When I still hesitated, he offered, "You really can't hurt yourself in this thing. It's going to distribute your weight over so much surface area, there won't be much pressure at all on the injury."

The thought of putting weight on this foot that I had been protecting with every ounce of my energy was just terrifying, and it took me several seconds to slowly lower the boot to the ground and begin shifting weight.

"There you go. Now let the boot do the work and roll along that big rocker as you take a step."

And so I did. I finally transferred all of my weight onto the booted foot and took a step. The pressure was intense, but it was more strange than painful. My foot hadn't borne any weight at all in about ninety days, and I could feel every bone and muscle strain. But it worked, and I made it the couple of steps across the examination room to a chair where I could rest.

With a big smile, I sat tiredly and listened to our final instructions for going home: Only walk in the boot for now, and for anything more than a few steps, use a cane for extra support. Time, too, to get started with physical therapy, so find someone you like and get going. Watch yourself, don't overdo it, but it's time to start trying to get that foot (and body) back into shape.

I heard the instructions, and they all sounded helpful, but I wasn't really paying attention (luckily, Sadiye was, and was able to repeat them to me later). I was content to bask in the glory of my newfound ability—putting one foot in front of the other, the same thing that my toddler could do, and yet it still felt like such an accomplishment. I had come out of a month of excruciating withdrawal and taken my first steps all in one day, and it was just almost too much to bear. I was so profoundly happy.

The joy of that day was captured on digital media a little later, when we stopped at a favorite French bakery for our celebration lunch. After I very slowly, very carefully walked from the car to the sidewalk outside the restaurant, I asked Sadiye to snap a quick picture to document our day of success. In the image, I'm wearing the scruffy beard of someone who hasn't left the house much in the past several weeks, but it can't hide my giant smile as I raise my arms victoriously, standing on my own two feet.

That was a good day.

CHAPTER 6

Dependence and Addiction

For many weeks, my overriding emotion was gratitude—gratitude of a sort that I had never experienced before. I was grateful to Sadiye for carrying me through my battle with opioid dependence, and to Sinem for giving me a reason to fight; I was grateful to be alive; and I was grateful for *wanting* to be alive. So filled with joy and gratitude, it took a while before righteous anger could fully take root.

But take root it eventually did, and as time passed, I became more and more distressed at what had happened to me. The distress came from a sense of betrayal: my doctors were supposed to make me better, and they certainly weren't supposed to hurt me. They are healers, whose oath begins with those well-known words, "*Primum non nocere*," or "First, do no harm." And yet, they had given me a medication that would, if not properly managed, cause serious suffering, and then abandoned me. How could this have happened?

At this point, I know that I might come off a bit dramatic. It certainly seems my doctors screwed up somewhere, and I got hurt. But it happens. People mess up, other people get hurt, and many times, it's much worse than what I experienced. I made it through, and I'm little worse for the wear. So perhaps I should just get over it. Right?

Indeed, this exact train of thought occurred to me many, many times over the months following my opioid withdrawal, and it led me to keep my suffering a humiliating little secret. The number of people on earth who knew what I had gone through were countable on my two hands. But the anger didn't go away. Something didn't sit right with my dismissive explanation of, "It happens." Something felt very wrong about the way I had been treated, and it didn't have only to do with me—what began to feel so wrong about my experience of pain management was how unconcerned my doctors were about such a serious and predictable harm. The question that slowly emerged, and which haunted me for months afterward, was, "Whose responsibility was I?"

Sadiye and I discussed my withdrawal *ad nauseam*, and we slowly began to get far enough away from the trauma of it to tell close friends and family. In discussing it aloud, we began to find a language and a framing that made sense to us: no one knew whose job it was to take care of me, and I slipped through the cracks.

But putting our hypothesis into words like that would outrage anyone who cared about us: "How could you slip through the cracks? It's not as if they haven't done this before!" Friends would get worked up and start to yell. It wasn't long before our very smart, kind, and wonderful inner circle would make the obvious connection that we hadn't fully made yet, saying things like, "In the midst of an opioid epidemic, these doctors are handing out drugs like candy, and then cutting you loose?!" Sarcastically, they would finish, "How shocking that our country has a problem with prescription painkillers."

The more of these discussions we had, the more I began to be able to distance myself from my own personal suffering and begin to take an intellectual interest in what had happened to me. After all, I'm an ethicist by profession—a *bio*ethicist, whose very job it is to investigate moral challenges relating to medicine, science, and public health—and something had gone very wrong in my encounter with the health-care system. The question that practically raised itself, then, was: does my individual experience provide any insight into broader problems in medicine? And the nearly inescapable answer is that it does.

To be clear: I don't think this because I believe I'm special, and so people should listen to me. Indeed, the importance of my case is that I'm not special. Nothing about what happened to me was unique to my circumstances. Millions of people, from all over, are seriously or gravely injured and are inducted into the healthcare system in a way similar to me. They are given lots of opioid medications and will predictably be on them for weeks or months. And, like me, many of them will plan to be off the medication at some point. The mechanisms of *tolerance*, *dependence*, and *withdrawal*, though, make this exit from opioid therapy more challenging than simply stopping the medication when it's no longer needed: stopping the medication *hurts*, because the body has become accustomed to it. Which means that it must be someone's job to help patients escape the grip of this medication.

The complete unconcern of so many physicians—physicians at major hospitals in large American cities who are leaders in their fields—seems to indicate that my problem was not a one-off. The challenge here is systemic, baked into the way our health care is structured. The doctors who prescribed my medication somehow didn't see it as their job to help me get off that medication. While I found that surprising, they seemed to have a point: pain medicine is complex, and there is a specialty for dealing with that complexity. So I was sent to pain management.

The problem at that point was that pain management seemed to take its job very literally: both pain specialist teams we sought help from delineated their job as *managing pain*. They could prescribe these dangerous, highly addictive medications, but tapering and withdrawal management were not in their purview.

Again, this struck me as surprising, since this is the discipline specifically trained to deal with complex pain patients, and these physicians presumably know the most about the medications involved. When I spoke to the receptionist at the second pain management clinic, though, I heard something in her voice that finally helped me understand what might be going on. When she heard my desperation, what she heard was the need for addiction services. Although her specific guidance was the particularly unhelpful suggestion of a "methadone clinic" (more on that unhelpfulness later), what she led me to see was that for doctors, the problem of managing opioids is tied up in their addictive potential.

Opioids are complex drugs, and they're scary ones too. They're not only potentially deadly, they're also addictive; they most often kill by getting their hooks into someone who then feels like they *need* the drug, and so will take more and more of it. This property of opioids makes them disconcerting to work with, but it is also not always well understood. And, in my view, this is part of why patients like me are far too likely to fall through the cracks of our complex medical system.

When the receptionist at the pain management clinic suggested that I contact someone in addiction services, I remember being surprised by her recommendation for a very simple reason: I didn't think I was addicted to opioids. I had a violent physical reaction to stopping the drug, sure—but I didn't *want* opioids, take more than I needed, or use them compulsively. In short, I had internalized the basic distinction described in modern science between "dependence" and "addiction," and what seemed obvious to me is that I was dealing only with the former.

In order to understand the distinction between dependence and addiction, we need to return to some of the basic science of how opioids work in the body. Recall that the body's opioid receptors—which typically respond to the body's own opioids, such as endorphins—are responsible for both blocking pain and causing euphoria. When an artificial source of opioids is introduced, these receptors have both an immediate and a longer-term response. First, in the short term, they go wild, capable of both providing significant pain relief and releasing a euphoric rush the likes of which most people would never experience naturally; that is, you get truly "high"—a feeling that many describe as being wrapped in a warm, comforting blanket, with pain, worries, and stress melted away. Your entire body relaxes, and core systems like heart rate, breathing, and metabolism all slow down.

In the longer term, though, the brain tries to adapt to this new environment of opioid plenty so as to achieve normalcy. This is because the brain is, basically, a learning machine that responds to new situations by becoming accustomed to them and trying to reestablish its normal balance. The more times that a flood of opioids is introduced, the harder the brain works to adapt to this new situation, reacting less strongly in the presence of the opioid. The result is the phenomena of *tolerance*, which means that more of the drug is required to achieve the same pain-relieving or euphoric effects, and *dependence*, which means that removing the source of opioids induces withdrawal symptoms. Withdrawal is, to put it simply, the opposite of the drug's effects: symptoms typically include dysphoria, hyperalgesia (increased sensitivity to pain), restlessness and insomnia, as well as nausea and diarrhea.

After two months of escalating opioid therapy (escalating, we now know, as a result of tolerance), I was clearly dependent on the medication, so taking it away sent me into withdrawal. But this physiological dependence is not the same thing as addiction. Addiction is more—it involves something else. But what, precisely?

It turns out that this question is surprisingly hard to answer. Most obviously, addiction involves some kind of problematic behavior—often drug use, but sometimes nondrug behaviors as well, such as gambling or, depending on which expert you ask, maybe even sex. But the behavior itself does not characterize addiction; after all, very many of us consume drugs like alcohol without developing alcoholism and partake in gambling and sex without developing addictions to these activities.

So addiction involves more than partaking in certain behaviors.

And if we look to our preconceived ideas about addiction, it becomes clear fairly quickly what the difference between an addiction and nonaddictive behavior really is. In short, addiction is a *problem*. Whereas my drinking causes me no problems, drinking driven by alcoholism can destroy a life. Alcohol or heroin or even gambling, for someone with the relevant addiction, becomes the all-consuming focus of her life, replacing values like work, family, and health. Addiction, then, is not merely a habit; it's a harmful habit that can seem to change the very identity of the person suffering from it.

When the behavioral component of addiction is made explicit, it's easy to see why, as we saw in our earlier history lesson, addiction has often been taken to be a moral failing. Humans act for reasons, and we judge them, blame and praise them, and hold them accountable for so acting. Addiction, then, is basically an affliction during which people make bad decisions that hurt themselves and other people. When someone acts as though heroin is the only thing in the world that matters, and creates a life that reflects that valuation, it's understandable to take them to have revealed their bad character.

Thankfully, the science has moved beyond this view. That's not to say all of us have: the very intuition I just outlined is hard to resist. For those who have known or loved someone with an addiction, it can feel almost impossible not to blame them at least occasionally. After all, watching an addiction bloom is basically the process of watching someone repudiate an entire set of good, understandable values and replace them with a singular, destructive drive: pursuit of the desired thing.

Advances in psychology and neuroscience, however, have slowly led to a replacement of this older, "moral model" of addiction. We now know that certain people are more likely to develop an addiction, as a result of a complex interplay between genetics and their environment. And the development of the addiction itself leads to changes in the structure of the brain—changes in particular to the reward and motivation centers—that distort how someone with addiction sees good and bad things in the world, and how easy or difficult it is to act according to one's different values.

These insights into the science of addiction have slowly led to a medicalizing of the phenomenon, according to which addiction is an affliction that happens to people rather than a choice that people make. A benefit of this view is that it allows us to destigmatize addiction to a degree: it's not a moral failing, and so judgment is not the appropriate response. Indeed, if addiction is some kind of affliction that some of us are more likely to experience through no fault of our own (due to genetics and background), empathy is a much more reasonable response to addiction than is judgment.

The dominant scientific view of addiction today takes this move away from choice to its most extreme conclusion. As described in the bible of psychiatry, the *Diagnostic and Statistical Manual of Mental Disorders*, fifth edition (*DSM-5*), addiction should now be thought of as a chronic, relapsing brain disease, characterized by craving and compulsion—experienced as an inability to refrain from pursuit of the object of addiction, despite harmful consequences. Addiction on this model is often described by use of the "3 Cs": craving, compulsion, and lack of control. So those neural changes that science has discovered? They are appropriately called pathological, meaning that addiction is an actual disease. And the symptoms of the disease, thanks to the particular neural pathologies, involve a lack of control. To develop an addiction, then, is to become sick and as a result to be unable to pursue the life that one wants and values.

Although the brain disease model of addiction has taken center stage, it is not uncontroversial. The very motivation to see those suffering from addiction as suffering from a disease, and so deserving treatment rather than punishment, can be taken too far, critics say. Sure, by telling someone that they "have addiction," which is essentially like "having schizophrenia," we help destigmatize their condition. It's not their fault that they suffer from addiction, we can say, and so their inability to stop drug use isn't their fault. But doing this also undermines the possibility of taking responsibility for their own recovery—it undermines their agency altogether. The casualty of the disease model, according to this line of criticism, is our ability to recognize those with addiction as full persons, able to exercise judgment. Not only can this be demeaning ("You can't recover on your own—you need medicine, because you have a disease"), but it undermines the accomplishment of the millions of people who *do recover* from addiction on their own.

Many of the critics who have this sort of problem with the brain disease model think it should be replaced with something more like a "learning" or "developmental" model of addiction. This group includes scientists like Carl Hart and Marc Lewis, as well as journalist Maia Szalavitz. In Szalavitz's colorful language, telling someone with an addiction that they have a "broken brain" is both misleading and unhelpful. The addicted brain isn't broken—it's merely learned a devastating habit too well, or developed in a way that makes what we think of as normal functioning much harder. Rather than seeing the brain as broken and in need of a cure, seeing the addicted brain as problematically developed calls for further development. The appropriate response to addiction, on the learning model, is more learning. Addiction is the result of a brain learning bad habits, so the way to fix addiction is for the brain to learn better habits.

I will not, in this book, attempt to adjudicate between the brain disease and learning models of addiction. There is a deep and fascinating literature discussing whether we should call addiction a disease, and wading into it would be the goal of a very different book.

As a philosopher, though, I do think I can help us understand why the stakes seem so high in this debate. While criticism and defense of the brain disease model often take the form of a debate in science, it's important to understand that our models of addiction are not wholly *scientific* theories; they are at least partly *philosophical* theories.

Take the *DSM-5* definition again, particularly the 3 Cs: addiction is defined by the inability to control compulsive behavior, even in the face of negative consequences. So was I ever addicted to opioids? Well, that depends on whether I experienced uncontrollable, compulsive urges to pursue the drug, even as it harmed me. But whether or not I could control my actions—let's put it a little more baldly, whether or not I was *free to act* how I wanted—is not a scientific question; it's a philosophical one.

Central to our understanding of addiction, then, is the thorny, very difficult set of issues surrounding when beings like us are able to make free decisions. And, completely unsurprising to a moral philosopher, the question of whether or not someone is acting freely when they pursue their addiction is intimately tied to whether we hold them responsible, blame and shame them, and so on.

The radical reaction against the moral model of addiction, then, rejects the idea that addicted behavior is free by going all the way to the opposite end of the spectrum: addiction is an affliction that is completely outside one's control. At least part of the criticism of this broken brain model, then, is the philosophical one that you can't escape from moral judgment without sacrificing the freedom to encourage and celebrate recovery. Everyone agrees now that the addicted brain is different, and that this helps us to explain the harms of addiction; but whether we call that change a disease that must be medically managed or a problematic development that we should address through further, corrective development helps us to understand how much responsibility to assign to those suffering from addiction.

Even though I don't know whether it's more helpful and appropriate to call addiction a disease, I do believe that we can be more careful about our philosophy of addiction, regardless of that decision. This is because we do not need to completely undermine the agency of someone with addiction in order to empathize with them, and to move away from a model of blame and punishment.

Consider an important study that Carl Hart describes in his book *High Price*. In a safe, residential setting, he offers people who are addicted to crack cocaine either a hit of free, pharmaceutical-grade cocaine or $5. In this setting, study subjects quickly become careful, calm reasoners, taking the drug some of the time but often opting for the money. They do not, as our intuitions about someone with a desperate addiction might suggest, merely go wild smoking the drug constantly until it kills them.

Surprising though some people find this conclusion, it really shouldn't be. Most people with an addiction to, say, heroin, don't shoot up in front of their boss, nor do they make a desperately needed buy if they realize that the seller is an undercover cop. Further, when provided with important services, many people who use drugs are perfectly capable of choosing to use clean needles, test their drugs for the presence of fentanyl, and, eventually, seek treatment.

Someone with an addiction, it turns out, is perfectly able to make at least some choices freely, at least some of the time. Having an addiction is not the same thing as being a robot or a zombie.

This does not mean, however, that the choices of someone with an addiction necessarily reflect their values. The language of "compulsion" and "inability to control" are intended to make clear that addiction seems to undermine our ability to refrain from drug use, even when it's obvious that this use is harmful.

Several philosophers describe models of our values and desires that are helpful in understanding what's going on here. Perhaps most famously, Harry Frankfurt describes a view in which we all have immediate desires—desires for sleep, pizza, binge-watching Netflix, and, for some of us, alcohol or other drugs like opioids. But we also have "higher-order" desires—desires about which of our immediate desires should actually move us to action. Although I certainly harbor Netflix desires, I also have the higher-order desire that I don't cave in to Netflix when I have work to do. I want my desire to be a good scholar and writer to "win out" and lead me to write instead of binge-watch. These higher-order desires, then, are more representative of who I am, such that putting off TV for the sake of work is a vindication of my real identity.

Of course, not all philosophers agree with the details of Frankfurt's view, but the general model that distinguishes between higher-order, or more central, desires and values and those that are more peripheral is a popular one. On this sort of view, we can make sense of what it means to be weak-willed—or as philosophers like to say, "akratic" (from the Greek *akrasia*, for "weakness of will"); sometimes, it turns out, my work loses out to Netflix. But we can also understand why we think that's a deviation from who I really am—because I in fact care more about my writing than about television.

This sort of model also helps us to understand what happens in addiction. Addiction comes with incredibly strong desires that pull people toward some behavior, but we most often recognize that the person wrestling with this affliction doesn't actually value the object of addiction more than anything else. Most of us value family, friends, work, and all sorts of other commitments incredibly highly, but addiction leads us to act as though those weren't our values. But if this isn't merely weakness of will (people who use drugs habitually aren't just succumbing in the way I succumb to Netflix), then there must be something wrong. And the science confirms this: the addicted brain has developed circuitry that makes those lower-order desires—which we do not, on reflection, endorse—pull us with incredible strength toward action. The addicted brain, in other words, has an incredibly hard time doing what the rest of us do fairly effortlessly, which is aligning our desires with what we genuinely value.

This difficulty *undermines* the agency of someone with addiction, in the sense that it challenges their ability to act as they want. It isn't hard for me to decide not to have a drink tonight if I have a lot of work to do or want to be awake early tomorrow. But for someone with alcoholism, that might be intensely difficult. Whereas I have something like the normal range of ability to act on my higher-order values, the presence of addiction puts a massive weight on the scale, pushing toward pursuit of some very particular behavior. And since the higher-order values are the ones that more represent who the person is, an addiction is a genuine challenge to one's identity in that it leads them to act contrary to what they care about. As philosopher Brendan de Kenessey puts the point: when addiction leads someone to abandon his family or lose his job, it's not that he's changed his values; it's that he—the part of his mind more representative of who he is—has lost the battle to his supercharged cravings.

Focusing on the difficulty of acting in line with one's values, rather than on the impossibility of doing so, does what I think we must do: it explains simultaneously why empathy is the appropriate response to addiction and why we should also bolster and recognize the exercise of agency when it's possible.

If you have the kind of brain that doesn't make pursuit of some drug feel virtually irresistible, then you are incredibly fortunate. That makes acting in line with your values much easier than it could be. And so when we see someone in the grips of a heroin addiction, our response should be empathy for her plight. After all, in order to do the central task of identity building that we all take for granted—the acting on one's central values—she would need to move motivational mountains. Failure to do something so hard is understandable, and we should want, more than anything, to help her if we can.

If she's able to find her way to recovery, though, we don't give the credit only to doctors or medicine. Because what she had to do was incredibly difficult, and she did it. That's an amazing achievement that we should recognize on the millions of occasions where it does happen.

So is this challenge to free will the kind of thing that warrants calling addiction a brain disease? I don't even know how to go about answering that question. But what does seem clear is that it's an "affliction," an unfortunate "condition," and related to one's health. After all, as we'll discuss in more depth later, addiction is treatable with medication, and so locating the affliction within medicine doesn't seem unreasonable. But that terminological debate doesn't seem to be what's most important to me. What's most important is to recognize that addiction is a behavioral affliction that sufferers experience as a threat to their very ability to act freely on their central desires and values.

This takes us back to why I didn't think I was addicted to opioids. I had a house full of pills—with doctors pushing more on me—and I didn't find it difficult not to take them. Well, at least not profoundly difficult. Not in a way that felt like it threatened my ability to act freely. They would have alleviated my suffering, sure, and so I wanted them. But I was able to reject that lower-order desire in favor of higher-order ones, such as getting healthy for my family. No, compulsive pursuit of the drugs despite bad consequences just didn't seem to be my problem.

The best explanation of my situation is that I was *dependent* on opioids, and so not taking pills hurt; but I wasn't *addicted* to them, and so I didn't feel compelled to take them. Why, then, did the woman at the pain clinic recommend that I go to addiction services? What about my situation made her think that was where I would receive help?

In fact, the tendency to push patients like me off onto addiction medicine is entirely understandable, once we get a sense of how addiction has been (and still is, in many ways) perceived by the public. And the story of this public perception takes us back to the character of the "junkie."

The junkie, recall, was a creation of the popular imagination in the early twentieth century, during the first days of narcotic prohibition. In reaction to the epidemic of addiction, overdose, and death that had plagued the country upon the release of Heroin, the U.S. government launched a prohibitionist series of policies that eventually led the politicians and the public to demonize those who fell under the spell of drugs. By making drug use a crime, the government turned those who used drugs into criminals, and their inability to quit using despite the consequences was evidence of their corruption. These creatures were too weak, and their resulting addiction was a moral failing. They couldn't control their own behavior, and they were not to be pitied or helped but judged and avoided. The image of the junkie that sprang up was the sweaty, shaky, desperate man, willing to do anything to relieve the pain of his withdrawal—the "dope sickness."

This image of the junkie does two things: it runs together elements of biological dependence with addiction, and it stigmatizes the whole package. And this is not surprising, as the science of the time did not see addiction as its purview. Addiction was the result of choice, not disease; if one got hooked on drugs, there was no language to distinguish between "chemical hooks" and "psychological hooks." In the view of "civilized society," the addict did something bad, wrong, and stupid, and then was too weak to stop. The language of the junkie helped the rest of us to maintain a sense of distance and superiority. *We* weren't like *them*.

The field of addiction medicine slowly developed over the second half of the twentieth century, and the idea that addiction is a disease began to take hold, eventually becoming dominant. But the legacy of the junkie still haunts us, and in fact the language is still widely used. America's so-called War on Drugs, ostensibly to remove the supply of addictive substances that could corrupt innocent people, treated those suffering from addiction as criminals rather than victims. Taking illegal drugs was a sign that one deserved jail, not treatment. And while many of us would like to think that this view is now, finally, solidly in our rear-view mirror, U.S. politicians and lawmakers continue to find it hard to abandon old habits. Following his appointment by Donald Trump in 2017, then–Attorney General Jeff Sessions made clear his own view that the War on Drugs isn't over, and that the United States needs to return to the aggressive policies of previous decades.

Even clinicians and practitioners of addiction medicine have a hard time avoiding language that shines a light on our sordid history: we call the urine that comes back positive for illicit drugs "dirty," and we encourage or require patients to get "clean and sober"—the implication, of course, being that the life of addiction is dirty and therefore bad.

The legacy of the junkie is so deeply entrenched in the public imagination that it is all but impossible for most of us to avoid. There is a deep current of disgust for and distrust of those who use drugs in America. And there I was: shaky, sweaty, desperate to be relieved of the dope sickness, sounding for all the world like an addict. A junkie. And doctors, like everyone else, despite the science that tells us to be compassionate, don't want to deal with junkies. Thank God, then, that there's a medical specialty to deal with them.

As a result of the tight relationship between dependence and addiction, and the stigma that comes along with both, we might expect that addiction medicine is, in fact, the field that knows what to do with patients like me. The problem, however, is that the same stigma attached to suffering from addiction is attached to treating addiction, and so treatment for substance use disorder is consistently devalued, understaffed, and massively underfunded. Every treatment center I called had an extensive waiting list in order to be seen, and some had strict requirements in order to be put on the waiting list. For instance, one clinic insisted that patients had to have been addicted to high levels of opioids for more than six months before being placed on the waiting list. Basically, the demand so far outstrips the supply of addiction treatment that patients are triaged, with only the most severe cases even getting an opportunity for therapy.

These clinics are simply not set up to help patients like me.

Whereas I needed assistance weaning off opioids, many addiction clinics specialize not in weaning patients, but instead on transitioning those who have used opioids for a long time onto the safer, ultra-long-lasting opioids methadone or buprenorphine. The goal of this treatment is to engage the brain's opioid receptors so as to prevent withdrawal, but to do so in a way that lessens the euphoric highs that drive addictive behavior. When it's successful, it allows patients to stabilize their behavior, giving up the single-minded pursuit of drugs and resuming a normal life. I will discuss methadone and other treatments in more detail in the final chapters, but we should preview here that this is precisely what such treatment centers *ought* to be doing. Although prescribing one kind of opioid to patients addicted to another kind of opioid might seem strange at first glance, this sort of medication is the gold standard for treating opioid use disorder.

When I called the first clinic in my area, the receptionist kindly, but directly, told me that tapering is not their job. Exasperated, I asked whether she had any idea who I should call for help. She suggested that I try general practitioners. "Have you tried your family doctor?" she asked politely. After all, those docs prescribe opioids all the time. "Surely," she said, "the doctors who prescribe so many pills must know how to manage them."

Right?

The year of my accident—2015—nearly a quarter-billion prescriptions were written. That's more than *620,000 each day*. So it's not as if the need for withdrawal management should be surprising. And yet, it's apparently no one's job.

When I began to tentatively ask physician colleagues what they thought of this manifest lack of skill in managing opioid weaning, I received a surprising response from more than one of them. Sheepishly, a general internist said to me, "Well, withdrawal isn't fatal, is it? I mean, we're taught that opioid withdrawal is uncomfortable but not dangerous—not like alcohol, say, or benzos [benzodiazepines]."

The person who said this didn't know my story yet, but he was conscious enough of how cold it sounded that he did seem embarrassed to offer it as a justification.

I thought to myself: sure, uncomfortable. That's definitely how I would describe my experience. Except for that whole "wanting to die" part.

The explanation bothered me so much that I decided to run it by a friend and colleague who's also a general internist (he did know my story at that time). I asked him if all doctors who deal with benzos know how to safely wean them, and he said yes. I asked if every doctor who deals with alcoholism knows how to safely taper alcohol, and he said yes. I asked if every doctor who prescribes opioids knows how to taper them, and he said "clearly not." Although he, himself, knew how to manage chronic opioid therapy, he said it was an accident of where he trained and his patient population. When I suggested that physicians see opioid tapering as less important to know because it's "uncomfortable but not dangerous," he immediately said that he's certain this is the case.

Trying to channel his colleagues, he offered, "If you don't know how to taper benzos, you'll kill someone. If you don't know how to taper opioids, your patients might suffer, but they'll survive. Right or wrong, the latter is optional in a way the former isn't."

This sort of reasoning is obviously problematic: doctors are supposed to protect their patients from harm—not only fatal harm. The moral malpractice is even more severe than that, though. Mismanagement of opioid therapy doesn't only risk harm in the form of withdrawal. Importantly, it can also contribute to addiction. While I have just gone to some lengths to show that dependence and addiction are not the same thing, what's important to note is that they can be related: dependence and fear of withdrawal can drive addiction.

The easiest way to understand how this works is to go back to the way that addiction changes the reward and motivation centers of the brain. A common way of understanding it is that addiction "hijacks" the brain's normal process of pursuing good things (reward) and avoiding bad things (punishment) and begins to create pathological circuits that turn one's focus, attention, desire, and energy to the object of addiction, while at the same time undermining one's ability to resist.

While some of us are more susceptible to addiction than others—differences, scientists believe, due to both genetic and environmental factors—no one starts out life suffering from addiction (although newborns can come into the world *dependent* on opioids as a result of a mother's use during pregnancy—this condition is called neonatal abstinence syndrome—there is no such thing as an "addicted baby"). Remember: the brain is a sophisticated learning machine. The process of developing an addiction is simply the process of pursuing rewards and avoiding punishments, with some rewards and punishments making it more likely than others that the brain changes become pathological. This is why some critics of the brain disease model focus so much on the learning aspect of addiction: addiction is basically the process of learning some habit.

So, for instance, the euphoria experienced as a result of dopamine released during gambling or sex, if experienced regularly enough, is sufficient to lead to addiction in some people. But the euphoria of oxycodone or heroin is in a different league altogether, setting off a chemical reaction in the brain that is unmatched by natural experience. If an orgasm lights a euphoric fire in the brain, an injection of heroin sets off an atom bomb. Thus, although those predisposed toward addiction are more likely to become addicted to gambling or to heroin, exposure to heroin is more likely to lead to addiction than is exposure to gambling.

Unfortunately, opioids have one more trick up their sleeves for driving addiction. Not only are they unmatched in their potential as rewards, but they also cause dependence, and so quitting opioids is a punishment. Whereas sex makes us happy, we don't become biologically dependent on sex such that not having it physically hurts. The double-edged sword that accounts for the incredibly dangerous nature of opioids is that taking them makes the brain very, very happy, while taking them away makes it miserable. The reward system, then, is powerfully pushed toward pathological, addictive patterns. And this takes us back to the particular danger of tapering mismanagement.

To see just how bad my doctor's advice was, let's imagine that my life had gone quite differently. Suppose that instead of having the family that I do, I was single and childless. Everything else about me was the same, but I had never married and I lived alone. Already we know that the aftermath of my motorcycle accident and the stages of recovery would have been much, much harder, but suppose that I had made it through. And then, just as happened in real life, my medication was badly managed and I went into withdrawal.

In a classic, but now-outdated, model of addiction, this fact of altered relationships shouldn't make a difference. Addiction is caused by the properties of some chemicals, which get their hooks into one's brain. Maybe some of us are more or less susceptible to these chemical hooks, but the cause of addiction is basically biological. Dozens of studies of rats in the latter half of the 1900s purported to prove this model: no matter the rat, if you put it in a cage and then offer it the opportunity to gain access to morphine or cocaine by stepping on a pedal, the rat would stomp that pedal all day, every day, sometimes until it died of starvation. Drugs cause addiction, and so having access to a drug is the primary variable determining whether one becomes addicted.

And yet not everyone who takes heroin becomes addicted. And some who do develop an addiction quit on their own. The flood of heroin-addicted veterans coming back from the Vietnam War made this point powerfully, as somewhere around 75 to 80 percent of them were able to leave their drug use overseas. If people were really like the experimental rats, these vets should have returned to the United

States, where heroin was still widely available, and stomped that pedal until doing so killed them. And to be sure, some of them did. But most didn't.

This sort of example led Canadian psychologist Bruce Alexander and his colleagues to reimagine the original wave of rat studies. Alexander's hypothesis was that the rats' behavior was at least partially a result of their environment—all of the studies had been conducted with rats in isolation cages, sometimes not even able to move due to the morphine-injection contraptions. Of course they chose the drug, Alexander thought; wouldn't you? But what if the rats lived in a wonderful complex designed to make rats happy; this led Alexander to the idea for creating what became known as Rat Park. Alexander suggested that if the rats had access to other rats and things to do, they would partake in less morphine.

The studies he conducted seem to support this hypothesis. Rats in Rat Park took significantly less morphine than did rats in isolation cages, and none of them died. Alexander's conclusion: one's environment is important in determining whether or not one is likely to develop an addiction. And while there is some controversy around the study itself, this basic idea is now well accepted. The human brain is much better at forming a pathological connection when it can focus on a single reward intensely. Distraction by other, competing rewards challenges the development of addictive pathways.

During my withdrawal, I spent much of my day thinking about my family—about my amazing daughter, and her wonderful mom, and how badly I wanted to get healthy for them. I wanted my life back; my idyllic, perfect, family-man life.

Take that away, and what happens to me? Of course I can't know for sure. Maybe I would have focused instead on my new career. That's totally possible. But maybe, I would have slipped further into the darkness. Addiction loves isolation, and I can just imagine the siren song of those pills on the table beside me, or in my pocket, calling out to me: *I can ease your suffering.* And then, my doctor gives me permission: "If it's that bad, Travis, just go back on the meds for a while. Try again when you're stronger." Maybe I would resist for a little while, but just maybe, with nothing else to focus on, I would eventually give in. With my deepest desire to be relieved of suffering having received the official blessing of the medical establishment, I would pop one of those shiny little white pills.

What would have happened if I had done that? Well, biologically we know: a flood of synthetic opioids would rush into my brain and spine, attaching to the receptors waiting desperately for them. And when that potent substance slid into the receptors, fitting perfectly like a lock and key, relief would course through my body. If it's like I remember it, the numbness would probably start in my mangled foot, settling the fiery pain. Then, as the relaxation washed up my body, I can imagine my restless legs would calm and my heart rate would slow. As the aches melted away, my brain would seem to float in a fog, and I would close my eyes and lay my head back. *Finally*, I would think. *Relief.*

And that relief is an incredibly powerful reward. Opioids relieve pain (reward) and they cause euphoria (reward), but they also relieve the suffering that taking them away causes (reward). The already strong connection between opioids and my brain's designation of "thing to be pursued" would strengthen further, and I would start thinking about the drug more. Especially when I tried to taper again. Perhaps a month later, I would decide to give it another try, convinced that I was ready this time, but of course (if I had the same bad, overly aggressive tapering recommendation) I would again immediately be made miserable by the withdrawal symptoms. And this time, I would know how to make it better. Every time the symptoms got bad, I might find myself compulsively thinking about that moment of relief when I abandoned the taper and saved myself from withdrawal. Maybe I would start obsessing over it, and with nothing else to focus on, I'd find myself making arguments for why I should go back on the meds again. After all, the doc said last time that if I wasn't ready, I could wait and try again.

Of course, if I were to succumb, then the whole process would repeat, and my brain would change yet a bit more. And each time I tried to quit, I would find it easier to convince myself to go back on the meds, as the motivation system in my brain became more and more corrupted by desire for the drug. Of course, perhaps I still would have found a way out. I'd like to think I would have. But perhaps not. Perhaps I would have given in each time. And we know where that story leads. It's led to the same place for millions of people. It leads to a sense of total loss of control, and to stigma, suffering, and eventually to helplessness and desperation. It leads to addiction.

To be clear, this alternate scenario is not designed to suggest that dependence *causes* addiction. In the actual world, I developed a profound dependence but avoided addiction. Most people who are prescribed opioids for any length of time will develop some amount of dependence, and very few of them will develop an addiction. But dependence is *related* to addiction because it adds another layer of reward and punishment to an already potent substance. If I had been unlucky enough to be vulnerable to addiction (whether due to genetic or environmental reasons), the suffering of withdrawal would have been just one more mechanism pushing me toward habitual use.

Thankfully, that's not what happened. I wasn't isolated, and my family gave me something to hold on to every day. And who knows what idiosyncrasies in my genetics or brain chemistry led me one way rather than another. Somehow, as a result of a hundred different pieces of discrete good fortune—because of features of my life that I had done nothing to earn—I didn't take any of the pills lying around my house. But I couldn't shake the anger at how close I had gotten to the edge. Somehow, in the middle of a national opioid crisis of epidemic proportions, my doctors had either turned their backs or pushed me in the direction of addiction. Something had gone very seriously wrong.

In the immediate aftermath of my encounter with the American healthcare system, I wanted a simple story about what went wrong—a particular person or group of people to be angry at, and maybe a catchy slogan that I could shout to encourage change. I felt wronged, and I wanted to know who was responsible and how it could have been prevented.

There is no such simple story, though. None of my doctors had bad intentions, and none of them were incompetent by today's medical standards. As I would hear from many physicians and researchers over the coming years, my experience was not that uncommon; and indeed, once you understand the forces surrounding opioid prescribing, it's completely unsurprising.

When I first began researching pain and opioids, I picked up Judy Foreman's important and comprehensive book *A Nation in Pain*, and in the middle of chapter 7, I came across a story that sounded disconcertingly familiar. Not in the details—the story was about a man whose pain from a rare autoimmune disease had led to his extended opioid use—but in a more general sense. Paul Konowitz was a physician, married to a physician, with lots of education and privilege between the two of them—even more than Sadiye and I had, in fact, since they both worked in medicine. And yet, when it came time for Paul to quit his opioid therapy, he could find no sound advice, and so he tried to taper himself, unsuccessfully, several agonizing times before finally stumbling onto a slow-enough regimen to make it through. As Konowitz told Foreman in an interview, "Doctors don't do pain well . . . They don't understand addiction, physical dependence, withdrawal. We had to figure it out for ourselves, and we had an advantage—we had the background and people to talk to."

Reading the story of Konowitz's miserable, fumbling taper, I knew that my friends and colleagues must be right: what happened

to me just wasn't that surprising. If this sort of case happened to people who are plausibly in the most privileged positions to know and to
find help, then how many patients have gone through this with zero
help and no voice for telling their story afterward?

Konowitz explains this kind of failure by reference to a knowledge gap—doctors don't "do pain well," and they don't understand
the mechanisms of dependence and withdrawal. And the data certainly seems to explain why this knowledge gap exists. In 2011, a
group of researchers at my home institute of Johns Hopkins published a study of pain education in the United States and Canada.
In an evaluation of more than one hundred medical schools, they
found that U.S. schools dedicated a median of just *seven* hours
to pain education, and only four medical schools had a required
course on pain. Many of the medical schools reported *no teaching* on pain at all. As Foreman reports for darkly comic juxtapo-
sition, a separate study out of the University of Toronto showed
that Canadian-trained veterinarians receive eighty-seven hours of
pain education.

Given the lack of education in pain medicine, we shouldn't be
surprised at comments like Konowitz's that doctors "don't do pain
well." As the existence of the broader opioid epidemic seems to be
making clear, many physicians lack the basic knowledge of even
when to prescribe opioids (and to be clear, this isn't always their
fault—remember that many were basically taught to give opioids to
anyone in pain). In recent years, many physicians have "come out"
as not knowing how to prescribe opioids. When I was first beginning
to research this topic, I closely followed the writing of Dr. Leana
Wen, who at the time was Baltimore's health commissioner and is a
brilliant commentator on our country's problems with opioids. On
September 26, 2016, she bravely and self-consciously tweeted, "It's
common medical practice to prescribe opioids for pain. I never had
a course on how to treat people with acute pain. #coveringopioids."
The fact that the further downstream skill of opioid tapering and

withdrawal management aren't well understood is not shocking. This lack of education almost certainly played a role in my experience.

That doesn't seem to be the whole answer, though. Lack of education seems like a good explanation of what went wrong with Dr. Roberts, who gave me the tapering regimen. He was charged with providing me guidance, and he clearly had no good idea of how to do that. But what about all of the other doctors I called? Most of them wouldn't even speak with me, and even my own hospitals and surgeons took a very "not my job" attitude about my particular need. It's not at all clear that lack of education was the problem in all of those cases.

One plausible explanation for at least some of the cases goes back to the discussion of stigma: pain patients—and even more so, addiction patients (or those who present as struggling with addiction-related problems)—are difficult and distressing, and many doctors don't want to deal with them. Pain patients are reporting on their subjective experience, and they could be lying to get drugs; and patients dealing with some aspect of substance use disorder are already identified as the kind of patient that doctors fear pain patients may actually be. The stigma surrounding addiction helps to explain not only why opioid use disorder is so massively undertreated but also why nonspecialist physicians don't want to touch those patients with a ten-foot pole. In short, as a pain patient who was struggling with the precise medications that are feeding an epidemic of addiction, it is not surprising that doctors who don't specialize in addiction medicine didn't want to deal with me.

There's a much more mundane explanation for what went wrong, though. Sure, doctors are poorly educated on pain medicine; and yes, pain and addiction are stigmatized topics within medicine. But it's also the case that I was a patient in a phenomenally complex medical system, with deep fissures between hospitals, fields, and individual doctors—fissures that can easily swallow the patients being tossed back and forth across their maw.

I was a patient of three different hospitals and somewhere around a dozen physicians; I underwent five surgeries over the course of as many weeks and had prescriptions written by who-knows-how-many clinicians (including at least one physician assistant—the clinician who often has the role of prescribing medication at discharge). At the end of two months, my trauma surgeon seemed to have a clear view of whose responsibility I was: the plastic surgeon's, because he had been the one most recently caring for me. In the game of patient hot potato, Dr. Roberts was stuck holding me when the timer went off, so managing my medication long term was his job.

But did he know that? Is that well-established policy? It sure didn't seem to be. No individual prescriber seemed to have a sense that I was *theirs*, and that sort of fracturing of care must certainly dilute individual doctors' sense of responsibility.

So physicians are poorly educated about pain, sure. And thankfully, there is starting to be some forward motion in rectifying that (although not nearly as much as you might hope). But the situation is much more complex than that. Pain patients have a problem that many doctors not only lack the education to treat, but they often don't want to treat them, and thanks to our complex, fractured medical system, many doctors have a ready-made excuse for not treating them.

The situation is a recipe for disaster, and at least part of the solution will need to be getting clear on *who is responsible* for patients like me.

CHAPTER 7

What Doctors Owe Patients

My doctors screwed up. Dr. Konowitz's doctors screwed up. And if our experience—our inability to get help despite all of our privileges—is any indication, then likely many other doctors have screwed up too.

The costs of these mistakes are not negligible. The suffering of unmanaged withdrawal is quite bad enough, but Konowitz and I represent the best-case scenario: we figured it out, or made it through with lots of luck and support. How many people have gone back to the medication, furthering a profound dependence or even leading to addiction? How many people have spent so long in their own little personal hell that the suicidal thoughts became real and entrenched, and eventually won out? These are terrifying possibilities that make the stakes distressingly clear.

What we don't know yet, though, is exactly who screwed up, and in what way. *Someone* should've helped me, and Konowitz, but who? And what precisely was their responsibility? If someone had a relevant responsibility—what in my professional life as an ethicist I often call a "duty" or an "obligation"—then we need to get clear on what exactly that was.

Importantly, the goal of this exercise is not for the sake of blaming. Of course, I've been angry and wanted someone to blame. But I'm not at all sure that blaming is helpful, which is why I've never used the real names of either my doctors or the hospitals in which I received treatment. Because the goal isn't to make a few physicians feel bad. The goal is to try to *fix* something that is obviously broken, and that is easier done through understanding rather than retribution.

In addition, the institutional explanations of the previous chapter help us to see why blame can feel inappropriate: my doctors were (I believe) well-intentioned, talented physicians; they were also part of a system that didn't help them properly identify or live up to their responsibilities. When good people don't live up to their responsibilities because they don't fully understand them, we soften our attitudes toward them. It doesn't mean that they did the right thing, but their failure is understandable in a way that makes the same level of blame less appropriate.

In other words, I'm not out to get doctors. But that doesn't mean we shouldn't discuss what they're doing wrong—and, crucially, how they can do better.

Without looking to blame anyone, then, my goal here is to try to figure out what doctors in fact owe their opioid therapy patients, and what any of us who might find ourselves in their exam rooms can expect (and, if needed, demand) of them.

It seems to me that the failure of my doctors is really pretty easy to pinpoint: they prescribed a medication that they either didn't know how, or weren't willing, to manage long term. And since that medication has long-term, harmful side effects, such prescribing seems to put the doctors on the hook for at least some of the suffering that may come about as a result.

If this seems reasonable (and doesn't it, for all the world, seem eminently reasonable?), then every one of my dozen or so clinicians over the course of two months screwed up. We called all of them for help, and none of them would provide it, despite having written at least one prescription for me. This is where we shouldn't mince words: a whole slew of doctors gave me a medication that they weren't willing to manage, and that was wrong. They simply should have done better.

Now of course, not all of these doctors played the same role: my trauma surgeon seemed to make the case, not unreasonably, that the plastic surgeon was something like my "managing" physician, since he had taken over prescribing once I was out of the hospital and in recovery. Once all of the chaos of hospital changes, multiple surgeries and surgical teams, and many nights on different hospital floors was over, Dr. Roberts was the one who emerged as my long-term prescriber. That's a pretty strong case for thinking he bears more responsibility than the others, who saw me for more limited periods during a chaotic time, in which I was continually being handed off. I'm sure that some trauma surgeons, ICU attendings, and other specialists who tend to see patients for only a limited window of their longer-term care would make the case that they have a much more specific, acute job: to fix the patient in front of them. They may contend that long-term medical management just doesn't fall on them.

If there are doctors who think this, then I should say up front that I understand. In a well-designed medical system, perhaps that's the arrangement that we would have settled on. But this is clearly not a well-designed medical system, and so we haven't in fact assigned the job of managing long-term opioid therapy to anyone. Although Dr. Roberts should have felt more responsible than the others, given his more extensive contact with me, it's just not clear that his contact lets any of the other doctors off the hook. Because here's the basic fact: they all prescribed a medication with predictable, harmful side effects and then weren't able or willing to help mitigate those side effects.

This is a failure, regardless of who else is involved.

We should further note what kind of failure this is. Protecting an opioid therapy patient from excruciating withdrawal isn't just helping—it's not acting out of the kindness of your heart if you're a prescribing physician. Sometimes we're allowed to not help others. Constantly helping everyone who needed it would require a massive change to the lifestyle of nearly everyone. But for the prescribing physician, managing a medication isn't optional in this way. It's a moral requirement.

Consider an analogy: Some of us wonder whether we are obligated to fight global hunger with our extra income, or whether we should stop by the scene of an accident to make sure everyone is okay. Although ethicists debate whether we have an obligation to help in such circumstances, it is fairly uncontroversial that any such duty to help is weaker than if you were responsible for the hungry person's field going dry, or if you caused the accident. Helping the victim of a situation that you caused isn't just being nice—you have a moral duty to mitigate the harm that you exposed someone else to.

Prescribing opioids and then leaving patients to fend for themselves is not merely "not helping"; it's causing an accident and then leaving the scene. Given the properties of tolerance and dependence, opioids taken for a certain amount of time will need supervised, careful tapering and, depending on the case, may require further medication or treatment. In the most difficult cases, exposing a patient to opioids will eventually lead to their needing treatment for opioid use disorder.

Now, the part of my example that is a bit unfair is that no one causes an accident on purpose for good reason, knowing that there may be an injury but judging it to be worthwhile nonetheless (except in action movies maybe). But if one did, that wouldn't change the nature of the obligation: having a good reason to cause an accident doesn't change one's obligation to help anyone injured by it. It changes how we view the initial action—we might say that it was an unfortunate necessity—but knowing that accidents can cause harm, you are obligated to help anyone hurt by your choice to cause one.

This is approximately what I think is going on with opioid prescribing: unlike causing an accident, doctors do in fact have good reason to perform this action regularly. However, prescribing opioids, especially in contexts where the patient is likely to be on them for some length of time (such as following trauma, multiple surgeries, etc.), exposes the patient to significant risk of serious harm, and so the doctor has a duty to mitigate that harm to the best of her ability.

Not only do I think this is about the most obvious claim I've ever made in ethics (and, since arguing ethics is my job, I've made quite a few such claims in my career), but I think we actually already accept this basic principle in medicine. Surgeons cause predictable harms of various kinds, and we take it that this fact gives them a variety of responsibilities. Indeed, the very use of opioids in the first place for postsurgical patients stems from the idea that surgeons have a duty to lessen the pain they've caused. Sure, they caused pain for good reason—that's basically just what surgery is—but it doesn't change the fact that they ought to lessen it if they can.

Postsurgical infection is treated similarly. Given that infection is one of the most consequential risks of undergoing surgery, surgeons go to great lengths to minimize the risk and then act quickly on any infection that does occur as a result of the procedure. Infection is a possible bad outcome of surgery, so surgeons do their best to mitigate those harms. And if an infection does occur and progresses beyond the abilities of the surgeon, she gets infectious disease specialists involved. Surgeons see both harm mitigation and a smooth handoff as part of their responsibility.

Or consider a different case of a medication with serious, predictable side effects: oncologists prescribe chemotherapy, which they hope will kill cancer cells but which also can make patients desperately ill. Indeed, the potential harms of chemotherapy can be so bad that not everyone thinks it's worth it to suffer those harms in order to obtain what can sometimes be a small chance at improved outcomes. As our ability to treat various toxicity-related side effects of chemotherapy has improved, however, oncologists have incorporated these treatments into their responsibility. There is undoubtedly good reason to give some patients chemo, but that doesn't change the fact that it can make them miserable; so any physician who prescribes chemotherapy is responsible for doing whatever she can to mitigate those harms. And as in the case of infection: the harms of chemotherapy can absolutely extend beyond the oncologist's ability to care for a patient. Cancer survivors may experience long-term harms from chemotherapy, in which case oncologists often must collaborate with other specialties. So they do. Both immediate and long-term harms of risky medication are recognized and attended to.

Recognizing that doctors have a duty to protect patients from the harms of medication that they prescribe will not, then, take a revolution in medical ethics. It's a totally sensible idea that almost everyone, on reflection, will accept. What it will take, though, is a recognition that this well-established principle applies in the case of pain medicine. Because that message clearly hasn't been communicated to all prescribers.

Saying that physicians ought to better protect their opioid therapy patients is one thing, but figuring out how to make it happen is quite another.

During the summer of 2018, I was invited to participate in a workshop at a world-class, private hospital, where more than a dozen clinicians and scientists (and one bioethicist!) would try to determine what surgeons ought to do about opioid prescribing in a few, specific cases. It was about the most friendly environment one can imagine for trying to establish responsible opioid management, as everyone there—including the surgeons—realized there was a problem and was ready to change their practice.

Indeed, the group was so willing to work toward better medicine that, when I presented my argument that prescribers must be willing to manage opioids long term and to follow up as necessary, the attendees immediately agreed.

I was floored. I made sure that they realized what I was saying—

that their surgeons would need to do something utterly beyond their current practice—and they simply agreed that it needed to be done.

Well, okay then, I thought. Maybe this will be easier than I anticipated.

Then we started working out the details, and thinking through just their particular hospital's protocols.

The first challenge is that surgeons don't actually tend to do the opioid prescribing when a patient is discharged. Instead, a nurse practitioner (a highly trained nurse who can write prescriptions under the supervisory authority of a physician) often handles this aspect of patient care. Surgeons don't even always see patients before discharge.

So the first question arose: Is it the nurse who is responsible for establishing a pain protocol, educating the patient, and responding to adverse outcomes from opioid use? Are the surgeons off the hook because they didn't sign the prescription?

No one in the room seemed to like the idea that the surgeon should be able to delegate this responsibility to the prescribing nurse, and so one physician commented that the relevant pain management follow-up should be incorporated into the patient's next appointment. After all, I was told, all surgical patients need to come in to be checked on at regular intervals.

"So how soon do you all see the patients after surgery?" I asked, hoping that this would be a workable solution.

But for the procedures we were discussing, the patients often didn't come in until one month after the procedure.

"One month?" I repeated. "I'm sorry to say, but that's just too long. If the goal is regular follow-up, then we need to know how the patient is doing regarding the pain protocol during the most acute recovery phase. Are they sticking to the plan? Are they off the meds? Are they taking more, and perhaps need a pain management referral? These questions can't wait for a month. At one month, if they've been using the medication aggressively, they will have already developed some tolerance and potentially a significant dependence."

One of the surgeons jumped in, "Oh, well we definitely talk to the patients before one month, we just don't see them. The nurses typically call on a schedule to check in."

"That's great," I responded. "Do we know what that schedule is? Do the nurses ask these questions? Are they informed of the intended pain management protocol?"

There were a few seconds of silence before one of the surgeons said, "I really don't think so, but we clearly need a nurse in on the discussion. Further, we need to establish a script so that we can collect the relevant information."

The question that we seemed to be rediscovering is: Who is responsible for managing pain medicine? Ostensibly, I was in the room to try to convince the hospital and its clinicians that *they* were responsible—that their patients deserve such care and that they're obligated to provide it. But even when they readily agreed, there was a live question as to who is best placed to provide that care and what they needed in order to provide it. As we quickly discovered, the details matter. Because, best of intentions aside, if no one trained to think about responsible pain medicine talks to surgical patients for an entire month, there will be some number of problem cases that aren't caught for far too long.

Now some healthcare contexts might seem easier than others when it comes to assigning responsibility. Primary care doctors, who have a well-established relationship with a patient, seem to be directly responsible for managing any opioids they prescribe. Understanding even this is progress, and it is almost certainly the case that very many such docs are not living up to this responsibility. After all, we've already seen that pain education is limited, many doctors were trained to prescribe without much concern, and pain is a difficult and stigmatized condition to treat.

When we enter the world of surgery and other complex care

situations, though, the cases get even more complicated. Our healthcare system is deeply fractured between disciplines, teams, and hospitals, leading to many opportunities for there to be failed handoffs of patients.

In short, even if I'm right that doctors ought to manage their patients' opioid therapy better, they work in a system that makes living up to the obligation much more difficult than it should be. If we, as a society, want doctors to do better at taking care of their opioid therapy patients, we probably shouldn't have them work within a system that makes doing it so intensely difficult.

Among the lowest-hanging fruit in terms of making meaningful change regarding opioid management is basic education. Looking back at both my case and the case of Dr. Konowitz, significant suffering could have been prevented if someone had known enough about long-term opioid therapy to warn us about dependence in advance, and then help us through the withdrawal process in the least painful way possible. Although managing opioids in the most difficult cases can be incredibly complex, and probably requires specialized knowledge (we'll come back to this), the basics of tapering are not that complicated.

By early 2017, I had published my first academic essay about my experience and the issues that it raised, and someone at the CDC came across it. In response, the CDC Injury Center tweeted out my essay, commenting, "Our #opioid Tapering Pocket Guide offers tips in situations such as this one."

Their pocket guide is just a few simple recommendations, based on the limited evidence that we have about opioid tapering. These recommendations include the advice to "go slow"—specifically: "A decrease of 10% of the original dose per week is a reasonable starting point. Some patients who have taken opioids for a long time might find even slower tapers (e.g. 10% per month) easier." (In fact, a 2018 study demonstrated that pursuing an even slower taper increased the likelihood of success.) Additionally, physicians should "adjust the rate and duration of the taper according to the patient's response," and they should never "reverse the taper; however the rate may be slowed or paused while monitoring and managing withdrawal symptoms."

In short, there is now simple, easy-to-find guidance available for determining the basic pace of tapering a patient. In my case, Dr. Roberts's taper was much, much too aggressive; and then when I became very sick from the withdrawal, he suggested reversing the taper (going back to the previous dose) rather than slowing down. Now that we've looked at the basic mechanism of addiction, in the previous chapter, it's easy to see why reversing a taper is not recommended, since relieving withdrawal through a higher dose is a powerful reward. The key, then, is to go slow enough to avoid the worst punishment of withdrawal, without increasing the reward from taking that medication in a way that could help push the patient's brain toward addictive patterns.

Of course, there are many complexities that can be added, and these can be found in the medical literature and in continuing medical education courses that are, now, finally beginning to pop up. While researching this book, I took one of these courses developed and taught online by Dr. Anna Lembke—pain and addiction specialist and author of the insightful book, *Drug Dealer, MD*—and she went through an extensive set of strategies that physicians can use to help mitigate the worst withdrawal effects. One of her central lessons to doctors new to the skill of opioid tapering is simple: Tapering is likely to be uncomfortable even in the best cases, miserable in the worst, and many patients will find it difficult. Going slow will help a lot of patients, but others will need medication in order to make it through the tapering. Some medications, such as clonidine and lofexidine, can be helpful for symptom management (although, like all medications, they are not without their own side effects); other patients may need to transition on to buprenorphine, which is a long-acting opioid similar to methadone. These patients start to blur the line between treatment for withdrawal and treatment for opioid use disorder. (Such patients are sometimes said to suffer from "complex persistent dependence": they do not exhibit the behavioral signs of addiction, but they are far too dependent on the medication to wean directly and can suffer from extended withdrawal effects.)

It's probably not reasonable to expect every physician who prescribes opioids to know as much as Dr. Lembke does; after all, that's why she's an expert. Surely, though, anyone who prescribes opioids should know at least what's in the CDC pocket guide. Given the stakes, that doesn't strike me as too much to expect.

Those who prescribe a lot, such as surgeons and pain medicine doctors, probably ought to know significantly more, such as how to deal with typical problem cases. For instance, several physicians who deal with opioid tapers mentioned to me that a distressing number of chronic opioid therapy patients get most of the way through the taper and then abandon the effort. The cruel joke of withdrawal (clearly evident in my own experience) is that it gets worse as you get closer to the end, because you eventually get to the point where the dosing of the pills means that you can't taper as slowly; and eventually, you have to drop from some medication to no medication. So the percentage reduction goes up toward the end, making the withdrawal more severe.

I'm obviously sympathetic to the worry that sufficiently bad symptoms can drive patients back to the medication: if my withdrawal had lasted one more night, that would have been me; those pills were on my nightstand, and I was ready to take them. So what should a physician do in such a case? I certainly don't know the answer, but I'm not a medical doctor and I don't prescribe opioids. For those who do prescribe a lot, this seems like the kind of thing we should want them to know.

Unfortunately, the challenges get even more significant. When I began my research into problems with how physicians manage opioid therapy, I was thinking of my own experience as the problem. And it is *a* problem: patients get injured, suffer acute pain due to trauma or surgery, get prescribed a bunch of opioids, and end up with a heightened risk of dependence or addiction due to physician inability or unwillingness to counsel and wean the patients. But I only had half the story. Patients like me are new to opioids, and we present one kind of challenge. There is another population of opioid therapy patients out there, and they are much more vulnerable than I ever was.

In late 2016, Dr. William B. Weeks—a physician and researcher at Dartmouth—published an excruciatingly personal essay in the very academic *Journal of the American Medical Association (JAMA)*. The essay was titled, "Hailey," which was the name of Weeks's little sister.

The beginning of the story traces a narrative familiar to those who have wrestled with chronic pain: Hailey was, by Weeks's account, a smart, energetic, lovely person—a lawyer who served the disenfranchised and a lover of animals. But after a back injury, she slowly changed. The pain was debilitating; she took increasing doses of many kinds of medications and eventually found herself on very high doses of opioids and benzodiazepines.

That's when her longtime physician—a caring and well-intentioned pain specialist—was diagnosed with Parkinson's disease and decided to quit practicing. After giving Hailey a list of possible physicians who could take over her care, he wrote a final month's set of prescriptions.

Hailey met with every single recommended physician, and at each meeting she was told that she would not be prescribed her current, very high doses. She felt, as I had, completely abandoned by the medical establishment as doctors took one look at her chart and said, "Not it." When her bottles of pills began to get light and she became more desperate, she started weaning herself and went into terrible withdrawal. The symptoms quickly became unbearable, and with no other option, she went to the emergency room to get more pills; there, she was identified as a drug-seeker and told that she would not have any of her prescriptions refilled. Sick and in pain, she became belligerent, was involved in an altercation with a nurse, and was charged with assault. Her downward spiral led to her being discharged from the hospital into police custody.

Four days later, she was found dead in her jail cell.

Hailey's autopsy report suggested that "opioid and benzodiazepine withdrawal were possible causes of death." As noted earlier, although opioid withdrawal tends not to be fatal (the very rare exception to this comes in the form of death due to dehydration from unremitting vomiting and diarrhea), benzodiazepine withdrawal can be, and so some combination of the two may be what ultimately killed Hailey. Although it wouldn't be recognized by any system for cataloging causes of death, I would advocate for a more dramatic—but more honest—note in her report: "Cause of death: medical abandonment."

Stories like Hailey's bring our embattled attitudes about pain and opioids back into the discussion, revealing how our current fear of opioids can affect withdrawal treatment. Because the worry about physicians' unwillingness or inability to properly manage opioid therapy raises one concern in patients like me—patients who are put on opioid therapy for periods long enough to risk dependency but with a clear end goal in sight—but a very different concern in what are often called "legacy patients," or those patients who have been prescribed high doses of opioids for years or even decades.

Legacy patients who are doing well on opioid therapy have been living in fear ever since America began to turn the corner on opioid-prescribing trends: these patients were prescribed high and escalating doses during years of an "opioids for everyone" mentality, but now they worry that their doctors will cut them off, or, as in Hailey's case, that they will lose their doctor and no one will take them.

The medical establishment believes that many of these patients would be better off without opioids. It's difficult for stable patients to believe, but the limited evidence suggests that it might be true. Some of these patients are likely experiencing all of the side effects of opioid therapies (including hyperalgesia, the paradoxical consequence of opioids *increasing* one's sensitivity to pain) and getting virtually no benefit from the medication. Unfortunately, though, they won't be able to recognize that fact until after they go through the long, difficult tapering process (which can take many months or even years in the most extreme cases). And the symptoms of withdrawal will convince such patients that during the tapering process, they are getting worse (after all, increased pain is one of the symptoms of withdrawal). So for patients on high doses of opioids who believe they have a pretty good quality of life, losing access to that medication might well sound like going through hell with the possibility that only more hell lies at the end.

Legacy patients thus provide one of the most devastating challenges to our response to the opioid crisis. Doctors, many of whom don't really know how to manage tapers to begin with, are being pressured to taper patients who are (justifiably) terrified of tapering. That's a bad situation.

Although the evidence on long-term opioid therapy could lead a strong physician-patient team to decide that tapering is in the patient's interest, and thus to consensual dose reduction, much of the concern is around the idea of "forced tapering," or nonconsensual dose reduction. Since doctors have the prescription pads, they don't need patients' permission to reduce their dose.

Obviously, forced tapers have many terrible possible outcomes. One class of concern is simply that forced tapers cause avoidable suffering, and so they are wrong. The suffering at issue is the suffering of withdrawal, and it's avoidable because continuing the medication would prevent it. This simple view is strengthened by the idea that physicians are the ones who caused the massive dependence of opioid therapy patients through their aggressive prescribing, and so causing harm by cutting them off, without their consent, seems especially violating. If I were a legacy patient and my doctor wanted to cut me off or force a taper, I would feel completely justified in saying, "*You did this to me*, and I shouldn't have to be tortured because you suddenly decided, two decades later, that it was wrong." Even if the relevant "you" wasn't a particular doctor—even if the physician who started me on this path was retired, deceased, or had long ago stopped prescribing—I could imagine the anger focusing on the "you" of the healthcare institution. The pain we are expecting legacy patients to go through if we decrease chronic opioid therapy should not be overlooked.

Another outcome that everyone recognizes as possible is that cutting off patients with serious dependence on opioids risks driving them to the black market. Fear of withdrawal can motivate extreme behavior, and prescription pads are not the only place to get opioids. An additional danger here is that illicit prescription opioids are expensive, while heroin is cheap. But of course, heroin is much more dangerous, as it is increasingly laced with the superpotent drugs fentanyl and its analogues. As a result of these forces, those pushed into the black market out of concern for their dose may find themselves at a much higher risk of overdosing.

Such a development would not be surprising to those working in addiction medicine. Indeed, Dr. Weeks mentions in his essay that, in the wake of Hailey's death, he became a buprenorphine prescriber— buprenorphine being the long-lasting opioid used for maintenance treatment, similar to methadone. He writes, "Many of my patients have a similar story: they had an injury, were prescribed opioids, accelerated their use of the opioids, and were abruptly cut off, usually because of a change in clinician or because the original one got angry over the patient's accelerating opioid use and simply quit prescribing. Most of my patients turned to illegally obtaining the opioids; many of them reverted to heroin because of the high cost of pharmaceutical-grade opioids."

An unintended consequence of forcing legacy patients off opioids, then, may be an increase in the number of heroin users. As we try desperately to invest in policies that reduce the number of overdose deaths, adopting prescribing policies that push some percentage of prescription opioid users to heroin seems like a terribly self-undermining move.

Finally, though, Hailey's case raises the most disconcerting possibility: that abandoning or otherwise badly managing opioid patients can result in their death. In Hailey's case, withdrawal itself may have been what killed her, but there is a less direct way in which medical abandonment seems like a pretty reasonable cause of death.

Toward the end of summer 2017, I got a call from Bloomberg reporter Robert Langreth. He was working on a story about the harms of having one's opioid therapy abruptly cut off, and he wanted to ask me about my own experience. As we talked on the phone, I got more interested in his project, as it was the first time that I saw the obvious connection between my concern about withdrawal management and the problem presented by legacy patients. My initial concern had been about how badly managing the tapers of traumatic and postsurgical patients (who will need this service as a matter of routine) might actually contribute to the opioid epidemic by reinforcing dependence and even contributing to addiction (as bad tapers are abandoned and going back on medication rescues patients from withdrawal). What Langreth had plugged into was the fear of the existing opioid therapy population that they would have their medication taken away; in other words, bad tapers—driven by many of the same problems of education and stigma—may already be pushing chronic pain patients further into harm's way.

Langreth's article was published in November 2017, and it's a powerful piece of reporting. In it, he tells the story of Doug Hale, whose life took a similar path to Hailey's. Doug, too, was an active person with a full life, until a series of medical complications began pushing him down the long, difficult path of severe chronic pain. Over the course of more than a decade, he was prescribed powerful opioids for various medical problems, ultimately driving him to truly massive doses.

In 2016—twelve years after being initiated on opioid therapy— Hale reported uncontrolled pain and began upping his dosage on his own, leading to his running out of pills early. As a result, his physician first tried to decrease his dosage, and then, after he ran out early again, the doctor cut him off. There is some disagreement between Hale's wife and his physician concerning exactly how this parting of ways happened, but what's not in dispute is that the physician no longer felt comfortable prescribing at what were certainly dangerously high levels, and so he recommended that Hale get treatment from one of a number of specialists.

Hale tried a by-now-familiar set of options, seeing many specialists and going through his own personal hell as he withdrew. After going to a detox clinic, he was off opioids but still in the throes of the terrible sickness. He, like me, tried a methadone clinic, and he was given a similar response: they wouldn't enroll him because he wasn't "truly an addict." Hale tried one more time to get meds from his doctor, but the doctor refused; he later wrote in his medical records, in depressingly familiar language, that Doug Hale had fallen through "the cracks" of the healthcare system.

The day after that appointment, Doug Hale sat down and wrote the following letter, in his visibly shaky handwriting:

I Douglas Hale,

Canot take the chronic pain anymore. No one except my wife has helped me. The doctors are mostly puppets trying to lower expenses, and not expect any responsibility. Besides people will

*die and doctors have seen it all. So why help me. Im expendable
and no threat. This life has been taken by myself.*

Douglas R. Hale

*Tammi L. Hale
I love you forever.*

He then put the barrel of a gun in his mouth and pulled the
trigger.

I don't think the doctors in Hailey's or in Doug's case were evil.
They were probably all well-intentioned, good physicians—like
mine. But they were put in an impossible situation by the way we, as
a society, are reacting to the opioid crisis, combined with the way in
which the healthcare system treats opioid therapy. As a result, Hailey and Doug are dead, and there are almost certainly more cases like
theirs. As we think about the dangers of opioids (which we *must*),
we must also think about the dangers of mishandling opioids and
withholding opioid prescriptions. The fact that we have prescribed
aggressively for decades means that we must deal with opioids in a
more nuanced way than if we were simply deciding, for the first time,
when to use these powerful medications.

In short, we can't think about the opioid crisis as raising only
the question of "When do we prescribe opioids?" It also raises the,
in some ways much more difficult, questions of "How do we manage
necessary opioids?" "When is it appropriate to end opioid therapy?"
and *"How* do we end opioid therapy once it's deemed appropriate?"

On the one hand, the lessons of this chapter can feel really distressing. The opioid crisis already seems to many people to be a nearly in-
surmountable problem. Prescription opioids still kill far, far too many
people, and we've been trying to turn that ship around for years now.
Apparently, we can't even do something that sounds pretty straight-

forward, like prescribe fewer opioids. And now here I've told some really harrowing stories about the much less obvious mistakes that doctors are making regarding opioid prescribing. How do we expect our healthcare system to get better at the rather nuanced activity of managing opioids if it can't even get better at not prescribing far too many?

Although understandable, I think this reaction gets things exactly backward. The prescription opioid crisis was never simple to begin with. "Prescribe fewer pills" is a terrible goal to give doctors because it makes no reference to the particular patient in front of them at any moment. Some patients will benefit from opioids and some won't, and so what we really want doctors to do is to prescribe fewer *inappropriate* pills, while continuing to prescribe when doing so is responsible. But that, of course, is a much greater challenge. As we try to recover from the era of far-too-liberal prescribing practices, we must be careful not to be reactionary, urging doctors to simply stop using this important medical tool. There is nothing simple about that challenge.

The opioid crisis doesn't merely raise a problem for opioid prescribing; it raises a problem for opioid *management*. In fact, we can do better than that: it raises a problem for *pain management*. What the opioid crisis makes salient for medicine is that we aren't particularly good at treating pain. We view pain with suspicion, and doctors take reports of pain more and less seriously depending on who is making those reports. We swing wildly back and forth in our embrace of the most powerful medications we have because of their addictive properties, but we have not yet done well at using them according to evidence. And when patients do develop problems with pain medication, we are far too likely to stigmatize and even abandon them. We don't have a prescription opioid problem; we have a pain problem that opioids happen to play a significant role in.

That's a helpful clarification, I think. But it's also overwhelming. The problem is so big. How in the world do we do better?

PART III

CHAPTER 8

Recovery

On the afternoon of August 25, I hobbled around the living room excitedly, trying to pick up a bit before Sadiye got home. My blue Triumph Motorcycles T-shirt—now a relic of a past life—was damp with sweat from the physical therapy session I'd just left, and the cane in my right hand was the only obvious indication of my handicap. The blue jeans I wore largely hid my atrophied legs, and over the past week, I had replaced my large plastic boot with oversize Crocs for shuffling around the house. Each day brought a new achievement in getting back some degree of normalcy, from driving myself to appointments to taking a few more wobbly steps while leaning heavily on my cane.

Today was different, though. Today I had something important to show Sadiye, and I wanted everything to be perfect. In the weeks since coming out of withdrawal, I had developed a singular focus on gaining back as much function as possible, spending hours each day with my physical therapist, in the pool, and doing exercises on the living room floor (often with Sinem lying beside me, mimicking my motions and counting my reps). Dr. Patel, ever the pessimist, had continued to caution me that just because I was able to walk in the boot didn't mean that I would eventually gain back much more function. I may never walk without assistance, or cover much distance, he would tell me. Only a couple of weeks after his last such pronouncement, today was the day that I would prove him wrong.

When I heard Sadiye's Camry pull up just outside, I hurriedly grabbed my gym bag off the floor and picked up a throw pillow that might get in the way of my demonstration. I quickly scanned our tiny living room to see if anything else was amiss. And then, leaning heavily on my cane and flexing my ankle to keep it warm, I hobbled over to the front door to greet my family.

"Well, you look chipper," Sadiye called from her parking spot, twenty feet away. She pulled Sinem out of her car seat, locked the car, and started up the steps to where I was waiting for them.

"I *am* chipper," I said, smiling. "Because I have something very cool to show you."

"Oh?" She gave me a furrowed brow. "That sounds mysterious."

I smiled mischievously and ushered them in through the door. "Okay, you stand over there . . . No wait, maybe over here, the light's better." I babbled like an amateur film director.

"What are you doing?" Sadiye laughed at me.

"Just wait, just wait. It'll be worth it, I promise." I was grinning like an idiot. "Okay, yeah that's good. Now here, set down Baby Girl and take my phone. I want you to take a video."

"Okay . . ." she said, as she slowly peeled our clingy daughter from her torso and set her on the floor to inspect the assortment of toys that had fallen under the futon. "And what, exactly, am I recording?"

"Well me, of course." I looked at her aiming the phone at me. "Are you recording?"

On the video, you can hear Sadiye say, "Yes."

"Okay." I stood still for a minute, looking somewhat apprehensively at Sadiye, who was probably ten feet away. And then, tentatively, as if coaxing myself through each movement, I picked my cane off the ground and tossed it onto the couch.

Sadiye inhaled sharply. Sinem started to whine from the floor, but Sadiye kept her eyes and the camera trained perfectly on me, waiting to see if I was really about to do what she thought I was going to do.

And then, carefully, tentatively—a little fearfully—I put my fragile left foot in front of my body and started to shift my weight onto it. No boot. No cane. My physical therapist had convinced me that today was the day to try this, but so far I hadn't done more than stand without my cane, shifting weight back and forth between my feet. I wanted Sadiye to be there when I really tried to walk.

Slowly, deliberately—not allowing myself to limp or shuffle—I lifted my right foot to take a step, leaving all of my body's weight on the foot that, just three months ago, had been blown apart. I felt the pressure on the weak bones rolling throughout my foot as I moved forward, and there was certainly pain, but nothing sharp—no cracks, no screams. I completed the step, took another one, and looked up at Sadiye.

In the video, you hear her slowly let out the breath she'd been holding, and at first it sounds like she's about to say, "Oh my god." But as she's overcome with emotion, the noise just becomes a scream of victory and encouragement. She begins to walk backward with the phone, willing me to keep walking toward her, and I do, finishing the distance of the room by throwing my arms up in the air as if I had just won the Olympic four-hundred-meter dash.

And that's the end of the video, as Sadiye dropped the phone to come give me a hug and help me to a dining room chair as I ran out of steam. I sat down, out of breath but overjoyed. She looked at me proudly, and then said what we were both thinking:

"'Never walk without assistance' my ass."

In the weeks and months and eventually years after the injury and my struggle with opioids, life would be punctuated by moments of celebration like this: my first steps; the first time I left my cane in the car; my first "jog" (that's a pretty generous word for it—something of a walking-speed shuffle that made me sweat); hanging up my cane for good; and hopefully more to come. But it was also punctuated by exhaustion, frustration, and regular setbacks. It turns out that trauma is serious business, and recovery can do more than take years. It can become the new normal—just the way life is now. Even as I write this, another year is going by, and I am marking new abilities and new distances. Those gains are certainly slower than they were at the beginning, but they're ongoing.

That first year, though; that was especially hard. I had been away from work for months, and the semester was starting up. As director of my institute's master of bioethics program, I was the official adviser and primary faculty member for three new graduate students starting in September. That brought activities and deadlines that simply weren't very negotiable. Lectures had to be delivered, grades had to be given, and I had to drive to campus.

My joy at having escaped the grip of opioid dependence was hard to hold on to in this environment. My life was pain and exhaustion. Being free of opioids meant constant, significant pain, and ibuprofen and acetaminophen only just took the edge off. The pain sucked every bit of energy from me, down to the bones, each day, and I would come home to collapse in a heap.

After only a couple weeks of going to campus irregularly, I began to get sick. I caught strep throat, got over it, caught a cold, and it lingered. The cold turned into another throat infection, which also stuck around. Every time I thought I was recovering, I would push too hard, my energy level would drop through the floor, and I would get sick again.

In October, I traveled for the first time, flying to Houston for an academic conference. My dear friend Miriam—a physician herself—agreed to be my travel buddy, carrying my things and helping me secure wheelchairs and assistance when needed to get around. The trip was overwhelming, and within two days of returning I started to hear my lungs crackling. That was the first time I got pneumonia that year. It wasn't the last.

Probably the most difficult part of those first months was the tension between recovery and setbacks. I wanted *so badly* to be "normal" again. I had thought that my life was over, and then I'd been given something like it back, and I was desperate to make what I had into what I remembered. Part of what that meant for me was a hunger to make visible improvements: to use my knee-scooter less and rely on my cane, to take steps without my cane when possible; I even bought different color Crocs so that they would blend into my professional attire and make my deformed left foot less obvious.

A strange thing happens when your disability begins to become invisible, though: people stop recognizing your limits (which was exactly what I wanted) and start demanding more of you (a side effect I hadn't foreseen). So every time I made an advance, I signaled to my outward environment that I didn't need others to worry about my pain, my limitations, or the general lack of energy that recovery meant. In a perverse way, my ambition to get back to normal was undermining my own progress.

Still during this period, virtually no one knew of my struggle with opioids. At the time, I wouldn't have identified the cause of that as "shame"; it simply felt very private. But why was it so private? My friends and colleagues knew all the gory details of my exploding foot, so if the opioid dependence was just another medical problem, it likely would have been a major topic of conversation.

It wasn't, though. Some of our close family knew, and only a very few friends. Toward the middle of fall, however, I realized that would have to change. Because as time went by, it brought me closer to something that I had intellectually known I would face but had managed to avoid really thinking about: yet another surgery.

The plan had always been for one more plastic surgery. When the surgical team covered my foot wound with flesh from my thigh, they used quite a lot of skin and fat. After all, it's better to have too much and need to trim it off than to have too little. So I had a very deformed foot that would never fit into a normal shoe. This sixth surgery, then, was for the sake of "shaping" the foot now that the swelling had gone down and the surgeon could see just how much excess tissue there was. It would involve removing extra fat, pulling the skin down tighter over the new, slimmer design, and cutting away the excess dermis.

Although it was nothing compared to the surgeries I had been through, it would be very, very painful. And so, it would require pain meds.

As I started to face this reality, I asked my doctor friend Miriam if it would be possible for me to undergo the surgery without taking opioids. She looked at me very seriously and said, "Travis, you *really, really* don't want to do that."

I believed her. But I also really, really didn't want to take any more drugs.

So I did the only thing I could given those two competing goals: I called off the surgery.

I didn't do so rashly. Sadiye and I scheduled a follow-up appointment with Dr. Patel to get his opinion. As an orthopedic trauma surgeon, he didn't do any plastic surgery himself, so it seemed like perhaps he would have less conflict of interest; he had no dog in the fight, so to speak, so I wanted him to tell me if I would have less function if I didn't have another surgery.

When he saw my fully healed "flap" and saw me walk in with my cane, he was clearly taken aback. My foot had recovered "exceptionally well," he said, and my level of function was "truly remarkable." So I asked him my question: did I really need another surgery?

"Absolutely not," Dr. Patel answered with authority. "Surgery is an opportunity for infection and adverse outcomes. You are incredibly fortunate not to have experienced any bone infection after having an open wound for nearly a month, nor any major complications from a serious limb-salvage situation. There is no need for another surgery, and I would advise against it."

I practically melted. I was so relieved. I now had an official medical recommendation for avoiding the thing I was terrified of. Timidly, I asked, "Dr. Roberts seems to think that my functional gains will be limited if I don't do this; are you worried at all?"

"Not even a little bit," he replied. "This surgery would be cosmetic. It could allow your foot to look more normal, yes, and you could fit into a broader array of shoes. But it would not be functional."

Done deal, I thought with relief. No surgery for me, and I don't have to worry about having another bottle of oxycodone in my house.

I shouldn't have celebrated so quickly, though. We had an appointment with Dr. Roberts later in the week, and I victoriously announced my decision to him.

"What? No. That's not right," he told me. He asked what exactly Dr. Patel had said to discourage the surgery. When I relayed the conversation, he responded, "Okay, he misunderstands. This is really not a major surgery. There will be no bone exposure, so you won't be at increased risk of osteomyelitis"—the medical term for bone infection—"and what I don't think he appreciates is the functional cost of not getting you into supportive footwear." He looked at me seriously for a moment. "You need to understand: this is not merely cosmetic. Without this surgery, you won't be able to wear normal shoes and your gait will suffer from it. Trust me: you want this surgery."

I was exasperated. I *didn't* want this surgery, and I especially didn't want it from him. Dr. Roberts, after all, had been the one to give me the much-too-aggressive tapering plan, and although he was certainly not the only one to leave me hanging, he got the lion's share of the blame in my mind. I had considered changing surgeons, but I didn't want my anger to get in the way of getting the best treatment. The fact was that Dr. Roberts had been in the room when part of my thigh became part of my foot, and that meant that he knew exactly where everything was. Although a new surgeon would have my medical records, no one else would have the intimate knowledge of the inside of my body. So I had committed to sticking it out with him—but only if I truly believed that I had to.

As if reading my mind, Dr. Roberts said, "Travis, this won't be like last time. I know you're worried about taking the pain meds, but this is so much more minor than what you've been through. We're talking about low-dose Percocet [oxycodone/acetaminophen] for a few days—two weeks at the most. You'll be fine."

On this particular issue, however, I did not trust him. And so I was not appeased.

"Look, you and Patel need to work this out," I finally responded. I'm a generally nonconfrontational person, and I don't always stand up for myself when I should. But I was scared and exhausted, and I didn't know how to adjudicate this competing information. "I don't know if I'm willing to go back on the pain meds or not, but I do know that I'm not scheduling that surgery until I have a coherent recommendation. The payoff has to be worth my—to be frank—absolute terror; and until Patel agrees that this is more than cosmetic, it doesn't pass that test. So call me when you've reached consensus. Until then, I'm not scheduling the surgery."

Dr. Roberts looked taken aback for a minute by my assertiveness, but he recovered quickly. "Okay, I think that's a reasonable plan," he said. "I'll call Dr. Patel tonight, and once I explain the surgery to him, I'm sure he'll agree with me."

I hoped against hope that he was wrong—that any recovery potential I had was independent of whether I got this last surgery.

He wasn't wrong, though. The next day, I got a call from both my surgeons. They had come to an agreement about the surgery: it was highly recommended and carried relatively little risk.

I was going back under the knife.

"So how do I handle this?" I asked Miriam. She is a pediatric intensive care unit doc, so she doesn't work on cases like mine, but she is also a trusted friend, and one of the only physicians I had absolute faith in who knew my whole story. "You told me before that I really don't want to do this surgery without meds. But I'm terrified. What's my move?"

Miriam took a deep breath. We were walking to our normal lunchtime haunt—a café one block over from our department home—and she was taking slow, measured steps to keep pace with my shambling progress. "I told you before," she said, "this won't be anything like last time. Yes, you'll need meds, but at low doses for a short time. I really think you'll be okay as long as you're alert to the need to use as little as possible. But,"—she paused—"I'm not a pain doc. And you're a professor at Hopkins. Surely you can do better than me. What about Dr. Erdek—that guy who came and gave a talk last year? Why don't you reach out?"

My brain—after all these months, still occasionally fuzzy from the anesthesia and trauma—lit up a bit. She's exactly right, I thought. I *do* know a pain doc. Michael Erdek was a practicing interventionist at Johns Hopkins's Blaustein Pain Treatment Center, just down the road from my office. When I had met him the year before, I discovered that he was more than just a sharp physician; we had also geeked out a bit about philosophy, as he used our discussion to exploit the fairly rare opportunity (in his clinical life) to discuss philosophical groundings for medical ethics. "That's a great idea," I finally said to Miriam. Although I was still a bit shy about the prospect of telling a new person my most intimate of struggles, I knew I needed help. And here I had access of the kind very few other people have.

As if sensing just a bit of hesitation, Miriam prodded, "Do it, Travis. He'll have ideas and strategies, but he'll also be able to give you clearer advice about just what kind of meds you'll need and what the risk will look like. My guess," she added, "is that his advice will be very reassuring."

And Miriam, my insightful friend, was right. The next day I

emailed Dr. Erdek, and he graciously agreed to see me for a consultation. We got the appointment on the books, and I began to relax.

When the appointment day came, I had serious *déjà vu* as I sat down and filled out the office paperwork that asked me to rate my pain on that good ol' 0–10 scale. As someone who wasn't constantly in terrible pain, I felt silly even putting anything down: I knew what real pain was like, and my dull background bone pain didn't qualify. Although I still hobbled around on a cane, wincing when I pushed too hard, I think I marked my pain down as a 1 or 2 that day, embarrassed to even act as though it was the reason for my visit. After all, I wasn't there for meds or therapy, I was there for advice.

I spent a lot of time with one of the physician residents, who listened to my story in detail, asked probing questions, and discussed the details of my upcoming surgery. She already had some ideas by the end of our conversation, but the final evaluation would come from Dr. Erdek himself, her attending physician.

When he came and joined us for the last part of the discussion, I somewhat shyly thanked him for taking the time to talk to me and apologized for taking him away from other patients. But he put me immediately at ease, reassuring me that this sort of advising was a good use of his time and that he was confident we could come up with a sound plan for the next surgery. But what he said first stuck with me perhaps more than any of the rest: "I'm sorry for what happened to you," he began. "And while I can say that your experience fortunately isn't the norm, I also have to say that it's not all that surprising."

I was stunned. Here was a Johns Hopkins pain doc confirming my fears about the deep structural issues in pain medicine. "I'd begun to suspect as much," I said. "But it's really horrifying that physicians can prescribe dangerous medications and then just abandon their patients."

"Yes, well, the good news is that there's no reason to think that will happen again," he said. "Your surgeons and colleagues are correct that this next procedure will be significantly less serious, but you also have something else you didn't have last time: the knowledge and experience to take charge of your own pain therapy. You're right to not want to be on medication any longer than you need to, and the goal will be to follow through on that plan."

He said this with so much confidence that I immediately began to feel relief. We did discuss a strategy for further minimizing opioid use, which would be to supplement with other serious prescription (but non-opioid) medications, but I was wary. Perhaps I was irrational from the fear, but I wanted to take as few pills of as few medications as possible. So I asked him a very straightforward question: "If we stick with just opioids, and I ask Dr. Roberts to prescribe a low-dose pill, say five milligrams of oxycodone, could I survive just taking a few of those in the worst moments after surgery, but committing to be off them within a week or so?"

Dr. Erdek responded carefully: "Yes, you could of course survive. It would likely be very uncomfortable. And you don't want to be in so much pain that it inhibits your ability to rest and heal. But," he continued, "I think you could follow that plan, and if you stuck to it, you likely would experience no dependence or withdrawal effects."

Then it's done, I thought. That's the plan. As few pills as possible, and then hopefully, never again.

With a weight having been lifted off my shoulders, I thanked Dr. Erdek and his resident profusely for listening to my scared questions and for so patiently advising me while other patients in the office were probably suffering from truly devastating pain. I didn't feel like I deserved so much of their time and attention, but I was so very grateful for it.

I had a plan.

On December 30, 2015, I went back to the hospital to undergo my sixth surgery. It would be relatively short (compared to the others), and I would be discharged the same day. That certainly didn't fully alleviate my fear of the pain and the medication, but it allowed me to at least convince myself to move forward—to sign the consent paperwork and let the anesthesiologist sedate me. The whole thing felt so routine by now: undress and put on the hospital gown; wait in the bed; have short conversations with the surgeon and anesthesiologist; finally, tell them I'm ready to go; watch the anesthesiologist press the plunger on the first sedative and start counting backward from one hundred. And then nothing.

As predicted, the surgery was incredibly painful. When I woke up and the anesthesia began to wear off, I immediately forgot my commitment to simply deal with as much of the pain as possible and called a nurse to ask about medication.

"We're trying to get you ready for discharge," the nurse said, "so we're not going to use any IV meds. You will be going home with Percocet, though, so I can bring you your first dose of that if you want."

"Yes, please," I responded without hesitation, grimacing as the pain flared up.

This momentary embrace of opioid therapy was not, however, a sign of trouble to come. As the two Percocet slowly washed over me and the acuteness of the pain faded, I regained some ability to think about how I wanted to deal with the pain. "Only when absolutely necessary," I thought to myself. "This *will not* be like last time."

I wish I could tell you that, having recommitted to this plan, it was easier than I expected and I just muscled my way through some minor discomfort. But that's simply not true. The pain was horrible, especially because it was so *sharp*; the tug of freshly cut tissue pulling against dozens of stitches was so much more invasive than the duller bone and joint pain I had become accustomed to, and I was miserable. I kept thinking about the confidence of the doctors as they told me how much more minor this procedure would be compared to my weeks of trauma surgery. "Well, sure," I thought, "compared to those"; but it was *not* an objectively minor procedure.

For close to two weeks, my life once again revolved around pain relief treatments—but this time, of a very different kind. I took ibuprofen and acetaminophen around the clock, carefully staying under the maximum daily dose; iced on a schedule day in and day out; and took a Percocet or two when I simply couldn't stand the pain anymore.

At the beginning, that meant a dose of opioids at least two or three times a day. It was more than I wanted, but I just couldn't stand it. Maybe someone else would be able to. But I couldn't. So I'd reach for the bottle.

After the first five days or so, though, I noticed that I wouldn't get so desperate so early, and I rarely took more than two doses a day: one to sleep at night and then the occasional rescue dose. Although I was incredibly focused on minimizing my use of the prescription pain meds, I don't remember having the cognitive focus to really evaluate how I was doing, or whether I thought I was succeeding at my plan. All I knew was that I hurt a lot, because I wouldn't medicate the hurt until it became unbearable. I was acutely aware of how easy it would be to take a lot of opioids. They worked, and without them, life was so hard. But no matter how bad the pain was, it was never as bad as the worst moments of withdrawal. And that was my motivation.

I do remember those two weeks feeling like they lasted forever, but they didn't. On the fourteenth day, I nearly made it without Percocet but eventually caved and took one late at night when the pain was keeping me awake. That nighttime dose was fairly common during the third week.

But at some point, I fell asleep without it, marking my first day without any opioid painkillers. I made it through that day with ice and over-the-counter medication, and when I woke up the next morning, no shivers, no sweats—no withdrawal. I had officially gone through the surgery and recovery without redeveloping dependence. I had used the drugs when I most needed them, but without them destroying my life. And while that would almost certainly not seem all that impressive to the millions of patients who have done the same thing without even trying, it was crucially important to me.

Somewhere deep down, I think I hadn't really believed that I could take those pills and make it out unscathed. Some deeply irrational part of my brain, formed through fear and desperation, had come to see these pills as a kind of dark magic. Surely they would ensnare me again, regardless of what I did.

But opioids aren't magic. They're just medicine. And like virtually any other medicine, they can be both beneficial and harmful. Yes, they can get their chemical hooks into your brain and cast you into the hell of withdrawal; and they can sedate your body's systems to such an extent that they cause death. They can also, it turns out, alleviate desperate pain. And with care, they can do the latter with less risk of the former.

Almost immediately after taking my last pill and realizing that I was okay, I knew that I wanted to spend some time thinking more about this dual feature of opioids—that they can both help and harm. What I was discovering about opioid use was, at its core, an issue in bioethics, and that just happens to be my job. I had experienced both the benefits and burdens of opioids firsthand, and I was beginning to get the sense that I had learned something important along the way. I wasn't yet sure what it was, but I wanted to find out.

In the basement of Deering Hall, the building where my faculty office is located, is a well-appointed conference room in which my institute hosts speakers and holds faculty meetings, and it's where I teach courses for our graduate program. On April 7, 2016, that conference room was packed full of some thirty of my colleagues in bioethics, medicine, and public health—dozens of the leaders in my field, decades my senior, intimidating in both their brilliance and stature. And I—nearly against my own will—was about to tell them a very personal story.

Several weeks before, I had gotten sucked down a research rabbit hole, reading tragic story after tragic story about opioid therapy patients who had been badly managed by their prescribing physicians. Although there was a growing academic literature and the occasional think piece about how physicians should prescribe fewer opioids, I was becoming more and more irritated by the lack of attention paid to the actual *management* of the medication once prescribed. I said to Sadiye more than once, "People act as though prescribing the pills is the only point of contact between physician and patient, and the only way to stem the flow of pain patients into the opioid crisis is to reduce raw prescription numbers. Does no one think that perhaps, just *perhaps*, it's also the doctor's job to manage the medications they prescribe and ensure that acute pain patients have a pathway off the medication?"

I was clearly not dispassionate about the issue, and I was becoming more frustrated the more I thought about it.

During this same time period, I began to regularly think about a discussion I'd had with a colleague in public health—an assistant professor named Dr. Brendan Saloner—who just so happened to work on issues concerning addiction, healthcare policy, and, currently, the opioid crisis. I'm not quite sure why, but he was one of the first people outside my inner circle to whom I decided to tell my story. Sitting in a Starbucks in Silver Spring, Maryland, Brendan had lots of thoughts about drugs, addiction, and America's current crisis. But he also made one comment that stuck with me. "Travis," he said, "your story is important."

I wasn't convinced this was true. It was too intimate, too idiosyncratic. Sure, it was important *to me*, but why would anyone else care about it?

"If you think you could bring yourself to share it," he said, "you might be able to really add something to the discussion." He even had some advice about where I might be able to publish an article that included both my experience and some ethical and policy analysis.

I don't think I really expected to follow through, but I couldn't shake the conversation afterward. So I began to write, and the writing was therapeutic. It gave my research direction, and I was learning things about America's problems with addiction, pain medicine, and much else. And there was certainly no harm in writing; after all, I didn't have to publish if I didn't want to.

But I kept thinking about Brendan's total confidence that this mattered. And every time I got really frustrated while reading about our broken medical system, I would think about Brendan's comment: "You might be able to really add something to the discussion."

That's what I was thinking about in the early spring of 2016, when I got an email from my institute's administrative director, asking for faculty to volunteer to speak at the April research retreat. The goal of these retreats is for faculty to present "works in progress," or scholarship that they are still thinking through, in order to receive feedback from the group. Having just started at Hopkins in 2014, I had only been to a few of these, but I had found the faculty discussions to be both insightful and warm. I knew it was a friendly, collegial environment, precisely the kind of environment in which one might first share his amateur attempt to turn a terrible personal experience into research that mattered.

Before I had time to think too deeply and to second-guess myself, I hit reply to the email and requested that I be added to the agenda. When asked for a title for my presentation, I responded, "Prescription Opioid Withdrawal and Physician Responsibility."

By the time it was my turn to present on April 7, I deeply, deeply regretted my decision.

At this point in 2016, I had been teaching at the university level and presenting my scholarship for a decade. I wasn't a particularly nervous person to begin with, and after so much experience, speaking was simply my job. And yet, as I leaned heavily on my cane to push myself up from my chair, my legs were weak and I genuinely thought I might not be able to walk to the front of the room.

"I can't do this," I thought to myself. But I knew I would.

I slowly limped to the front of the room and warmed up for the talk, thanking everyone for indulging me. "Those of you who have seen me present before," I began, "were probably very surprised to see the title of my talk on the agenda. You may be thinking, 'Travis has absolutely no background in clinical ethics, so what does he think he's doing?'" The room chuckled a bit. "And you would be right about that: I have no idea what I'm doing." The chuckle turned into a louder laugh.

I was loosening up. "That's why I need you. I've started to believe that I might have something worth saying on the question of today's talk"—I looked at Brendan for a second—"but I'm outside of my comfort zone. So if any of you have advice for this very new, perhaps ill-advised project, I would receive it gratefully."

And with that bit of self-handicapping out of the way, I began the most terrifying talk of my career. Even at the beginning, as I described some of the basic facts about the opioid crisis, the nervousness threatened to choke me. I had prepared for this, though. Since I knew it may be hard to get through, I had brought a printout of the paper I was working on—the article in which I told my story in some detail, and tried to draw a lesson or two from it. When it came time to tell my story, I paused once again.

"I really want to get through this, and it's time to tell you a story—to give you a case study in the ethics of opioid prescribing. But as I think you'll understand in a minute, this is going to be a bit hard for me, so I'm going to break one of the central rules of presenting, and I'm going to read this part to you. Because,"—I really couldn't believe I was about to do this—"I'm pretty intimately involved with this particular case study. That is, the case study is me."

So I pulled out my paper, and I began to tell my story: the failure of my doctors to advise me, and then a week-by-week breakdown of my withdrawal symptoms. As I got to the latter half of the story, my whole body shook, and I was quite sure that my voice would give out and I would shatter into a million pieces. Here I was, telling a room full of the people I most respect in my field my most intimate of stories. I felt vulnerable and exposed, and like I may have been crossing some sort of line. But my voice didn't give out, and I didn't shatter. I managed to get through the story, and when I took a deep breath to recenter myself before diving into the analysis of the "case study," you could hear a pin drop in the room.

I talked for a few more minutes, articulating what I called a "badly needed principle in medical ethics." The principle, I argued, was easily defended on any plausible moral theory, and it went like this: "A physician who prescribes a medication with predictable and harmful side effects is obligated to work to mitigate those side effects, or at least to ensure that the patient has access to someone who will work to mitigate those side effects." So an obvious implication is that anyone who prescribes opioids is obligated to work to mitigate the harms of dependence and withdrawal (or, further: addiction and overdose) or to make sure that the patient has access to someone who will.

As I said in my presentation on that day: this seems like just about the most obvious moral claim I've ever defended, and yet my experience indicates that at least some physicians need it spelled out. I closed by thanking Brendan for pushing me to pursue the project, and I thanked Sadiye and Sinem for—as I put it then, and as I still believe—saving my life.

I had managed to stand for the whole presentation, leaning heavily on my cane, and as I wrapped up, I melted into a chair to begin the discussion portion of the event.

I don't remember every question asked and comment made, but I remember that my brilliant, experienced, powerful colleagues were as warm and supportive as anyone could ask. And I remember two particular discussions.

Immediately after I finished, Dr. Nancy Kass—a senior public health ethicist—raised her hand and said something that I'll never forget: "Travis, go ahead and write that paper with the moral philosophy and the new principle—it'll get published, and that's great. But," she pointed at me with confidence, "that's not what's most important here. Everyone—*everyone*—needs to hear your story. Stories matter. Stories can make a difference."

That moment, building on the discussion with Brendan, marked the turning point in my understanding of how to work to achieve meaningful change. *Stories matter*, I would continue to think to myself over the coming years.

The next person to ask a question was Dr. Jeff Kahn—my faculty mentor and the person who would, in the coming years, become the next director of my institute. Jeff had been so, so supportive during the previous year, helping me to arrange my life so that I could keep my brand-new job while healing from home. He was the one who asked the question that would come to occupy me for months.

"Why didn't you come to us?" he wanted to know. He paused to let me think about it for a minute.

"I really don't know," I practically whispered.

"I guess I want to invite you to think about this for a minute: You're faculty at Johns Hopkins University, you have colleagues and friends who know people in one of the best hospitals in the country." For just a second, I thought he was asking only the personal question—that he just wanted to know for himself why I didn't let them in. But he continued: "There's a really important piece of your story that you didn't note here, which is that you are among the most privileged people to whom this could have happened. If you couldn't save yourself from suffering, how are we supposed to expect that everyone with even fewer resources will make it out unscathed?"

Then I understood. It had taken me a minute, but I caught up:

he wasn't asking me to explain to them why I didn't let them help me; he was asking me to reflect on the reasons that I kept my struggle a secret, and to recognize that any challenge I faced would likely be amplified for others.

Although I had explored some of these pieces on my own, Jeff's question shook me to my very core. I didn't actually know why I had never called him, or any of my physician colleagues. And I was definitely aware of my privilege, and horrified at the thought that most patients have even less access to good pain care than I did. But I hadn't put those two thoughts together until just then.

What Jeff suspected immediately is that, whether I had ever articulated it or not, some of the stigma associated with opioids, dependence, and the relation to addiction infected my behavior. I, like so many others, turned inward during my struggle, allowing my life to become defined by solitude and darkness. If there had been more light shone on the problem, maybe I would have just reached out immediately, as I regularly have during my time at Hopkins when I've had other medical questions (one of the benefits of working with clinicians is getting to pick their brains when I or a family member have health issues). If opioid dependence and withdrawal hadn't, at some level, seemed shameful—if it had been just another element of my healthcare experience—how differently might things have gone?

I know that I learned a lot from that first time sharing my story, and as I went on to tell it publicly, dozens of times, I would continue to learn from every audience. But the takeaway that I will never forget from my wonderful colleagues was simple:

Tell the story. Shine a light. Don't let the suffering of people like me exist in darkness anymore.

CHAPTER 9

Pain, Drugs, and Doing the Right Thing

Over the last couple of decades—as America conducted what some have come to call a "War on Pain"—patients who sought medical attention for injury, illness, trauma, chronic pain, or surgery were often given opioids. Many of them were given huge amounts of opioids, and some of those patients are still on high (and increasing) doses today. These are the legacy patients discussed earlier.

But the vast majority of opioid patients experienced the analgesic benefits of their medication and simply stopped taking it when the pain receded, never suffering any ill effects. Their bottles of Percocet or Vicodin likely continue to sit in a medicine cabinet (just in case!), raising another concern about diversion—that they may be stolen for misuse or for sale, typically by family members; but the patients themselves are doing fine. Without giving it any conscious thought, they did what I did for my sixth surgery, using the medications when needed and stopping them when not.

A very small subset of the population, however, entered a dark period of their lives. Some developed opioid use disorder and fed their addiction through ever-increasing doses of prescription medications, while others were eventually turned away by their fearful doctors. These victims of abandonment have faced and continue to face a choice: go through the hell of detox and try to enter recovery or turn to the black market. For those who choose the latter, heroin and illicit fentanyl become increasingly attractive options, due to cost and availability. Tragically, those who go down the path of opioid use disorder don't all survive. And those who do survive may come out the other side only after destroying their own lives and the lives of friends and loved ones while deep in the throes of addiction.

The question facing us now, as a society, is precisely this: how do we get the benefits experienced by the first group while minimizing the harms experienced by the second? Or, as I can't help but see it: how do we save people from my initial experience with opioids (or much worse), while promoting the kind of pain care I received for my later surgery?

Throughout this book, I've alluded to different kinds of pain that might be treated with opioids. For instance, the modern pain movement was helped along by focusing on the needs of cancer patients at the end of their lives. Since these patients were suffering horribly, and fear of addiction seemed perversely puritanical when facing death, the idea that such patients should have access to whatever medication makes their suffering more manageable, including opioids, strikes most people as utterly reasonable.

However, in the history sketched earlier, cancer and end-of-life care was the camel's nose under the tent. Pharmaceutical companies and eventually an entire generation of pain advocates moved from the claim that opioids are appropriate in that limited case to the much more contentious (and ultimately problematic) claim that opioids are appropriate in a wide variety of cases. Our enthusiastic acceptance of this refrain depended on the idea (which companies like Purdue Pharma were happy to peddle) that opioids aren't that addictive or dangerous.

Of course, that claim was false. Opioids are devastatingly addictive and dangerous, and the extent of America's drug crisis is the proof. But as the swinging pendulum metaphor suggests, it's also not the case that we should simply go back to the prohibitionist policies of the mid-twentieth century.

In short, the challenge we face is the need for nuance. The benefit of opioids doesn't mean that we should take them like candy, and the risk of opioids doesn't mean that we should lock them away and forget about them.

Nuance is always harder than simplicity, though. Treating pain well requires knowing when opioids will actually help more than they'll hurt, and that requires a lot of data—data that we didn't have until distressingly recently. Now that we're starting to get it, though, we must rethink our use of this deadly-but-powerful pain medication.

Many of us have a story about treating moderate acute pain. We break a bone, go to our doctor or the emergency room, and the physicians start to work on the repair (setting or casting the bone) while also addressing our pain.

Another common example is dental work. Tooth pain is really not fun, and dentists cause a lot of it—pulling teeth, performing root canals, and the like. For years, during the heyday of the War on Pain, dentists also treated pain aggressively. In fact, in 2011, dentists were the second-highest prescribing group of clinicians (behind family physicians) and wrote a full 12 percent of immediate-release opioid prescriptions in the United States. Patients would go in for an extraction and walk out with a bottle of Vicodin or Percocet.

Although these sorts of moderate acute pains can be disruptive and uncomfortable, it's important to recognize that they also aren't genuinely severe pains. Nonprescription painkillers often take the edge off quite effectively, and the more disturbing levels of pain tend to last only a few days. It's for this reason that the American Dental Association, recognizing dentists' role in the opioid crisis, issued guidelines for dental pain management in 2016. While these recommendations do not prohibit the use of opioids, they do recommend that dentists adhere to the CDC guidelines and that they try NSAIDs (such as ibuprofen) first. Likely as a result, prescribing by dentists in 2017 fell to 8.6 percent of national opioid prescribing—an improvement, for sure, though still nearly as much as that prescribed by pain management (8.9 percent).

It's hard for many of us to imagine that nonprescription painkillers can actually be helpful for disruptive acute pain. After all, we take Tylenol and ibuprofen for every minor ache; surely a broken bone requires something stronger. This question about the effectiveness of nonprescription medications is a place where we really need data, and we're finally beginning to get it.

In 2017, a group of researchers did the first randomized clinical trial comparing the effectiveness of opioids to a combination of acetaminophen (Tylenol) and ibuprofen for moderate to severe "extremity pain"—arm, shoulder, leg, or hip pain—in the emergency department. Their findings, published in the *Journal of the American Medical Association (JAMA)*, were impressive. In the words of the researchers, "For patients presenting to the ED with acute extremity pain, there were no statistically significant or clinically important differences in pain reduction at 2 hours among single-dose treatment with ibuprofen and acetaminophen or with 3 different opioid and acetaminophen combination analgesics." In other words, Tylenol and ibuprofen worked just as well for this sort of pain as did low-dose opioid painkillers. Regardless of whether it might *seem* like we need something stronger than over-the-counter meds, the data suggests that we don't really—they can work just as well as the heavy hitters for some acute pain.

Shortly after learning of this sort of data, I found out that I needed to have a wisdom tooth extracted. Never one to miss out on a learning opportunity, I asked my dentist, "So will I need opioids to recover from the extraction?"

My kind, young dentist didn't miss a beat. "You know, we used to think that you did, and we'd send patients home with bottles of

Vicodin for every little procedure. But it turns out that you really don't need them, and I don't know if you've heard anything about this on the news, but opioids are really quite dangerous. We're trying to make sure we don't prescribe them unless they're really necessary."

"You know, I do think I've heard something about that," I replied. I was glad to hear both that change was occurring and that my particular dentist had such important information.

Unsurprisingly, the extraction was quite unpleasant, and the pain was definitely disruptive. I took Tylenol and rested. Would I have preferred to just sleep comfortably through that pain? For sure. But I could make it through, and the Tylenol definitely helped.

The universe must have a sense of humor, though, because about three days after my tooth came out, the severity of pain went through the roof. The side of my face looked suddenly swollen, and I went from uncomfortable to miserable. I called the dentist and he told me to come in, after which he confirmed my suspicions: I had developed an infection in the socket and needed antibiotics. He asked about the pain, and I was honest.

"It's a lot worse," I told him. "It went from manageable with Tylenol to pretty miserable."

"Okay," he responded. "Remember that conversation we had about Vicodin? Well, I said we try not to prescribe it except in those cases where it's really needed. And until these antibiotics kick in, I'm afraid you might need it. So why don't I send you home with a few pills?" He wrote a scrip for twelve tablets of the low-dose hydrocodone mixed with acetaminophen and told me that I should be back to normal levels of postextraction pain within a few days.

Although I wasn't thrilled at the thought of hydrocodone in my house, I also no longer thought of opioids as black magic that would inevitably pull me into a tailspin. Having taken Percocet for my last surgery, and then having quit as soon as possible with no real dependence or withdrawal, had marked a significant turning point in my attitude toward pills. Not to mention that the pain really was quite bad, and it's exceedingly hard to resist pain relief when being bombarded by serious acute pain.

I accepted the prescription.

The experience of escalating dental pain helped me to think through the challenge of nuance in pain management. My thoughtful dentist avoided using the meds willy-nilly, but he still saw them as a tool in the toolbox when things got worse. In his eyes, opioids are neither a cure-all nor are they evil; they are to be respected for their power, but they can ease some of the suffering that his procedures cause. Could I have made it, even with the infection pain, on Tylenol alone? I'm sure I could have, and perhaps I should have. But the pain was disruptive, and my dentist's view of the usefulness of a dozen Vicodin tablets did not seem unreasonable.

I took two of the pills that first day, and one the following day. Then the pain began to recede. I switched back to Tylenol.

The kind of moderate to severe acute pain described above is very different from severe chronic pain that weighs on a patient and disrupts one's life. Some of the most common forms of chronic pain include lower-back pain and joint pain. These sorts of deep, disruptive pains—evidence of arthritis, injury, and often just a lifetime of some form of neglect or abuse—are a large part of the reason that family physicians are the only category of clinicians who have outprescribed dentists in terms of immediate-release opioids. Americans see their family docs because they hurt, and for years, those docs have written millions of prescriptions for oxycodone, hydrocodone, fentanyl patches, and more.

On the one hand, it is completely understandable for a chronic pain patient to ask for something stronger than over-the-counter pain meds. The pain doesn't let up for these patients, and they can see their lives dwindling to a smaller and smaller level of activity. Many quit or lose their jobs, are unable to play with children or grandchildren, and are tortured by relentless pain.

On the other hand, though, long-term opioid therapy raises se-rious challenges. After all, the major risks of the medication include tolerance, dependence, and addiction (all of which occur over time), as well as overdose, which is more likely to occur as the dosage gets higher. So just in terms of the basic mechanism of the medication, if a patient is on it for weeks or months, she will develop a tolerance, requiring a higher dose for the same analgesic effect. She will also develop a dependence—as I did—meaning that when she tries to stop, withdrawal symptoms will provide a major obstacle. Since the body's respiratory and other systems do not become tolerant to the dose increase as fast as they do to the pain-relieving or euphoric ef-fects, increasing the dose increases the risk of overdose. And finally, the euphoric effect on the brain's reward system makes the drug pow-erfully addictive.

In short, putting patients on opioid therapy with the intention of leaving them on it for any length of time is, even just based on the medication's properties, more worrisome than using it for short-term, acute pain relief.

It seems, then, that what is desperately needed in this space is data on how effective these medications are for chronic pain as well as how dangerous they are. Only then could we make an evidence-based decision concerning their appropriateness—and only then could the patient herself make an autonomous decision regarding whether she wants to take certain risks for the prospect of certain benefits.

Up until very recently, however, we did not have this evidence base. In fact, for more than two decades of aggressive prescribing of opioids for chronic pain, we had virtually no high-quality evidence of their long-term effectiveness in the chronic pain population. What we did have, of course, was overwhelming evidence of the risks of using opioids in this population—especially as the years wore on. As a result, the language that began to pop up in guidelines and reports concerning prescription opioid use was something like the following:

there is virtually no high-quality evidence that opioids are effective for the management of chronic pain, and there is extensive evidence that they raise patient risk for a multitude of adverse outcomes, including opioid use disorder, overdose, and death.

That is not exactly a ringing endorsement.

In 2018, the evidence base for opioid use in the chronic pain population got worse. For the first time, researchers completed a twelve-month, randomized clinical trial (the gold standard for scientific evidence) comparing the use of opioid therapies to non-opioid therapies such as acetaminophen and ibuprofen. The patients in the study suffered from two forms of common chronic pain: lower-back pain and arthritic knee or hip pain. Some of the patients received opioids, while others did not. And at the end of the twelve months, the patients in the different groups were compared to one another. The result? The group taking opioids did not have increased function or decreased pain over their non-opioid counterparts. Indeed, those on opioids had slightly *more* pain at the end of the twelve months, as well as significantly more side effects.

This is incredibly important evidence, and it came far, far too late in the game. Although it doesn't mean that opioids are never indicated for patients suffering from lower-back or arthritic joint pain, it does cast serious doubt on the practice of using opioids as a standard treatment. What doctors can honestly say to patients complaining of those ailments is that opioids are simply not good medications for their ailment, and so given their risks, many other alternatives should be tried before discussing the appropriateness of opioid therapy. As the CDC puts it: opioids should not be considered first-line therapy for chronic, noncancer pain.

In the spirit of nuance, though, we should remember: patients aren't data points in a study. Patients are the living, breathing, unique individuals standing in front of their doctor. Sometimes, a patient with excruciating, debilitating back pain may try every therapy in her physician's repertoire, all to no avail. She may, at the end of this macabre circus, be depressed and even suicidal from the unrelenting pain and loss of function. Such a case raises difficult questions for doctors, and some of them may write prescriptions for opioids; and some of those patients who receive opioids as a last resort may get their lives back. All of that is consistent with the data above, and with the idea that opioids should not be first-line treatment for most chronic pain.

In general, the growing evidence base and the recognition of medicine's recent history of overprescribing are leading us to reduce reliance on opioids for moderate acute pain and for many forms of chronic pain. The ideas explored so far can be summed up as follows: non-opioid therapies work surprisingly well for both acute and chronic pain and have less severe side effects for most people. If opioids are necessary for acute pain, they should be used in very small doses for the least amount of time possible, and for chronic pain, they should be used only after other therapies have been exhausted.

This disjunction between modest acute pain and chronic pain, however, leaves out a big, important class of pains that very many people will experience at some point in their lives: postsurgical and traumatic pain. This class is characterized by truly severe acute pain that, in the worst cases, will last for weeks or even months while multiple surgeries are required to stitch someone back together. In short, the kind of pain I experienced for months after my foot was crushed and while physicians continued to cut, poke, prod, and stitch my exposed wounds. Virtually no physician will tell you that major surgery or trauma should be suffered through without opioid therapy. But if traumatic and postsurgical pain can last weeks or months, then this class of patients will face some of the same risks as chronic pain patients. In short, surgery and trauma raise a specific challenge because physicians are likely to see opioid therapy as necessary for this level of pain, but the timeline of recovery can extend to such a degree that it starts to blur the line between acute and chronic pain therapy.

Recent findings confirm precisely this worry about exposure time postsurgery. In a paper for the CDC, researchers looked at initial opioid prescriptions for more than a million patients, and then looked to see what predicted whether these patients would still be on the medication one and three years into the future. The study found that patients prescribed even just one day of opioids had a 6 percent chance of still being on opioids one year into the future. Much more disturbing, though, was how aggressively that number jumped when the initial prescription was longer. More than 15 percent of patients prescribed opioids for ten days continued use for a year or more, as did a full 30 *percent* of patients who were given a prescription for more than a month.

In early 2018, another group of researchers looked at opioid prescribing specifically for surgery patients and found that length of initial opioid use also predicted *misuse*—defined here as opioid dependence, abuse, or overdose. Perhaps most shocking is that patients given a refill of their opioid medications were at *double* the risk of misuse, and that each additional refill increased the risk of misuse by approximately 70 percent. Further, each additional week of opioid use increased the risk of misuse by 34 percent.

In short, the evidence on this question is in: longer exposure to opioids, along with increased dose, increases the most serious risks associated with opioid use. And so while prescribing opioids at all is a significant decision (remember: those given a single day's prescription had a 6 percent chance of still using opioids a full year later), reducing the exposure time can make a real difference to a particular patient's risk profile. My dentist, then, had very good reason both for not wanting to prescribe opioids at all (preventing that initial exposure risk) and for giving me a small number of pills when he decided that I was going to need something stronger while the antibiotics took effect (indeed, as I discovered, he could have given me fewer). Twelve pills, it turns out, is significantly different from thirty or 120 pills in terms of probable outcomes.

What, then, do we do about major surgery? And about trauma? Do we know how many pills are appropriate for getting an average patient through recovery from different procedures?

My first piece of data on this question was a pretty personal one. A bit more than two years after I fought my own battle with opioids, my mom's knees—having been on a long, slow decline into uselessness—gave out completely. She needed new ones. And bilateral knee replacement, which is just medical jargon for "two new knees," was going to hurt. A lot. Being my mom, and having watched what I had gone through, she was not looking forward to the procedures.

In preparation for her procedure, we did a lot of talking. She talked to her surgeon; I talked to my friend and colleague Dr. Casey Humbyrd, who is an orthopedic surgeon at Hopkins; and we got her psychologically prepared. Her surgeon told her, "For two weeks, you're going to hate me. But after that, you're going to love me." That is, that this was really going to hurt, but that it would be worth it.

I asked Casey to tell me what reasonable, cautious use of opioids for bilateral knee replacement looked like. She responded, "I tell my patients that they get two weeks. They get two weeks on the meds before I start getting on their case. And they tend to need it. But I also tell them that I expect them to start working hard to wean themselves off after that, and that I'll be following up with them. Most are able to do it."

So that's what I told Mom when I called her after talking to Casey: "You get two weeks before I'm on your case."

When she got home from the hospital, Mom had with her a bottle of 120 Norcos—7.5 milligrams of hydrocodone mixed with acetaminophen. When she was conscious and alert enough to relay that to me a couple of days after the procedure, I wasn't surprised, but I wasn't happy.

"Just to be clear, Mom, that's four pills a day for thirty days. I *really* hope you don't need that many," I told her, worriedly.

"Okay, okay," she replied. "But I'd rather have too many than run out." I was sure that was true as a report of her preferences, but I was also sure that this sort of justification was part of the problem. Until recently, opioids could not be prescribed remotely, and so getting a refill required a new trip to the doctor. This was inconvenient for all patients and can be very hard for some (the elderly, those with mobility restrictions, those without a lot of help during recovery). Physicians, too, don't want to be bothered by a follow-up visit just for more pills. Easier to send them home with more than they'll need.

Although I worried about the number of pills in that bottle, my mom is tough as nails and relied on the Norcos as little as possible. She was miserable for the first several days, and she probably took three or four pills a day. By the time I flew to Indiana to take care of her over the second weekend while my sister was at work, she was shuffling around on her walker pretty good and experiencing less pain. We spent a lot of time talking about the path to getting off the meds completely.

"You're almost at two weeks, Mom," I'd say, nervously glancing at the calendar. I felt obnoxious and overbearing, but I also simply couldn't stop myself from saying something. I knew far too well what the cost of too many pills could be.

"I know, I know. I think I'll be able to get away with just a pill to help me sleep and maybe one after physical therapy starting next week," she responded. I was relieved to hear that she had a plan, and I relayed that strategy to Casey. She confirmed that this was a totally reasonable timeline.

Mom stuck to the schedule. We video-chatted every day after I flew back home, and I'd judge both how much she was grimacing and how sedated she looked. She slowly gained more energy, and she would do more moving about as we chatted. In the middle of week three, she took her last Norco pill.

Sometime later, I asked her if she would count how many pills were left in her bottle. I was confident that she hadn't used anywhere near the full 120, but I wanted to know just how many extra she'd been given. She texted a little while after I asked, writing, "Have 73 of 120 remaining." She had used well under half of what she'd been prescribed.

I should have been surprised, but by this point, I'd begun to see the data on overprescribing for surgery. Practitioners in all different fields are starting to examine their prescribing practices, publishing what the average prescription is for a given procedure and then attempting to find out how many pills patients actually end up taking. Results like my mom's are not uncommon.

A particularly striking result was published in 2017 by a group of researchers at the University of Michigan. Their study looked at a particular procedure—gallbladder removal—and found that the average postoperative prescription for this surgery was about 250 milligrams (measured in morphine equivalents, for the sake of standardization). When the researchers interviewed patients, though, they discovered that the average amount of medication taken was only *thirty milligrams*. As a result, the group produced a prescribing guideline that included an educational component. It informed patients that they likely would need only a few pills for a handful of days, and that they shouldn't take the pills unless they really needed them. In the months following the implementation of this guideline, the average amount of opioids prescribed dropped from 250 to 75 milligrams, and with *no increase* in refill requests.

Just because opioids are seen as necessary in cases of surgery or severe injury, then, does not mean that we can't make very real progress. Being exposed to opioids at all puts one at risk, and the evidence suggests that the length of exposure increases risk to a remarkable degree. As a result, we simply cannot justify sending more opioids out into the world than are needed—we can't allow doctors to routinely write prescriptions for 120 pills when sixty will do, or for thirty pills when three to five will do.

And just in case it seems far-fetched that opioids can cause problems in a matter of weeks, there is a small coda to my mom's story. Late in her third week after surgery, we were chatting during our daily call and I asked if she was sleeping okay.

"Oh, not great," she replied. "I don't feel all that good. And my legs are kind of jumpy when I lie down. I think they're just restless from all this time doing nothing."

"Mom . . ." I started slowly. "Do they feel twitchy, like you really have to move them; like your muscles are building up electric energy or something?"

"You know, that's exactly how they feel," she replied.

"You're in withdrawal, Mom!" I was exasperated. "Did that symptom not sound awfully familiar to you?"

"Well, I guess," she started. "But it's really not that bad. Just annoying."

"That doesn't mean it's not withdrawal, Mom. It's just more minor than mine was because you were on fairly low-dose opioids for a shorter amount of time."

I'm not sure she was convinced during that first conversation, but the jitteriness persisted over a few days and bothered her more as she lost progressively more sleep. Later that week, she was getting genuinely tired and frustrated, and she called to ask me what I thought. I asked her when she had taken her last pill, and we did some math.

"Well, predicting isn't an exact science," I told her. "But my symptoms abated almost exactly a week after I took my last pill. That matches the common withdrawal timeline in much of the literature. My guess is that by Thursday"—it was Tuesday when we were talking—"you'll sleep through the night. Just a couple more days; you can make it."

Friday morning she called: she had slept restfully through the night and was feeling much better.

Mom's withdrawal wasn't terrible, and if she hadn't known my story, she may never even have figured out that's what it was. Re-covering from surgery, after all, is painful and uncomfortable for lots of reasons, and it's not always obvious how to pull apart those dis-comforts. But understanding how quickly dependence can form is crucially important for understanding why larger prescriptions might predict long-term use: stopping the pills can cause withdrawal, and withdrawal causes increased pain and discomfort. It's not exactly a surprise that more people will continue to take a medication when stopping that medication makes them miserable.

The bad news is that American physicians do not, as a whole, appear to be using opioids well. We've already learned that, beginning in the late 1990s, physicians began aggressively overprescribing. But the outcry over an opioid epidemic has been ongoing for years, and prescribing peaked between 2010 and 2012. So we might expect that docs know better by now and are treating pain in a more evidence-based manner.

And indeed, some are. Many of my colleagues and the clinicians that I meet at conferences are engaging in novel strategies to use opi-oids more appropriately. The data, however, suggests that practice, overall, is slow to change.

There are certainly straightforward changes that we could make. These are the "easy solutions," in the sense that they are low-hanging fruit—obvious, and shocking that we aren't doing them already. For starters, clinicians need to reduce clearly inappropriate prescriptions: moderate acute pain that can be effectively treated with acetamino-phen and ibuprofen simply should not be treated with opioids. That is an exposure point that we can avoid. And, as we've already discussed, opioids should not be first-line therapy for chronic pain. Although terrible, recalcitrant chronic pain may sometimes, in close and careful consultation with a specialist, be appropriately treated with opioids, that just shouldn't be the primary tool in the physician's toolbox.

Severe acute pain, though, is likely an appropriate target of opioids. But there are still, in this case, obvious improvements to be made. We need evidence for how many pills are likely needed for all procedures, and we need physicians to follow this evidence. The Michigan Opioid Prescribing Engagement Network (OPEN), whose researchers conducted the gallbladder study discussed earlier, is leading the charge in this area: not only are they filling in the evidence base, but they are using that data to provide concrete guidance. On their website, OPEN maintains a set of evidence-based recommendations regarding how many pills of different kinds should be prescribed for many different surgeries. The battle now is to get an entire population of surgeons to use those guidelines, even if it means radically changing their habits.

Just because it will often be appropriate to use opioid therapy for major surgery or serious injury doesn't mean that nothing can be done to mitigate the risks in these cases. In much of the discussion of the prescription opioid problem there seems to be a view that the only way to reduce the harms of opioid use is to reduce the amount prescribed. Once we concede that opioids may reasonably be used in some cases, it's as if we're supposed to give up on that patient, thinking, "Well, I guess we'll just have to risk it this time."

This is an absurd position, though. The act of prescribing isn't the only relevant act when a patient is put on opioid therapy. One of the most shocking features of my initial healthcare experience was that no one ever told me to worry about dependence or addiction, nor did anyone carefully manage my prescriptions. That was obviously a problem. And one of the major differences between that experience and my later one was that, in preparation for my sixth surgery, I asked to be educated on what would be necessary and what my outcomes might look like. This kind of patient education is crucial, and it occurs in the context of other medical interventions: we collect "informed consent" from patients, which is supposed to mean that they indicate their understanding and free endorsement of a treatment plan. Why did my prescribers not think that a similar level of understanding and consenting was required for the dangerous pain medications I was on?

As part of that understanding between physician and patient, there should be an "exit strategy"—a plan for getting that patient off the medication. This will often involve only a plan for some number of days of use and perhaps a modest taper. But the longer the patient is exposed, the more complex the exit strategy may be. Dependence may be severe enough, as in my case, so as to call for specialized knowledge of tapering. Or it may be even more severe, as in the case of someone who was on the medication for many months or even years. If the dependence is bad enough, and withdrawal is crippling despite the best efforts of the physician, then the patient may need help from someone in addiction medicine who has a broader set of tools available.

Of course, pursuing appropriate opioid prescribing doesn't mean that we get to forget the lessons of the book's previous section: pain is real, and opioids work for some people. In addition, we've used this medication for decades, which means we have an entire population of legacy patients, some of whom are stable on very high doses of opioids. Nothing that I'm saying here implies that clinicians should be allowed to be callous regarding patient pain, or regarding the suffering that comes from forced or aggressive tapering.

America's millions of pain patients, all of whom are unique individuals, and the unknown number of legacy patients, are a reminder of that critically important goal: nuance. Our response to the opioid crisis cannot be ham-fisted or uncareful, lest we risk solving one health crisis by exacerbating another. Thus, while educating physicians and trying to inculcate a culture of ethically responsible prescribing may seem like obvious strategies, they're likely not enough. How does medicine face the reality of real pain and suffering and a legacy of opioid overuse within the context of a national epidemic?

The high-level solution to this desperately difficult problem, according to many physicians and experts, is genuinely "multimodal" pain care—that is, pain care using many different modalities, or strategies, that relieve pain via different pathways. In the context of most acute and chronic pain, this means utilizing some combination of nonprescription pharmacological approaches such as acetaminophen and NSAIDs, along with physical therapy, exercise therapy, yoga, cognitive-behavioral therapy—even meditation and acupuncture. Sometimes prescription pharmacotherapy is appropriate, even when opioids aren't. The medication that I was on for neuropathic pain—gabapentin—is a non-opioid painkiller that is quite effective at treating some kinds of pain (as I discovered); the related medication pregabalin (Lyrica) has also been marketed to treat fibromyalgia pain. Although these medications still cause dependence and can be abused, they are taken to be less dangerous than opioids, and so seen as a helpful alternative therapy. And even if opioids are deemed appropriate in any given case, utilizing these other modalities can reduce the reliance on opioids, keeping the dose down to a safer level and preventing escalation.

In the surgical and traumatic context, multimodal pain teams are increasing the use of local and regional anesthetics. Some of these are fairly well known, such as lidocaine (local) and epidural (regional). But some extremity injuries or surgical interventions can also be aided by nerve blocks, which essentially "turn off" the pain-sensing nerves in an area of the body, preventing those pain signals from being sent to the brain.

In short, we have a lot of pain therapies—many more than I've mentioned here—and are researching more all the time. You would be forgiven for wondering why this isn't simply the answer. Why, that is, do we not just change the way we treat pain, utilizing all of these other modalities and relying on opioids less?

It's a good question, and the answer is both complex and depressing.

In April 2017, I was invited to speak at an anesthesiology conference on the opioid epidemic. As I was quickly learning, physician organizations have been scrambling to discuss potential solutions to the crisis, and I would regularly receive this sort of invitation to give my perspective as both a bioethicist and a pain patient. The presentation itself went fine, and I learned a lot about the role of anesthesiology in pain management by listening to these physicians, but my real education came during a break between sessions.

After my talk, I was getting some coffee in a dark hallway of the university hospital where the conference was being held when a physician approached me to ask some follow-up questions. As we chatted, a couple of other docs joined us, and we began to discuss alternative pain therapies for postsurgical patients. Relishing the opportunity to pick this group of experts' brains, I told them the story of how I had really been quite miserable after my free flap surgery, and that one of the therapies that helped me to recover was IV acetaminophen (IV APAP, as they tend to call it—APAP being short for the chemical name of acetaminophen, or acetyl-para-aminophenol).

"You know, I was surprised that they only approved me for three doses over twenty-four hours," I told them. "Actually, it was so helpful that I asked a resident why I couldn't have more—I swear it took the edge off as effectively as morphine for at least a short amount of time. If I'm remembering right, the resident said something about the limit probably being there to protect me from liver damage."

One of the anesthesiologists in the group chuckled.

"What, is that not the real reason?" I asked. "I remember pushing the resident a bit, since it wasn't obvious why it should be more dangerous in IV form than in pill form. I mean—it's just Tylenol, right?" The doc who chuckled looked at the other two, who gave wry smiles.

"It's because it costs a hundred bucks a pop," he finally responded.

One of the other docs in the group took over: "It's a great drug, but it's prohibitively expensive, and so we have hospital orders not to use it." I think my mouth was actually agape. He continued, "It'll be off patent soon, and then it'll be standard of care."

These guys were so sure of themselves, immediately, and they each knew that the others knew. Which means that this was common knowledge among anesthesiologists. They know that there is an effective, non-opioid painkiller, and they use it as little as possible because of its expense.

"But wait a minute," I said slowly, trying to catch up. "I don't get it; doctors do expensive things all the time, like put my foot back together. Hospitals are happy to pass the charges on to me or my insurance. Why not in this case?"

Another doc jumped in. "Bundles are part of the problem," he said. "In an effort to contain spiraling healthcare costs, surgical packages get bundled together. The hospital gets paid a set amount for a surgery—say, a knee replacement—regardless of how much it costs them to do it. So using expensive therapies over cheap therapies costs the hospitals money. Some of our hospitals basically have standing orders on IV APAP. You don't use it at all, or if absolutely necessary, you use it for one day."

I thought about my three doses. My pain doc had needed me to get back ahead of the pain, and I wasn't making it through between doses of hydromorphone. So he splurged on a few doses. And then I didn't get it again.

Incredible.

It's important to note that this conversation took place in 2017. Later, I would do my homework on the topic of IV APAP and find out that it was quite a hot topic. The brand name, Ofirmev, had seen two major price hikes in recent years, from $13 per vial to about $45. And while that may not seem prohibitive (and it is not the "hundred bucks a pop" that the doctors quoted me), it's orders of magnitude more than cheap, generic opioids. In fact, an FDA analysis of price trends for opioids reveals that the cost for generic opioids has been less than 2.5 *cents* per morphine milligram equivalent for more than two decades—a dose literally costs pennies. Ofirmev was already an expensive alternative, then, and after the price hikes, it was stratospheric. And as I would also learn later: certain patients aren't allowed to be billed at all for IV APAP under the federal drug rebate program. So if a patient uses this expensive medication, the hospital may end up eating 100 percent of its already high cost. Widespread use by hospitals, then, could literally cost millions of dollars per year in revenue. It's no wonder that hospitals aren't big fans of this medication, nor is it any wonder that the Ofirmev issue was on these anesthesiologists' minds—in 2017, this was big news.

It's still a bit shocking, though, that hospitals would pass on an effective, non-opioid pain treatment due to costs. After all, it's not like hospitals are unaware of the toll being exacted by the opioid crisis; nor are they unaware of the effectiveness of the medication. Their own doctors know that it can be effective (it'll be "standard of care" once it's off patent), and there is literature to support this observation. Indeed, multiple studies of IV APAP have concluded precisely what I experienced—that it can be as effective as morphine in reducing certain postoperative pains.

On the one hand, this presentation of the information makes hospitals seem downright evil: Ofirmev works, but they're greedy, so they withhold it. But the picture is a little more complicated than that. While there are studies demonstrating effectiveness of IV APAP, there are other studies that seem to show that it's no more effective than oral APAP—which is to say, Tylenol in normal pill form. In short, the data is confusing, and it's totally unclear whether IV APAP is supposed to save us from the opioid crisis or if it's a total rip-off, costing hospitals massive amounts of money for little or no benefit.

This confusion runs deep. At another conference, in a room full of surgeons, anesthesiologists, and other physicians, I asked what the role of IV APAP should be. And in that one room, with only a few dozen physicians, one immediately said it should be relied on more heavily, as it works wonders in her practice; after which another doc immediately raised her hand and said that, actually, she has a study coming out in the next year showing it to be no more effective than oral Tylenol for a certain set of procedures.

Conflicting data on the table, the group simply moved on, deciding not to make a determination regarding the medication.

I have to say, though, that I don't find the data all that confusing. Different pains respond differently to various medications, and so each study is relative to a particular pain or procedure. It may well be that limb trauma is well treated by IV APAP (that was both my experience and is supported by the literature), whereas total joint replacements are treated as effectively by oral Tylenol (the conclusion of multiple recent studies). And individual patients, too, sometimes differ. Just because IV APAP worked as well as morphine for me, in a limb-salvage situation, doesn't mean it would work as well for my mom during her recovery from double knee replacement.

So what should hospitals do? Well, the argument being made right now is that hospitals have to contain costs, and since the evidence doesn't support IV APAP use (at least, not unilaterally), it's irresponsible to use it. But that feels a little too convenient for the hospitals. In my case, I was *telling them* that a safe, nonaddictive medication was effective for my pain, and that I preferred it to the high doses of opioids I was receiving. In effect, I told them which data point I was. *I'm one of the people helped by this medication.* And they wouldn't give it to me—perhaps not because of any one doctor's decision but instead because of a hospital rule.

And that seems like a problem. I wanted a non-opioid that was effective for me, and I was denied it and given more opioids instead because it was easier to have a cost-cutting rule that simply said "no." And the defense of such policies is that IV APAP is not a "magic bullet" to reduce opioid use, since it doesn't work for everyone all the time. But that's no defense. Because there are no magic bullets. The argument is *not* that widespread use of this medication would solve the prescription opioid crisis. It might, however, help; and in the context of prescription opioids, "might help" ain't nothing. So sure, the expensive formulation of Tylenol in IV form won't solve the problem of postsurgical pain relief, but it appears to be a totally reasonable candidate for sometimes reducing our reliance on opioid therapies. And it's being overlooked, in the midst of a crisis, due to cost.

As it turns out, cost is the depressing theme in many of the pressures and incentives that lead to aggressive opioid prescribing. Physical therapy (PT) is another disheartening example. Although my PT was fully covered by insurance during the year of the accident, what I didn't realize was that this was only because I had already hit the deductible (and indeed, the out-of-pocket-maximum) on my insurance plan. My many months of intensive physical therapy, therefore, cost me nothing.

When the calendar ticked over to 2016, I discovered that this wouldn't always be the case. After my first several sessions, I got a bill for $100. When I called the insurance company, I was informed that PT was covered at a significantly lower rate until I hit my annual deductible, which is several thousand dollars. My prescription reimbursement, however, did not change. While working hard at physical therapy—something I was willing to do—would cost me several thousand dollars over the year, my copay for most prescriptions was $5 to $15.

After fighting with the insurance company and finally realizing what it would cost, I quit PT. I committed to doing the exercises at home as best I could, but I knew that I wouldn't push myself as hard or get the same benefit as I would from the therapists. At that point in my life, however, that was the trade-off I decided to make. Which makes it eminently understandable why others make this trade-off. After all, very many people would have even more trouble than I did covering that kind of expense, and we can't forget that what you get for that money is the privilege of working hard and hurting (because, let's be clear, physical therapy *hurts*). So do you want nearly free pills or expensive and time-consuming pain? The incentive structure here isn't great.

The situation gets even worse when we start to discuss less-traditional therapies. Despite an evidence base supporting exercise, yoga, mindfulness meditation, massage, and acupuncture (more on this later), many insurance plans cover none of these expenses, so taking up a new lifestyle to combat pain can get expensive.

From the physician's perspective, trying to teach patients about different pain therapies and counsel them regarding lifestyle choices can be time-consuming and difficult. In an era of managed health-care systems, where doctors are allotted mere minutes to spend with patients, these sorts of deep, difficult discussions can seem like a luxury that doctors can't afford. While there are some excellent, multimodal pain clinics in the United States, and physicians who work there are able to take the time to develop and discuss this sort of individualized treatment plan, most patients are not seen by those few clinicians. Most patients are seen by family physicians, urgent care clinicians, and ER docs, who have neither the time nor the expertise to sit down and have a thirty-minute conversation about alternative pain therapies and lifestyle choices.

Add to all of this the fact that many patients don't actually want these long, difficult conversations with doctors about alternative pain therapies. The American public has, after all, also been the audience for pharmaceutical marketing, and we, too, have internalized the message that there is a pill for every pain (and, further: if you don't get a pill, your pain isn't being taken seriously). We expect doctors to prescribe us something to feel better, and physicians are acutely aware of this expectation. We want a pill, and they know we want a pill. And that backdrop makes any discussion of non-pill alternatives even more difficult than it might otherwise be. If I come into a doctor's office hurting, expecting her to fix it, and she sends me away telling me to exercise, see a physical therapist, and perhaps try massage, I might leave pretty unhappy—especially if I can't afford those alternative treatments.

Although you might think that it's okay for patients to leave unhappy, and that physicians should just be prepared for that, there's one more wrinkle in this dynamic: we live in a world of business- and people-rating. If I feel slighted by my doctor, I can go online and leave her a scathing review, which can hurt her business.

Hospitals also rely on patient surveys for feedback on their services, and pain is one of the issues raised on these surveys. As a direct result of the last decades' War on Pain, hospitals want patients to rate physicians on their pain care, and these survey results matter. Reimbursement can now be tied to these survey results, and so survey scores can affect a hospital's bottom line. It's thus not surprising that physicians fear patients giving them negative feedback if they don't write for opioids, and their employers using this feedback in decisions about pay or promotions.

So patients at least appear to have significant power over clinicians, in that they can rate them for the public as well as for their bosses. And these mechanisms matter for clinicians' very livelihood. Sending patients away upset and dissatisfied sure seems like it could be bad for business. And while we may think there are very good reasons for the system to be set up that way (as a disincentive to bad behavior), these same incentives can make it profoundly difficult for doctors to act *well* in those cases where the right behavior will not be appreciated by patients.

Money also gets entangled with prescribing incentives in another, distressing way, which is that it can flow directly from the pharmaceutical industry to doctors. It is common practice for physicians to accept various kinds of payments from pharma, ranging from the fairly innocuous meals ("I'd like to tell you about our new product over lunch") to lavish dinners, speaking fees, and all-expenses-paid trips to beautiful resorts to discuss topics like pain management. The resulting conflicts of interest have raised enough concern that the

Affordable Care Act (the ACA, or "Obamacare") included some-thing called the Physician Payments Sunshine Act, which required all makers of drugs, medical devices, and biologics to report any pay-ments made to physicians. Payment reporting began in August 2013, and the data is now publicly available online—indeed, you can find out whether your physician has received any such payments by sim-ply going to https://openpaymentsdata.cms.gov and typing the phy-sician name into the search box.

This data has enabled researchers to look more closely at the influence that pharma money has on prescribing. Although most people, I think, would expect that being paid by pharma increases the chances that a doctor will prescribe that company's brands (after all, if it didn't, companies wouldn't spend the millions of dollars that they do), some of the results are truly shocking. One study, jointly performed by Harvard's T.H. Chan School of Public Health and CNN, found an incredibly robust correlation between pharma payments and opioid prescribing. According to the study, the more a doctor prescribed, the more likely it was that the doctor was getting paid by a drug company. As reported by CNN, "Among doctors in the top 25th percentile of opioid prescribers by volume, 72% received payments. Among those in the top fifth percentile, 84% received payments. Among the very biggest prescribers—those in the top 10th of 1%—95% received payments."

Further, those who prescribed more got paid more. Compared to the typical doctor, a doctor in the top 5 percent of national prescrib-ers received twice as much money from drug companies; one in the top 1 percent of prescribers received four times as much; and one in the top 0.1 percent—the very highest prescribers of opioids in the country—received an average of *nine times* the amount of pharma money as the typical doctor.

It is simply difficult to look at this data and believe that pharma money isn't influencing how some of these doctors prescribe.

While the amounts of money in the Harvard/CNN study are distressing, a separate study showed that even very small amounts of money transferred from drugmakers to doctors are associated with changes in prescribing habits. According to a recent paper in the *Journal of the American Medical Association (JAMA)*, receipt of a meal costing less than $20 was positively correlated with increased prescribing of the drug being promoted during that meal. And further meals, or meals costing more than $20, were then associated with even higher rates of prescribing.

We might be tempted to give doctors the benefit of the doubt here, and think something along the following lines: they have busy lives and only so much time to learn about new drugs. Encounters like paid lunches are educational opportunities for physicians, and if they are convinced by the data given them by pharmaceutical reps, there's no reason why they shouldn't start prescribing more of the promoted drug.

Although this reasoning is tempting, we might also hope for a more rational educational system for doctors. If physicians need to learn about opioids (and for all the world, it seems like they do), they should learn from some sort of formal continuing education, not from direct marketing. And it turns out, doctors do, in fact, take continuing medical education (CME) courses to stay abreast of pain and opioid therapies. The hitch? These are often paid for by pharma too. In some ways, this is an even more insidious form of influence, because CME courses are a normal (indeed, required) part of a clinician's life, and there is often no indication that a given course has been paid for with drug company money. But according to an investigation by *Mother Jones*, many of the most popular CME courses about opioids are funded by a conglomerate of drugmakers, including Purdue, Pfizer, Endo, and Janssen.

Added up, what all of this means is that practicing thorough, multimodal pain care is difficult, time-consuming, and expensive—

both for physicians and patients. Writing a scrip, however, is what doctors are trained to do. It's quick, easy, and leads to a happy customer. Moreover, a physician may be financially rewarded for writing particular prescriptions. This set of forces acting on both sides of the clinical encounter is undeniably powerful, making the status quo of aggressive prescribing far too easy, and challenges to that status quo genuinely difficult.

The challenges I've laid out for practicing responsible pain medicine are massive, structural issues and will not be solved by any one individual clinician. Problems involve everything from reimbursement structure to physician conflicts of interest, the valuation of multimodal pain therapy, and the very idea of our market-based, hyper-specialized, complex healthcare system—not to mention American attitudes toward pain and medicine (but we'll come back to those in the final chapter). Although there are things individual physicians can do in terms of responsible opioid prescribing and management, the complete solution will not be laid at the feet of practitioners. This is a problem with our very system.

Further evidence of the structural nature of the problem is the fact that a less opioid-focused view of pain therapy will be harder to achieve in some places than in others. My colleagues at Johns Hopkins have a number of incredible advantages, one of which is the ability to refer patients to one of our pain treatment programs. Something similar will be true in most urban centers, or near major teaching hospitals: physicians can off-load genuinely complex cases onto specialists who can practice careful, multimodal pain medicine. Or, better yet (since those specialists have limited bandwidth), they can partner with local pain docs, both providing better care to their patients and learning sophisticated pain medicine practice.

What about my friends and family in the small towns of Indiana, though? When they need to see a physician, how likely is it that their doctor will know a pain specialist right down the road who can handle complex cases? Especially given the geographic spread of the opioid epidemic, we need any solution to our aggressive opioid pre-scribing to be practicable in West Virginia, the rural Northeast, and small towns across the country. How can we structure health care such that humane pain care is available everywhere?

Given the scale of the problem, I can't lay out a precise solution in these pages. I can't, that is, say that careful, compassionate pain care during an opioid crisis is achievable if we simply pass some par-ticular piece of legislation. But as someone who thinks about ethi-cally appropriate action and policy for a living, I can say something about the form such a solution will take.

In short, we only really need two things—but they're two very big things. First: we need physicians to be allowed to (and required to) treat pain based on their best judgment. But second: we need their judgment to be good—far better than it is today.

The first point is a counterproposal to the ham-fisted legislative reactions to the opioid crisis discussed earlier. As lawmakers find themselves ever more scared by the drug overdose crisis, they react by trying to restrict prescribing. But, as I noted then, we don't want to arbitrarily restrict prescribing—we want to restrict prescribing *when appropriate*, which requires judgment on the part of the physi-cian, based on the individual human standing in front of her.

However, the past decades have taught us that many clinicians do not understand pain or opioids in anything like a sophisticated way, and that cannot be allowed to continue. Medical schools don't emphasize pain education, despite pain being a prominent cause of seeking medical attention, and so we end up with clinicians making *ad hoc* judgments based on who-knows-what influence. But, as we've just seen, many of those influences aren't great for rational, respon-sible prescribing. We don't want docs to give out more opioids out of fear of negative survey results, out of ease, time constraints, or because it's what the latest pharmaceutical rep recommended.

In short, clinicians need to be much better educated about pain management, and specifically about the risks and appropriate uses of opioid therapy. But this training must not be paid for by the very companies producing those medications.

Move one step up from the clinician encounter, though, and we see another problem: even if physicians get better at treating pain, it won't matter if patients can't access the recommended treatment. And so we also need a serious revision of current reimbursement policies so that it is just as affordable to do the right, sometimes hard thing (say, pursue physical therapy) as it is to fill a prescription for Percocet.

None of these are concrete, actionable policy recommendations. Getting to that point will require sustained engagement with experts from all different arenas. But seeing where we need to go is an important start. Expertly treated pain is the goal, and the road there involves building capacity in both the expertise (physician training) and treatment (availability and reimbursement of both opioid and non-opioid treatments).

A lot of America is in pain, and a lot of America is on opioids. The former is clearly bad, but the latter isn't necessarily a good solution to the former. We now know that opioid therapy isn't nearly good enough to warrant the level of prescribing seen over the last two decades, but simply stopping the flow of pills isn't the right answer either. The problem we find ourselves facing requires care and nuance, and that's never easy.

It is, however, absolutely necessary. Responsible prescribing practices aren't optional—it's not like it would be good if we could do it but okay if not. Physicians are trusted with prescription pads in order to protect us, and we need them to do that. That doesn't mean never pulling out those pads, but it does mean doing so thoughtfully, writing words like "hydrocodone," "oxycodone," "fentanyl," etc. only when there is good justification. It also means taking responsibility for patients after they leave with that piece of paper, managing the medication long term. We, as patients, need doctors to protect us from the very medications they prescribe.

This burden on clinicians would exist even without the opioid crisis, but the epidemic's existence throws such responsibilities into sharp relief. We're thinking more about pain management than we might otherwise because one of the central tools of the trade is killing us.

Fixing pain management will not, however, solve the opioid crisis. Given the role that pharmaceuticals played in creating America's problem, you would be forgiven for thinking that this was our main task: fix overprescribing, and the crisis will end.

If only it were that easy.

CHAPTER 10

America's *Three* Opioid Epidemics

The language of the opioid epidemic began to seep into the American mainstream around 2011. Although a bit dramatic-sounding to many ears (at least at first), the U.S. government and then-director of the CDC, Dr. Thomas Frieden, suggested that the scale of the crisis, already by this point, justified such language. Around this time, drug overdose—driven largely by increases in opioid overdoses—took over as the leading cause of accidental death, killing more people each year than auto accidents. Over the following decade, such comparisons would get worse: the drug crisis would eventually become the leading cause of death (not just accidental death) for Americans under fifty years of age.

After this declaration of crisis, the death rate did not slow down; it *sped up*. While the overdose death rate increased on average only 3 percent per year from 2006 to 2014, it averaged a massive *18 percent* increase from 2014 to 2016, driven largely, still, by opioids. By this point, the drug overdose epidemic killed more people each year than ever died in a single year during the height of the AIDS epidemic—indeed, more Americans died in 2016 from drug overdose than died in the entire Vietnam War.

It is not, then, hyperbole to say that America is in the midst of an opioid epidemic. It is, however, misleading in one way: there is not *an* opioid epidemic, there are three.

The opioid epidemic that most people think about, thanks to the news and stories like mine getting attention, is the prescription opioid epidemic. We've learned a lot about this crisis over the course of the book so far, including its origins in the 1990s and the public health outcry that ultimately led physicians to at least begin changing their prescribing habits. The demographics of this epidemic are quite well understood: its victims are largely (though certainly not exclusively) white and more likely to be found in America's small towns, suburbs, and rural communities. Common profiles are the high school athlete who got hooked on OxyContin after a football injury, or the Appalachian laborer treated for low-back pain from a lifetime of physical strain.

This prescription crisis, however, did not *introduce* modern Americans to opioids.

East Baltimore, for instance—home to my office on Johns Hopkins's medical campus—has long struggled with opioids. But Baltimore's epidemic is not primarily driven by overprescribing of pills. Like New York, Los Angeles, and other major cities around the United States, Baltimore has dealt with opioids for decades; we just didn't hear about it as much. (More on that conspicuous silence in just a bit.) These urban centers have long been ground zero for an ongoing, underground heroin epidemic.

We know quite a lot about the demographic of this older crisis as well. Heroin use prior to 2000 was mostly a problem in larger cities, and the burden was disproportionally shared by minority communities. Access to these drugs was controlled by a criminal underworld frequently disrupted by gang violence, which enforced norms of a black market in the absence of the legal economy's laws and regulations. Many Americans who grew up in situations similar to mine—in the 1980s and '90s in small-town America—would have had no earthly idea how to go about getting heroin.

These two, fairly distinct, public health crises finally collided, however, when heroin began washing across the United States in the early 2000s—flourishing not only in America's big cities, but in its small towns, suburbs, and rural areas. As documented powerfully by Sam Quinones in his book *Dreamland: The True Tale of America's Opiate Epidemic*, the arrival of Mexican black tar heroin, which was dirt cheap and conveniently delivered by friendly dealers who didn't carry guns, changed the heroin game drastically.

Flooding the streets of America with heroin drove down the prices, disincentivized the use of dangerous cartels, and exploited a brand-new need: the addiction that was cropping up in every corner of the country, thanks to exposure to heroin's pharmaceutical cousins.

This third epidemic—a new heroin epidemic—no longer discriminates based on race, class, or geography. Cheap heroin makes sense to the high school athlete, addicted to OxyContin but cut off from prescriptions, and so it has spread like wildfire across those areas hit hardest by prescription addiction. Having rooted itself in those communities, then, heroin poses the same threat it always did to the cities where it was endemic: a robust supply of a dangerous substance can be accessed by anyone looking to self-medicate, not just the person already suffering from addiction.

As prices were driven down, the drugs also became more and more dangerous, laced with fentanyl and its analogues, affecting users from America's old heroin epidemic as well. Minority communities, which had largely been spared the worst effects of the prescription epidemic, began to see overdose death rates rise again as the heroin supply became more dangerous. Experienced users, some of whom had survived their addiction for several decades, could suddenly find themselves in mortal danger from a contaminated supply. In short, as the population of heroin users grew from those who typically started with heroin to include those who typically started with pills, the supply became steadily more dangerous, killing more and more opioid consumers of all types.

In one sense, then, it's understandable to call the crisis facing America now *the* opioid epidemic. However the history played out, we're now facing a country saturated with a combination of heroin and prescription painkillers, and a public health crisis of unprecedented proportions. We have to be careful, though, because failing to distinguish between the multiple epidemics can get us in trouble when we try to think through potential solutions.

Audiences react strongly to my story of prescription opioids, abandonment, and withdrawal. Family members, dear friends, colleagues, and strangers I speak with after talks often want to express sympathy and tell me how awful it is that I was treated the way I was. And somewhere in that conversation, many of these lovely, warm, sincere people will say something like the following: "The way you were treated is unbelievable. No wonder we have an opioid epidemic!"

No wonder indeed.

However, some of these sympathetic and well-meaning people seem to infer from my story that we can solve our country's drug problem by fixing pain care. The problem concerning opioids, they gather, is a problem concerning medicine; eliminate stories like mine and we don't have an opioid crisis. And this, I think, is a problem. While my experience can teach us about how responsible pain care should look, and perhaps how to make some progress against the *prescription* opioid epidemic, it does not, I think, tell us much about how to make progress against the other two opioid epidemics.

Starting in about 2012, opioid prescriptions finally began trending down—slowly at first, and then picking up steam; but as discussed, the overdose death rate has skyrocketed since then. This increase has been driven almost entirely by heroin and illicit fentanyl as the supply has become more and more dangerous. By 2015, prescription opioids were involved in less than half of all opioid overdose deaths (often in combination with other substances, such as cocaine and psychostimulants).

Now of course, that doesn't mean prescriptions aren't playing a role—remember that many new heroin users started their opioid use with pills. But it does mean that the existing population of people using opioids is using a lot of heroin; and it suggests that some pain patients are willing to transition to illicit opioids if they suffer from opioid use disorder and no longer have access to prescriptions. In this environment, it would be very difficult to reduce total overdose deaths by affecting only the supply of prescription opioids. Even if the number of pills put out into the world could be reduced dramatically (and we can't forget that doing so would risk harming both pain and legacy patients), this wouldn't affect heroin users and could in fact drive more heroin use.

It's certainly important not to recklessly contribute to new cases of opioid use disorder. One of the best reasons for physicians to be very worried about their prescribing practices is to protect new patients from unnecessary exposure to dangerous medication. But the opioid epidemic isn't a problem that can be solved solely by not adding any new people to it: there is a massive population of people suffering from opioid use disorder—2.1 million by one recent estimate—and a deep supply of dangerous drugs. Any solution will have to go far beyond preventing new cases of addiction.

How do we do that? Surprisingly, the answers are not all that mysterious. Although we may not know how to turn around an addiction crisis like ours overnight, public health scientists know a lot about how to help. The challenge facing America is not a lack of knowledge; it is, at least in large part, a lack of motivation.

At the most basic level, we need to do two things: first, provide evidence-based addiction treatment that is affordable and accessible; and second, keep those suffering from addiction alive until they are willing to use this treatment. We know how to make serious progress on both of these fronts and could start immediately with enough money and political will. Of course, we would not be able to save every person with opioid use disorder, but it would go a long way.

The gold standard for treating opioid use disorder is something called medication-assisted treatment, or MAT. Essentially, MAT combines traditional recovery strategies with one of three types of pharmaceutical therapies: methadone, buprenorphine, or naltrexone.

Methadone is what's called a full opioid agonist, which means that it acts on the brain like other opioids, activating opioid receptors and thus causing all of the effects of other opioids—both good ones like pain relief and bad ones like respiratory depression. The difference with methadone is that it is a very long-acting opioid that can be titrated very carefully to essentially "even out" a person's brain chemistry. With careful dosing, it can eliminate withdrawal by giving the brain what it needs but at the same time avoiding the intense highs and lows of other opioids, preventing the cycle of craving, compulsion, and destruction that defines the life of someone suffering from addiction. Methadone is used as a "maintenance" treatment, which means that it doesn't get someone off of opioids (at least not immediately), but it keeps opioids from ruining his life. If a patient is eventually stable and wants to wean off the methadone, that's great; but the primary goal is to eliminate the harmful behaviors associated with addiction.

Buprenorphine is a similar medication, but it is a *partial* opioid agonist. Unlike methadone, it doesn't fully activate the brain's opioid receptors, but it still gives the brain enough of what it wants to keep withdrawal at bay, while providing fewer "highs" than a full agonist. Buprenorphine can also be used for maintenance treatment or to mitigate the harms of withdrawal in a patient who is ready to taper off opioids altogether.

Naltrexone is completely different from the first two therapies—it's an opioid *antagonist*, meaning that it *prevents* opioids from interacting with a patient's brain chemistry. Think of it as a defender of one's opioid receptors: by planting itself in the way, naltrexone prevents other substances (like morphine or heroin) from engaging those receptors. When on naltrexone, opioids don't cause euphoria and so cannot feed an addiction. Essentially, it's a bulwark against relapse: by taking this medication, one makes it impossible to get high from opioid use, undermining any motivation to pursue the drug. Unlike methadone or buprenorphine, then, naltrexone must be used when a patient is already abstinent, since it does not treat dependence or fend off withdrawal.

The evidence in favor of MAT is overwhelming, with extant data suggesting that incorporating medication—especially methadone and buprenorphine—into addiction treatment significantly reduces mortality risk. The problem? All of these therapies are various combinations of rare, difficult to access, and prohibitively expensive.

Although some treatment options, such as methadone, are themselves quite cheap (methadone is a very old opioid and has been off patent for a long time), others can be very expensive. The thirty-day injectable form of naltrexone, for instance, is about a thousand bucks a month; and comprehensive, inpatient rehab can be tens of thousands of dollars for a twenty-eight-day stint.

Most important, though, is that the addiction medicine infrastructure is spread desperately thin. Results from a 2016 national survey suggest that only 10 percent of those suffering from substance use disorder actually receive treatment. Although there are almost certainly many complex reasons for this, lack of access is a major one. In cities like Baltimore, patients with opioid use disorder face long waiting lists when they decide they want to seek treatment, and every delay getting someone into treatment is an opportunity for that person's addiction to kill them.

An additional problem is geography. With many of the nation's epidemic hot spots sitting in small towns and rural locations, those looking for treatment may have to drive hours to find it. If their insurance doesn't fully cover the treatment, or if they don't have insurance, then the long drive may be for a very expensive service.

An obvious move toward saving lives, then, would be to simply make evidence-based treatment, like MAT, accessible and affordable. This by itself could go a long way.

However, not everyone with opioid use disorder is ready to seek treatment. And even those who are ready may well relapse at some point. Recall from chapter 3 that, according to most addiction medicine specialists, we should think of addiction as a chronic disease, or at least a chronic health condition. And like any such chronic health condition, it involves long-term (maybe even lifelong) management, with some expectation that the patient may take the occasional step backward.

What this means is that those with opioid use disorder may take a while to access treatment, even once it's available; and they may trip up at some point and relapse. For both reasons, a second part of addressing the opioid crisis is preventing individuals' addiction from killing them before they get treatment or when they relapse. In other words, what we need is a series of "harm reduction" strategies that make opioids less dangerous for those who do take them.

Down the road from where I went to college in southern Indiana is the small, seemingly sleepy town of Scottsburg. Having spent four years as a student and two years as an employee of Hanover College, I knew Scottsburg as the place where State Road 56 attaches to I-65, and for a good spot to get gas or maybe a bite to eat before pulling onto the interstate. It seemed like the last place in the world you would find a drug epidemic.

Less than a decade after I left Indiana for graduate school, however, this appearance would be proven deceptive. Scott County— home of not-quite twenty-five thousand people according to the U.S. Census—came to discover the prescription opioid pain reliever

Opana (oxymorphone), which residents crushed, mixed with water, and injected like heroin. Unfortunately, without access to clean needles, they shared, and so the addiction crisis that spread through the community like wildfire brought with it an additional health problem: human immunodeficiency virus, or HIV. Scott County, which had rarely seen a single case of HIV during the course of any given year, suddenly reported five cases at the end of 2014. Just a few months later, *eighty-five new cases* sprang up. Thanks to Opana and risky injection practices, my *alma mater's* neighbor was soon ground zero of a genuine epidemic.

Then–Indiana governor and soon-to-be vice president Mike Pence suddenly found himself presiding over a kind of crisis he never would have expected: a rural HIV outbreak. When he called advisers for help, he was immediately told by public health officials that he needed to get clean needles into the hands of people who use drugs. This, they told him, is an evidence-based strategy for combating infectious disease outbreaks secondary to injection drug use. In short, those who use drugs reuse and share needles because the law in Indiana prohibits possession and distribution of them. If given an opportunity to return used needles (keeping them off the streets) and obtain clean ones, people will share less often and the outbreak can be stemmed.

Pence, however, was not a fan of giving needles to people who use drugs. He, like many Hoosiers (not to mention other citizens around the country), saw programs like syringe exchanges as enabling or promoting bad behavior. Drug use is bad, the reasoning goes, so why on earth would the government want to give the people using drugs the very tools they need for the practice?

The answer, however, is that needle exchanges do not lead to increased drug use, and they do attenuate the harm that can go along with such use. Pence's advisers gave him this information and urged him to implement a needle-exchange program.

Facing the prospect of the outbreak reaching truly devastating proportions, Governor Pence, on March 26, 2015, reluctantly signed an executive order permitting a syringe-exchange program in Scott County. During the news conference announcing the order, Pence commented, "I will tell you, I do not support needle exchange as antidrug policy, but this is a public health emergency." He clearly wasn't happy, but—as they say—desperate times called for desperate measures.

Scott County's needle-exchange program is credited with eventually turning the tide of Indiana's HIV outbreak, but not before a total of 181 cases were confirmed.

Syringe exchange, like the one used in Scott County, is an example of a "harm reduction strategy," which is exactly what it sounds like: an intervention that has the goal of reducing harms that attend some behavior, regardless of whether one approves of that behavior. Seat belts, for example, are a harm reduction strategy: People will drive, and driving is dangerous. Some number of people each year will die in auto accidents. Since we can't, or won't, stop people from driving, seat belts can prevent at least some of the most serious harms from occurring. Other mundane examples include things like airbags and motorcycle helmets, while another example that tends to divide people is distribution of contraception and sexual education to minors. Although not everyone approves of empowering young people who have sex, helping them to do so safely prevents unwanted pregnancy and sexually transmitted disease.

A needle-exchange program constitutes harm reduction because it doesn't try to prevent drug use; instead, it tries to prevent someone's drug use from seriously harming them. And that, of course, is why some people (like Mike Pence) are uncomfortable with the strategy: it doesn't push toward or require abstinence from the dangerous behavior. In fact, since needles are required for injecting Opana or heroin or whatever, providing someone with a clean needle with which to inject drugs feels like *helping them* to do drugs. And if you think drugs are bad, this can feel dirty.

But the evidence is overwhelming that these programs work. According to a review of the literature by the Centers for Disease Control and Prevention, needle-exchange programs reduce the incidence of bloodborne diseases like HIV, hepatitis B, and hepatitis C, without increasing drug use or crime. In addition, the health benefits make them incredibly economically efficient. In short, the data is clear: needle exchanges are a powerfully effective public health intervention.

As a result, someone like Pence can feel backed into a corner and end up green-lighting a harm reduction program but not liking it. The extremity of the situation might call for it, but it feels to some people like they're doing something wrong. Although they embrace, within some extreme context, the particular harm reduction strategy, they continue to believe that there is something wrong with—as they see it—enabling someone's bad behavior.

There is another way to view harm reduction, though, and that is to see these strategies not as a necessary evil, but not as evil at all. This more radical view doesn't reluctantly accept only the particular harm reduction strategy (because desperate times and all that); it accepts what we can call a harm reduction *philosophy*, which fully endorses interventions that keep people's habits from harming them needlessly. Just as we don't think seat belts are a necessary evil— because driving isn't morally bad, and so helping people to drive more safely isn't wrong—needle exchanges also aren't a necessary evil.

The harm reduction philosophy embraces strategies like needle exchange because it takes a nonjudgmental view of drug use. Although many people believe that taking drugs is somehow *wrong*— morally prohibited, corrupting, or revealing of a bad character—the harm reduction philosophy sees the drug use itself as morally neutral. People are valuable and deserving of dignity, and that doesn't change if they choose to take drugs. After all, most of us take drugs. My own preferred chemical habit is coffee, which I am using at this very moment to keep me at my desk writing for a few hours longer. Relatively few people look askance at me for indulging in this particular substance.

The drug use, then, is not what's bad—what's bad is the drug use killing the user. What's bad about heroin, says the harm reduction advocate, is not the diacetylmorphine compound, the euphoria it causes, or even the dependence that one can develop as a result. What's bad about heroin, rather, is the disease and death that go along with unsafe practices, as well as the social impacts of an unchecked and single-minded pursuit of the next dose. Those consequences, however, can be addressed. It is within a community's power to reduce the risk that someone's drug use will result in their contracting HIV. In fact, it's even within a community's power to prevent some people from spiraling out of control or dying as a result of their addiction.

Note that this view can also be deeply tied to a realization that addiction is a health problem. A particularly powerful argument in favor of harm reduction is to show how the idea that we shouldn't "enable bad behavior" relies on the outdated notion that drug users are simply bad people—that the junkie or the dope fiend is a victim of nothing other than his own choices. But if addiction is an issue of mental health—which I've suggested is overwhelmingly plausible, whether we call it a "brain disease" or not—then the appropriate response is not judgment but health care.

When thought about this way, making available some forms of MAT—those therapies that involve methadone or buprenorphine—can be seen as a harm reduction strategy. After all, MAT explicitly doesn't get someone to stop using opioids; it provides them with an opioid that can attenuate the harms of their drug use. And this is precisely why some people—often the same folks who dislike programs like needle exchanges—also dislike MAT. It is why you sometimes hear a politician or antidrug crusader say something like, "Methadone just replaces one addiction with another." But such a comment reveals that the speaker doesn't fully understand what addiction is. Recall that addiction is a health condition defined partially by its negative *behavioral* components—the compulsive pursuit of a drug despite harmful side effects. If someone is able to give that up by taking methadone, then methadone is a pharmaceutical *treatment*; it maintains a physiological dependence but avoids the harmful withdrawal effects of abstinence as well as the behavioral components of addiction. This is why I say it allows people with opioid use disorder to take back control of their lives.

Another harm reduction strategy that gained significant support as the overdose crisis overwhelmed the nation is the distribution and use of the overdose-reversal medication naloxone. Naloxone (brand name Narcan) works by knocking opioids out of the brain's receptors, reversing the sedating (and euphoric) effects of opioids. Someone who might otherwise die if an overdose is allowed to continue can be brought back to consciousness and out of immediate danger by timely use of this medication.

Although naloxone is a prescription medication, it is such an effective harm reduction tool that many parts of the country have innovated to make it more widely accessible. In Baltimore in 2015, then–health commissioner Dr. Leana Wen wrote a standing prescription so that anyone could access naloxone, and she fought to get it into the hands of as many police, EMS, and citizens as possible. And cities and states across the country are doing the same. In an epidemic marked by hyperdangerous injection drugs, naloxone is public health's first line of defense. In fact, in April 2018, Surgeon General Jerome M. Adams released an advisory in which he recommended that "more individuals, including family, friends and those who are personally at risk for an opioid overdose, also keep the drug on hand."

Many people who support MAT, naloxone, and needle-exchange programs probably feel a bit like Governor Pence did—a little uncomfortable about supporting a behavior that they have problems with but willing to utilize the tools we have to combat an overwhelming public health crisis. Others who, on reflection, endorse the broader harm reduction philosophy tend to enthusiastically embrace these tools. Since drug use itself is not bad or wrong, they say, the fact that harm reduction strategies don't require abstinence is not a problem. Opioid use disorder is a health condition that affects some number of those who use opioids, and when an individual has this affliction, her life is beset by all sorts of risks and harms. We have the tools to reduce or eliminate those risks and harms, so we should use them. Harm reduction strategies are public health interventions like any other, promoting the health of the population.

In this moment in American history, it doesn't matter whether we embrace harm reduction reluctantly or enthusiastically; but we do, I think, need to embrace it. If you sympathize with the reluctance of Mike Pence, I get it: it's hard to shake the long historical narrative according to which drug use is bad, and so "helping people to use drugs" feels wrong. But just as he recognized the emergency of southern Indiana's epidemic, so too must we all recognize the emergency of America's broader epidemic. Tens of thousands of people are getting sick and dying as a result of their drug use, and they don't have to.

In fact, we know even more about how to stem the tide of America's drug overdose epidemic than I've let on. MAT, needle exchanges, and naloxone are a great start, but once we acknowledge the basic logic of harm reduction, we find that there is even more we could be doing to stop Americans' drug use from killing them.

On the north side of East Hastings Street, in Vancouver's Downtown Eastside, is a nondescript storefront alongside many others like it. The picture of a hypodermic needle on the front door gives the appearance of a medical facility, and that impression continues on the inside. Visitors come through the door, put their names down at the check-in desk, and wait to be called into the back.

Rather than the private rooms of a standard health clinic, however, the back room has a dozen "stalls," each with privacy blinders on either side, a metal desk, a mirror covering the wall, and a hard plastic chair. Across from the stalls is a long desk covered with medical equipment.

The facility is called Insite, and while its goal is definitely health promotion, it is not your typical community clinic. Its primary purpose is reducing the harms that often attend injection drug use (with secondary goals including things like connecting those who use drugs with health care, providing treatment information, and offering a safe space and community for people who might struggle to find either). The injection room—with its twelve stalls—is staffed by health professionals and full of sterile injecting supplies. Each visitor is offered a clean needle, a sterile cooker, a filter, water, and a tourniquet: everything needed to cook and inject heroin, available in a safe, supervised environment.

Insite, in other words, is a "safe injection site"—also sometimes called a "supervised drug-consumption facility" or an "overdose prevention site." Consumers of injection drugs can come here to inject drugs with sterile equipment, mitigating the risks of contracting hepatitis C or HIV through shared needles, and they are surrounded by trained professionals should they overdose. Staffers at Insite are equipped with drug testing strips that can test a consumer's supply for the deadly powerful opioid fentanyl, allowing the user to decide whether to decrease her dose in light of that knowledge. Should a visitor overdose anyway, the overdose-reversal drug naloxone is on hand. Since opening as the first safe injection site in North America in 2003, Insite has served more than three and a half million people, intervened in thousands of overdoses, and recorded not a single fatality.

To Americans, the idea of a safe injection site—where drug users can publicly do something that's not only illegal but which many people consider wrong—is anathema. Carving out a geographic territory where the rules seem not to apply, and where healthcare resources are spent on those pursuing "bad life choices" seems to be a sort of moral paradox. But for those who endorse the harm reduction philosophy, the appearance of paradox is easily dissipated: there's nothing wrong with the drug use itself, and so the fact that medical resources are being spent on people who use drugs isn't mysterious. They have a health need, which facilities like Insite provide. For those not quite ready to fully embrace the harm reduction philosophy, but who can see the rationale for Mike Pence's emergency needle exchange, it's hard to understand what, precisely, makes safe injection sites a bridge too far. A needle-exchange program acknowledges that we should prevent people's drug use from making them sick or killing them with HIV/AIDS but sends people who use drugs back to alleyways and shooting galleries to potentially overdose alone, where no one can help them. If the drug overdose crisis justifies providing clean needles, then it seems strange to insist that those needles be used in a riskier way than they could be.

To the extent that Americans are surprised by harm reduction strategies, we are actually a bit late to the game. The United States has slowly come around to the idea of needle-exchange programs, with close to three hundred open across the country by 2017. That number is absolutely dwarfed, however, by other countries. Australia, for instance, has more than three thousand needle-exchange programs—more than *ten times* the number in America—serving a population that is less than one-tenth the size. As a result, there is only one needle-exchange program for every thirty-two hundred Americans who use intravenous drugs; in Australia, there is a program for every thirty-one people who inject drugs.

Safe injection sites exist in dozens of cities around the world, with more being proposed all the time (including within the United States). And the reason is simple: they save lives and prevent suffering. As an added bonus, they also save money through decreased burdens on the healthcare system, while at the same time improving public order and increasing access to addiction and other health services by people who use drugs. By taking drug use off the streets, where it's most harmful, and connecting those who use injection drugs to safe equipment, public space, and healthcare information, safe injection sites are able to do a lot of good. Needle exchanges can prevent disease, and naloxone distribution can reverse some overdoses, but a brick-and-mortar site where people can come to use drugs offers the possibility of connecting them with people and resources rather than driving them ever further into the shadows. After all, the harder it is to see the person using drugs, the harder it is to save them.

Of course, if you go down this rabbit hole very far, it becomes very difficult to understand many of our current practices. What I've been suggesting here—alongside many in the field of public health—is that we should take a harm reduction approach to the injection drug crisis. Whether you buy into the *philosophy* of harm reduction, our current context of crisis justifies the basic strategy: we have to find a way to prevent our family members', friends', and fellow citizens' drug use from killing them. You may find this eminently sensible, or you may come to it reluctantly, as Governor Pence did. But either way, I think you should come to it.

Our jails, however, are full of people who were arrested for doing precisely what I am suggesting we explicitly help them to do—namely, for taking illicit drugs. If we follow harm reduction reasoning all the way to safe injection sites (which I think we should), then we are basically building a geographically limited decriminalized zone. Within the confines of those buildings, people will be protected while doing the precise thing that can get them arrested should they walk outside and do it on the sidewalk. The legal and moral stance we are taking starts to get very confusing.

In fact, if you really accept the harm reduction philosophy, then safe injection sites themselves—as I've described them—are a bit strange. They allow people who use drugs to inject their own, almost certainly contaminated, heroin while trained medical professionals anxiously wait around to prevent them from dying. But if you're allowing drug use, while trying to prevent that drug use from killing people, there is a much more straightforward way to do it: you could provide regulated, pharmaceutical-grade heroin. Then consumers know what they're getting rather than dipping into the Wild West of fentanyl-laced product on the street. And they don't have to steal or commit any other crimes in order to feed their habit. Whereas safe injection sites primarily reduce harm to the consumer, prescription heroin can also reduce other harms that attend opioid use disorder by undermining the incentive to obtain drugs illegally.

For exactly these reasons, prescription heroin is in fact used in several countries around the world. Vancouver itself has a small clinic, so at least a few Canadians who use drugs don't have to take their own supply to Insite—they are able to go to a healthcare facility to access pharmaceutical-grade diacetylmorphine. Switzerland has been using prescription heroin since the 1990s, while the United Kingdom has had "heroin-assisted treatment" (basically MAT using heroin rather than methadone or buprenorphine) for addiction since the early twentieth century. All of these sites boast impressive statistics, demonstrating that providing heroin to those suffering from addiction can reduce mortality from opioid use, reduce the need for criminal activity, and provide the kind of stable access that allows drug users to take back control of their lives. If harm reduction reasoning is valid, the case for prescription heroin is surprisingly strong.

These views are obviously at odds with the aggressive American criminalization of drugs, which helps to explain why we have been so slow to adopt harm reduction approaches. But now we have begun to adopt these strategies—often reluctantly—citing the scale of the crisis we're fighting. And the same reasoning that justifies needle exchanges and naloxone seemingly can (and does, in some countries) justify supervised consumption and even prescription heroin. Although prescription heroin may be a bridge too far for many Americans, discussion of supervised injection facilities is picking up steam across the country.

None of this implies that Americans are uniformly softening in their attitudes toward drug use, but these discussions certainly wouldn't have happened, say, in the 1990s (when there was actually a concerted effort to *ban* needle-exchange programs nationwide). In a recent study on the way the media reports on the drug crisis, a few of my colleagues at Johns Hopkins showed that between 1998 and 2012, there was evidence of a shift away from the idea that drug use should be solved by law enforcement toward the view that drug use can be addressed with tools from medicine and public health. It appears, that is, that there is at least some increase in our sympathetic response to those who use drugs. Rather than simply throwing them in jail, we're discussing getting them treatment and investing in their lives. We are beginning to recognize addiction as a health problem rather than a criminal justice problem, and so addressing it with evidence-based therapies rather than punishment.

In my view, this is an obvious improvement, and we need to invest in an even louder, more public discussion of a thoroughgoing harm reduction approach. It's time, I think, to abandon the idea that we will arrest our way out of drug use and addiction, and instead to take care of our friends and family members who need help.

I remember a question I got after one of my very first talks on the opioid epidemic. I don't remember which venue it was, but I remember who asked it: she was a black woman—middle-aged and petite, with kind eyes and a disarming demeanor—and she stood quietly for what seemed like a long time before she finally asked her question.

"Why do you think we're just now talking about opioids so much? I mean: all of a sudden, it's everywhere; you'd think we just discovered drugs in this country."

In hindsight, I know that I misunderstood her question. I gave her a very academic answer, trotting out some of the history we've already covered in this book: the role of pharmaceutical companies, the rise of pain as the fifth vital sign, etc. But she seemed unsatisfied. I wasn't even done answering before I knew that I had missed something.

After I finished, she responded, "That all may be true, but I want to suggest something else that you might want to think about a bit."

"Of course," I responded, always eager to gain new perspectives.

"It's because white kids started dying." She let that sink in for a minute, as I suddenly retraced the history in my head. "You see," she continued, "I've had an opioid epidemic in my community for as long as I can remember, but we don't talk about that one. It's a crisis now that white kids in West Virginia die from OxyContin instead of black kids in the city dying from heroin."

I was embarrassed for not understanding the force of the question, and I immediately backpedaled. "I see," I responded. "I see. Wow. I really appreciate the perspective, and I'm going to think about it more." Caught flat-footed, it was all I could say, but I remember her comment so clearly because it was the first time I heard the racial aspect of the crisis brought up.

It was not, however, the last time I would hear that point made. Because my kind, thoughtful interlocutor was exactly right about the demographic shift in drug use, as we've seen in this chapter. And so her suspicion that race has affected the way we react to the crisis is completely understandable. More than understandable: it's compelling. And as I've spent the last few years attending conferences and listening to speakers, this point has come up again and again. And far too many of the predominantly white experts are caught just as flat-footed as I was when confronted with this question. Far too many of us, that is, can get invited to give a talk about the opioid crisis without having considered its racial dimension.

It's certainly not the case that every particular reaction to the opioid crisis is *racist*. I'm talking about it now, and I wasn't in the 1990s. And I certainly hope this has more to do with the fact that

I was a teenager in the 1990s and completely unaware of most important things going on in the world. So I don't think the fact that I'm desperately searching for solutions to the opioid crisis only now means that I'm racist.

My interlocutor's broader point, though, is difficult to deny, no matter how uncomfortable it is. When heroin was doing the most damage to communities of color, the American response was aggressive criminalization. It is not exactly a cutting-edge analysis to point out that the War on Drugs disproportionately affected black men. And now that heroin has, mediated by pharmaceutical opioids, made its way into every nook and cranny of the United States, indiscriminately killing white and nonwhite folks alike, we're screaming alarm. Our response is outrage at any perpetrator we can find (pharma, for instance) and sympathy for those caught up in the grips of addiction. Whereas we jumped at the chance to throw black men in jail for possessing small amounts of drugs or drug paraphernalia, now we have books like this one, discussing the need to get people clean needles, a safe space to inject, and treatment when they're ready. It would take serious mental gymnastics to make oneself believe that race has nothing to do with it—especially in a country riddled with a history of racism.

I don't think the woman who posed the question to me intended to suggest that we should aggressively criminalize drug use by white people. Yes, that would bring our attitudes about drug use into alignment, but something tells me that wasn't her goal. It's not that sympathy is the wrong response to those struggling with substance use disorder; it's that it was the right response all along, and it's hurtful to people of color when we act as though we only just discovered this—now that it's an epidemic for white people too.

Many people, when confronted with the racial analysis of the opioid crisis, defensively point out that race isn't the only thing that changed between the old opioid crisis and the new, headline-grabbing epidemic. Importantly, they say, the mode of first exposure to opioids has changed as well: while heroin hooked people in the old days, the whiter epidemic of the new millennium is driven by reckless prescribing. This matters, I'm told on a regular basis, because the prescription opioid user becomes an "accidental addict." Patients trust their doctors, and so they have good reason to take whatever medications they were prescribed. Those who began their addiction with heroin, by contrast, *chose* their fate. They took risks, and the consequences are on them.

It's important to say at the outset that distinguishing people based on whether their addiction is "accidental" or not is a bit strange. I've never met someone—regardless of their mode of introduction to drugs—who went looking for an addiction. Rather, people take drugs for many reasons, some good, some bad, but typically because it offers something that they want or believe they need. Note that this is true for prescriptions as well as illicit drugs. I took opioid painkillers because I hurt; but heroin, too, is an analgesic (remember Bayer?), and there's no reason to think that many people who use drugs aren't killing pain—sometimes physical, but sometimes emotional or psychic pain as well. The framing of some addictions as "accidental" obscures the fact that we all choose to take drugs, or not, based on different reasons.

What this suggests people are really trying to say is that taking medication is reasonable, while taking heroin isn't; some of us take drugs for good reasons, while others don't. As a result, those who end up addicted from a prescription pad aren't *responsible* for the consequences in the way that those whose addiction stems from heroin are. Our sympathy, then, is tracking responsibility, and that's a defensible position. Disproportionate concern for today's epidemic is not racist, it's just moralizing.

Or so the argument goes.

I think there are lots of problems with this argument. The first one is that many of the Americans suffering from opioid use disorder, and whose addiction began with prescription opioids, did not get those prescriptions legitimately. When OxyContin burned its way through Appalachia, it quickly became a drug of abuse. Teenagers crushed it, snorted it, or injected it, and they only moved on to heroin once it became widely available and cheap.

The story is the same across the country. "Pill mill" operations, such as American Pain, in Florida (grippingly described in the book of the same name), dispensed pharmaceutical opioids like a drug dealer disguised as a clinical operation. Bad doctors and unscrupulous businesspeople made millions of dollars selling prescription opioids—as drugs to feed addiction, not as medicine. While there were certainly people like me who were exposed to opioids by their physicians and then developed dependence or addiction, there are many others who stole from family members' medicine cabinets, were given pills at a party, or bought them on the street.

The point here is *not* to try to convince anyone to have less sympathy for those suffering from opioid use disorder, but to point out that many Americans *do* have sympathy for the victims of today's epidemic, and that not all of them fit the model of the "accidental addict." Many were killed by the OxyContin they were exposed to at parties, or by the heroin they switched to after their Oxy habit became too expensive.

Further, many who began with heroin weren't acting fully autonomously when they started. Many of those suffering from opioid use disorder first tried drugs as a teenager, when the frontal lobes of their brains were still developing and they were not fully in control of their actions. The exculpating ability of youth is proven in many of our judgments and laws: the very reason that we take children under the age of eighteen to be minors, and to be dependent on their parents, is that we don't believe they are fully capable of making free, informed decisions just yet.

So some of those who became addicted to prescriptions made bad choices, and some of those who started with heroin didn't really (they weren't fully "choices," given their age). The responsibility argument, then, just doesn't work very well. It is simply not the case that current opioid users are uniformly innocent victims in a way that previous opioid users uniformly were not.

Perhaps we shouldn't have focused on responsibility to begin with, though. Even those who freely choose to use drugs—whether prescription or illicit—surely don't deserve to *die* for what they did. Even supposing that drug use is morally bad, and so freely choosing it makes one responsible in a way that matters: should the penalty for this transgression be life with Hep C, HIV, or an early death due to overdose? Death seems a pretty steep punishment for trying a substance that promised pleasure and then finding out (too late) that one has the sort of brain that makes giving up that euphoria exceedingly difficult.

The punishment doesn't seem to fit the "crime."

The question this line of reasoning leaves us with is this: aren't we simply better off expanding our circle of empathy and care rather than trying to figure out who deserves our attention? My inclination here is that our move toward understanding addiction as a health issue rather than a moral or criminal justice issue is a move in the right direction; we just made it too late, and to our terrible shame, in response to victims that those in power could better identify with.

The woman with the kind eyes seemed to have it right: our talk of responsibility doesn't really distinguish between the old opioid crisis and the new, which means it's hard to avoid her conclusion. America saw the devastation of opioid addiction when it found its way into the small towns, the suburbs, and the predominantly white families of those in positions of power. It was wrong, and we need to own it. But it doesn't mean that sympathy was the wrong response—only that it came too late. The way we move forward is by making sure that our newfound patience with and concern for those whose lives are being ruined by the pleasure molecule is distributed more evenly, and not in a discriminatory way.

In short, the racial aspect of the opioid crisis is a stain on

America's response. It shouldn't have taken a change in the demographic of the victims before those in power were willing to do something. But since it has, what we absolutely must do is ensure that our collective response to *the* epidemic is not a selective response to the *second* epidemic. Understanding the harms and horrors of addiction—even if prompted by the prescription opioid epidemic—needs to change our view of addiction and drug use for everyone. Insofar as we see this crisis as deserving resources, and its victims as deserving sympathy and help, we absolutely must not do so selectively. Treating some people as innocent victims and others as junkies is how we truly fall to the most biting racism charge.

In a strange way, then, the second opioid epidemic—tragic though it is—presents America with an opportunity: get better at dealing with addiction. Let's change the way we view drug laws, health care, and our very concept of what people "deserve." We shouldn't address addiction because some people *deserve* our help; we should do it because people are suffering, and helping them is within our power.

As one comes to understand the history and trajectory of America's drug crisis, it might start to seem unclear why we should even talk about prescription opioids. It turns out that the epidemic has shifted sharply toward heroin and illicit fentanyl, and there are millions of Americans already living with opioid use disorder. Curbing prescriptions, then, will not solve the epidemic. Further, the prescription epidemic has been seen as a white epidemic, and so continuing to focus on cases like mine—a white man who was harmed by prescription opioids—can risk furthering the historical injustice of seeing drug use sympathetically when it's a "white problem."

All of this is true, and it means we must proceed carefully. We shouldn't give the impression that solving the prescription epidemic will solve the broader epidemic, and we should demand justice for all communities devastated by drugs—both illicit and prescribed. But none of that means we don't have to talk about pain and painkillers anymore. We must, because this is still a part of our healthcare system that is profoundly broken.

However much it's the case that illicit fentanyl is destroying America, that doesn't mean that prescription opioids aren't also deadly. In 2016, for the first time in nearly two decades, the number of people who died from prescription opioids decreased. But it was still north of fourteen thousand, which is more than fourteen thousand too many. And this data isn't surprising, since doctors still prescribe opioids aggressively, often having received little or virtually no real training and without knowing how to manage the medication over its full course. We continue to lack a solid evidence base for much of the prescribing that is done, and the evidence base that we do have is woefully underutilized. The physician role, in short, still matters.

Not to mention that physicians are now on both sides of the harm that's possible from prescription opioids: they can prescribe them inappropriately, but they can also *discontinue* them inappropriately. The legacy patients who (justifiably) fear abandonment are some of the most vulnerable in this discussion. They were prescribed opioids aggressively, and in some cases inappropriately, which has resulted in dependence. Now, if they are forcibly tapered or abandoned by physicians, they face truly hellish withdrawal—a form of suffering that could completely understandably drive someone to take their pain management into their own hands by accessing the black market. Physicians must juggle their dual obligations not to prescribe recklessly, while also not allowing their patients to suffer needlessly.

Finally, the ethics of prescribing is simply important, even quite apart from the backdrop of an opioid epidemic. When doctors, whose very job it is to help us and protect us from harm instead hurt us, that matters. My physicians took an oath to "first, do no harm," but they prescribed me a medication that they couldn't manage, and they did harm me. As it turns out, I'm not the only one. So yes, most opioid overdose deaths now come from illicit drugs. But that doesn't mean that the harms of dependence, withdrawal, and addiction that attend reckless prescribing behavior don't need to be discussed.

Pain medicine in this country is deeply broken, and we need to talk about it. Pain patients, legacy patients, and patients at risk of developing an addiction are all vulnerable populations, capable of being harmed by bad practice and policy. Protecting these patients may help to address the opioid crisis, but it won't *solve* the opioid crisis.

We have to do it anyway.

Making a Difference

"Have you ever had acupuncture?" The man asking me the question was holding a sealed and sterile package of eight very tiny gold needles. When I slowly shook my head no, he followed up: "Do you want to?" His smile was a bit mischievous, and I had no idea if he was messing with me or serious.

Dr. Chester "Trip" Buckenmaier III is an intimidating man with a thick mustache who looks exactly like the U.S. Army colonel he was before retiring from that part of his life. Less obvious by stereotype is his expertise as an anesthesiologist for the military. And less predictable still is his enthusiasm for acupuncture. Gruff military men and Western-focused, military-trained physicians don't fit my stereotype for acupuncture evangelists. But Trip really is one, and the stories he can tell about his experience administering acupuncture are *awe*some, in the old, literal sense of the word.

Looking on as Trip needles me about needles is Lieutenant General Dr. Eric Schoomaker, the forty-second surgeon general of the U.S. Army. Like Trip, he is retired from the military but a practicing physician and professor at the Uniformed Services University (USU). And he, too, is enthusiastic about acupuncture, as he is about all manner of self-care in an age when health care must deal with more than simple disease management.

The only lifelong civilian at the table other than me is Dr. Neil Grunberg, a friend of a friend, who had been the one to suggest my visit to the Defense and Veterans Center for Integrative Pain Medicine (DVCIPM, pronounced "dee vee sip-um"), where the four of us now sat. Neil has a humbling number of advanced degrees and publications, and he is a professor in several departments at USU. They all wait to see whether I'll invite Trip to stick a needle in me while we get to know one another.

"Uhhh, sure, I think," I said, laughing nervously and wondering if he was really going to do it.

He absolutely did, walking over to me in two long steps, adjusting my head to position my left ear so that he could choose his injection point and then positioning the strange, short needle. I heard a kind of *snap*, and felt a small pinch in my earlobe. Trip turned around, tossed the small piece of plastic that remained into the trash, and sat back down.

"Can you tell that the needle is still in your ear?' he asked.

I was totally unsure. It was a strange feeling. My left earlobe felt hot, and I was certainly focusing on it, but no, it wasn't clear at all that something was in it.

The kind of acupuncture he just performed, he explained, is called auricular acupuncture (stimulation on the external ear surface), and the mechanism he used was specifically designed to be ultraportable and usable in nonclinical environments. Each small (about two inch) plastic container holds a *very* small, gold needle in its tip, which the container could inject just under the skin.

"How long will it stay there?" I asked.

"Several days, if you want it to," he responded. "They typically fall out in the shower or while you're sleeping. No big deal. The military guys like them because they look like earrings, but they can't be forced to take them out." He chuckled.

Although I tried desperately to pay attention to the conversation that unfolded afterward, I continually found myself distracted by what certainly seemed to be less pain in my bad foot. As my attention was drawn to my warm ear, I felt no pain at all in my usually stiff and achy foot, and I couldn't help but wonder whether that was really possible. Did this single needle stick really change my chronic pain level? If so, was it just placebo—that is, was it due to my brain expecting it to benefit me? And finally, if it was just placebo effect, did that matter?

I was having a hard time staying focused. Luckily, my new friends were compelling storytellers and teachers, and they eventually pulled me out of my head and back into reality.

Trip, Eric, and Neil sat at that conference table with me for three hours, explaining to me what they do and why they do it. The reason I wanted to talk to them is because, basically, military pain medicine is years ahead of much of civilian pain medicine in many important respects. The reason, Eric explained, is that they—the military—have gotten so good at saving soldiers' lives over the last decade and a half or so that we have a rapidly growing population of veterans surviving excruciatingly painful wounds and going on to live with serious, chronic pain. As body armor improved and our ability to extract wounded soldiers advanced, the kind of traumatic injury that would have killed soldiers a generation ago became survivable. More limbs were mangled or lost, but more lives were saved. Doctors like Buckenmaier and Schoomaker were charged with finding ways to improve the sort of care these soldiers received.

Although this information was all new to me, it actually had already earned them some limited notoriety. A powerful essay in *Wired* magazine had documented military pain medicine efforts, especially the regional anesthetic techniques used by Buckenmaier known as nerve blocks—the therapy discussed earlier in which nerves can be "turned off," preventing pain signals from being sent to the brain. Later, the documentary film *Escape Fire* dove even deeper, revealing the military's drive to control pain effectively, from the moment of triage through recovery, while minimizing the risks of aggressive opioid therapy. What both investigations revealed is that the hellish situation of war was driving pain care innovation, including not only expanded use of techniques like nerve blocks, but also eventually the use of acupuncture. *On the battlefield.*

This last point blew my mind. Yes, these men were really telling me that acupuncture is not only effective but so effective that they train people to carry these miniature sterilized needles for the sake of augmenting pain care at the site of battlefield injury.

I suddenly had a very different picture of what I had previously taken to be "alternative medicine"—or as too many people in my academic world may have thought of it: "fake medicine." Although I have already noted that there is evidence in support of acupuncture, up to this point I hadn't really believed that it could be so effective as to be endorsed by the military, which I don't think of as being a particularly warm-and-fuzzy institution—not the kind of place where I would expect an "alternative" therapy to be taken up.

But it works, and so the guys at DVCIPM stay busy, trying to think about pain medicine according to a different model. This is what really has them ahead of the curve. Their patients need a lot of pain care, so they have seen the inadequacies of the old model first-hand. Opioid-centric therapy—focusing only on getting that first shot of morphine as quickly as possible after trauma and then keeping the wounded soldier doped up all the way back to the States and through recovery—had resulted in too much dependence, addiction, severe chronic pain, and post-traumatic stress disorder (PTSD). And while the military certainly still requires a lot of morphine and other opioids, the more sophisticated approach developed by the folks at DVCIPM is improving the lives of wounded veterans.

Perhaps the most important thing I learned in my day sitting with these military doctors and researchers is that the very frame we have for pain is part of what drives bad solutions. Too many of us, too often, think of pain as something that needs to be eliminated, and so we focus on pain intensity, with the goal of no pain. This is precisely how we traditionally use that ubiquitous 0–10 scale: Oh, you have pain? Okay, how intense? Let's see if we can get that number down. And the patient thinks, "Yeah, down to zero."

A pain-free life, though, is not an appropriate goal. As Trip would tell me that day, "I can get anyone's pain to zero. It's just that you'll be lying on the floor, slobbering all over the carpet." And I immediately thought of my time in the hospital, where I essentially did precisely that (though on hospital bedsheets rather than the floor). Not that I blame myself for seeking serious pain relief immediately after trauma, but thinking only of intensity would drive me to beg for unconsciousness. If I had tried to take that reasoning and move forward into recovery, the goal of pain reduction would have been incompatible with living.

Indeed, I had unreflectively begun to endorse a more complex view of pain on my own. I explained earlier how, in those first days at the hospital, I devised my own rules for reporting my pain on the 0–10 scale, and they involved more than sensation—I was interpreting them as limits on functioning in the world. I wanted to be with Sadiye, and to be able to reason about what was happening to me. Seeking to drive the pain down too aggressively would make those things impossible; it would, that is, result in my slobbering on the floor.

In an effort to incorporate this insight into pain treatment, the DVCIPM team has released a new pain scale, which now strikes me as incredibly important. This revised pain scale is to be used with a list of questions, and together they link the intensity of pain to four other considerations: activity, stress, mood, and sleep. Each of these functional and overall well-being considerations is ranked, and the overall pain rating reflects not merely pain intensity but the effect of pain on one's life. Rating one's pain, then, is not merely an exercise in trying to subjectively evaluate just how bad it feels—it is about judging how the pain affects overall quality of life.

The revised pain scale represents, for me, an important step in moving away from opioid-centric pain care. As we've seen: opioids have many costs, even when they're effective; and it turns out that they're not as effective as we thought. Taking opioids can, in some cases, improve function and quality of life; but when they don't, they shouldn't be used. It sounds obvious to point out, but our obsession with a unidimensional pain scale and a medicine that can get us to zero, but with serious costs, has been a recipe for disaster.

What the revising of the pain scale really points out, then, is the role that each of us has to play in solving some of the overwhelmingly large and complex problems raised throughout this book. Sure, it's true for most of us that we can't (as individuals) force doctors to learn more about how to manage opioids, nor can most of us single-handedly increase access to treatment for opioid use disorder. But each of us can begin to question the views we hold that have allowed our current healthcare system to develop.

During the summer of 2017, my dear friend Colin Hickey needed to undergo surgery. Two of them, in fact. He had managed to tear the labrum of each hip (a cartilage ring around the hip socket), due to a combination of his active lifestyle of hiking, playing tennis, and dancing, plus a structural deformity. The surgeon needed to fix both sides, so he would operate on one side first and then do the other a couple of months later.

This sort of surgery is difficult to describe in terms of its "seriousness." On the one hand, it's minimally invasive. The surgeon is able to do the work with only very small incisions, so the outward appearance is of a fairly minor surgery. Once inside, however, he would have to repair the torn cartilage and carve down some excess bone to prevent the sort of friction that caused the tear in the first place. This makes it sound much more significant and explains why people who undergo this surgery have months of physical therapy and recovery, after weeks of extremely limited mobility.

After his first surgery, I visited Colin at his apartment, and naturally we swapped "war stories" of our injuries, surgeries, and recoveries. He was in pretty rough shape, able to move only very little, and was confined to his bed for most of the day. He looked pained but also completely alert. I asked him about his pain and meds.

"Yeah, they gave me a bottle of pills, but I don't want 'em," he replied. He, of course, knew of my own struggle with painkillers, and he looked at me sympathetically. "Obviously I know the risks; but I also just don't think I need them. It hurts, and it'll hurt for a while. But the first days were the worst, and I made it through. So I don't think they're necessary."

As usual with Colin, who is one of the most focused, thoughtful, straight-up *toughest* people I know, I was impressed. "So you didn't take any of the pills? At all?"

"Not a one," he replied.

Now I was definitely curious. This conversation was taking place at just about the point in my research where I was beginning to understand how little evidence base we have (or at least *had*, until recently) for our prescribing habits. "And how many pills did they prescribe? Of what?"

"Uhhh, I think it's like sixty, probably Percocet. They're right there on the table," he gestured. "Feel free to check 'em out."

He was right: sixty pills of 5mg oxycodone/325mg acetaminophen, and not a one missing. We chatted about his reasons for a bit, and it really seemed to come down more to his personal philosophy than his knowing what he knew because he happened to have seen his friend get hurt. Colin has always been something of an ascetic—he's a Colorado hippie who has been a complete minimalist as long as I've known him. He doesn't need *stuff*, and he isn't a huge fan of medicine. He's the kind of guy who felt rich while we were working for poverty wages as graduate students in Washington, DC. And while he would have, I think, taken the pills if he really thought he needed them, he just wasn't afraid of some pain, and he was willing to be uncomfortable and work hard.

I've always admired him for his dedication to a philosophically rigorous life, but I admired him even more after that day. There wouldn't have been anything wrong with his taking the pills, but he didn't need them. And instead of using them anyway, to drive his pain down from manageable to zero, he just stuck it out. When he went in for the second surgery some weeks later, he told his surgeon that he hadn't used any of the pills so he didn't need a new prescription. And he was right. When the summer was over, and both hips had been fixed, he was pushing his way through physical therapy and still had an untouched bottle of sixty Percocet.

Nothing about my admiration for Colin should indicate that I think all torn labrum surgeries should be performed without prescribing opioids for recovery. If you have had that surgery and you took some of the pills, I get it; I probably would have too. What I love about Colin's story, rather, is that it highlights the degree to which some pain can simply be dealt with. Not all of it needs to be, but some of it can be. Life hurts—quite a lot for some of us—but not all of those pains require pharmacological intervention. And importantly, our expectations can really affect how reasonable that suggestion seems. Part of why Colin was able to make it through that summer, I think, is because he doesn't expect life to be pain-free, and he's willing to put up with quite a lot. Perhaps more than should be expected of any of us. But it's important to reflect on what we *can* do in order to think carefully about what we *should* do.

As I was thinking about this very story, I ended up chatting with my mom on the phone, and we were discussing her knee replacement surgery. I told her how impressed I was by her recovery and how little medication she had taken. In response, she told me something I hadn't expected: "Well, you told me it was going to hurt—that it was really going to suck. And I knew that I didn't want to be on the meds for too long. So I went into it expecting for it to be pretty terrible. I was ready, I guess. And I knew it wouldn't last forever."

Watching these two people that I deeply care about—my mom and my friend—come to understand pain and medication differently has been very moving. Trauma caught me by surprise, and when I found myself in hospitals for weeks, on morphine and fentanyl drips, popping oxycodone, I hadn't prepared myself at all. It was all new and terrifying. I had one goal: avoid the pain. And only in retrospect can I realize that I carried that goal much too far forward into my recovery.

I wish someone had prepared me for the pain—told me that I would hurt and that it would be scary, but that I didn't have to let elimination of pain become my sole priority. In short, I wish I had been mentally ready to balance the need for pain relief against the risks and costs of medication. This leads me to think that one of our major goals for rethinking how we deal with pain is not a goal for physicians (although we've identified plenty of those); it's a goal for the rest of us. We need to foster a different relationship with pain and come to a more careful understanding of what we can live with and what we can't—what calls for pharmaceutical help and what might be manageable in other ways.

In many places around the world, but especially in America, we live in a "pill for every pain" culture. You have a headache? There's a pill for that. Sprained your ankle? Pill for that. Ongoing back pain? Yup, you guessed it, there's a pill for that. Our over-the-counter medications already capitalize on this culture, selling us acetaminophen, ibuprofen, and aspirin by the buckets. It's no surprise, then, that prescription pharmaceutical companies jumped on board as well. The basic strategy behind Purdue's marketing campaign in the 1990s and early 2000s was that OxyContin was effective (stronger than morphine, and lasts twelve hours!) and safe (less than 1 percent of patients develop an addiction!). So why restrict its use to cancer or palliative care? OxyContin is the pill for *moderate* to severe pain—the pill, that is, for nearly every pain.

The unfortunate fact that we've been uncovering, however, is that medications have side effects. The effects of opioids can be particularly devastating, but that certainly doesn't make it the case that all other painkillers are perfectly safe. Acetaminophen must be carefully limited in dosing to avoid causing liver damage, NSAIDs like ibuprofen and celecoxib raise one's risk of heart attack and stroke. The list goes on. This is not a unique feature of pain medication, of course; medicines, in general, have side effects. Deciding whether to use a particular medication for a particular ailment is always a process of weighing the risks and benefits.

This consideration of trade-offs is especially difficult for treating chronic pain. As we now know, opioids should not be considered first-line treatment for chronic pain, as they are both risky and may well be no more effective than non-opioid therapies. However, most physicians will also warn patients that a lifetime of any pain medication can be dangerous, given the side effects listed above. Determining how to proceed is truly difficult. Sometimes there are alternative interventions that can be considered, such as injections, nerve blocks, or surgery. And sometimes it is completely unclear what will be best for a particular patient.

Not all treatments for pain involve a pill (or some other medical procedure), however. A truly surprising amount of scientific data supports what we might think of as "lifestyle" therapies; or as some people call it: self-care. There are many such strategies, supported by varying degrees of scientific evidence, and more research is being conducted all the time. Looking at just some of the most common suggestions: exercise, yoga, and massage have all been shown to be beneficial for dealing with pain. And really, this shouldn't be all that surprising. After all, doing these things amounts to taking care of one's body, which can strengthen and heal weak and damaged tissue.

Additionally, cognitive-behavioral therapy (CBT)—a form of

psychotherapy that focuses on altering unhelpful cognitive patterns and behavior—has been shown to be effective for treating certain forms of chronic pain. Despite this evidence base, however, many people find such a suggestion offensive. If a physician recommends CBT to a chronic pain patient, the response may well be some version of "What? So you think this is all in my head? You think my pain isn't real?"

That pain can be treated with CBT, however, implies nothing of the sort. Chronic pain is often what's called "maladaptive pain," which means it no longer signals tissue damage or injury. Whereas acute pain serves as an alert that one's body is at risk, that same pain can transition into chronic pain that no longer serves that function. It's maladaptive rather than adaptive—pain that causes suffering but which plays no productive health role.

The evidence that CBT can successfully treat chronic pain suggests that therapy can help the brain and nervous system to correct this dysfunction. By pursuing psychological health, one can simultaneously promote pain relief.

And of course—going back to the guys at DVCIPM—acupuncture has also been shown to be effective in treating chronic pain. Although it's totally unclear (to modern, Western medicine) *why* it helps—that is to say, the mechanism of acupuncture pain relief is a bit mysterious— the evidence does suggest that it works. Indeed, some evidence suggests that it can work as well as pharmacotherapy for some pain and that the results are lasting.

The list goes on, and research is being conducted into all sorts of lifestyle interventions, ranging from mindfulness meditation to qigong and tai chi. In short, the evidence is mounting that changing one's lifestyle can constitute genuine pain therapy. Being more active, pursuing exercise and physical therapy, getting professional massages, going to therapy, and getting acupuncture all can be part of a lifestyle prescription. None of them are a magic bullet (sadly, we don't have one of those), but they are genuine treatments.

Of course, pursuing such a lifestyle change can be exceedingly hard and prohibitively expensive. Changing your entire life is difficult, and for some people likely impossible. And whereas pills are relatively cheap, the kind of changes I'm discussing here are not.

Despite my privilege, I don't do as well as I should. I try to exercise and regularly fail. I'm intimidated by yoga and bristle at the cost of most of the things on this list. But I will admit that, to the degree that I've been able and willing to implement self-care, my pain has gone down. I eventually stopped taking my pain medication (celecoxib), and I feel like I have less pain, better function, and better quality of life than I've had since the accident.

Is that placebo? Is my brain doing that to me because my research has led me to expect, and hope, that it might?

Does it matter if it is?

Look, it's certainly not the case that self-care is magic and will replace our need for powerful opioid medications. Some pain is devastating and life limiting, and sometimes that pain responds well to opioids. I am most certainly not recommending that we all just get up after an injury and "rub some dirt in it." That's not the answer, and not my suggestion.

But we can be part of an important culture change. We can stop demanding from our doctors a pill for every pain, and we can try to take seriously the nonpharmacological treatments they suggest. In fact, until the medical community completely catches up, we can even keep tabs on them, like Colin did. The surgeon was ready to give him two large bottles of pills, and that laid the burden on him to say "no thanks." We can ask whether sixty pills is really necessary, or whether just a few might do.

In short, each one of us can make a difference. Not by trying to eliminate opioids from pain medicine but by formulating an attitude and a set of expectations that makes it easier for clinicians to use those powerful tools responsibly.

Mother's Day has always been an important day in our house, but it has taken on even more meaning since 2015. Just two weeks before Memorial Day weekend, it was a gorgeous day that year, and we made the most out of it. Our then one-year-old daughter and I had taken Sadiye to a local winery for a lovely, extended picnic out on the grass, pairing wine for the adults and juice for the kiddo with cheeses and breads. And there had been dancing—*lots* of dancing—to the live bluegrass of a sweet, talented local musician.

Being the twenty-first century, and armed with iPhones as we were, that day at the winery had been well documented, with high-quality family photos and goofy dancing videos. The one that is forever seared into my brain is of Sinem, so young, bouncing on her mom's knee, shaking her goofy little head to the guitar player's rendition of "The Devil Went Down to Georgia." That video, like that day, was so filled with joy that it practically leapt off the screen. And when I landed in the hospital two weeks later, and began my long journey of recovery, it was the last video on my phone.

I watched it a lot early on, when I spent so much time in the hospital alone, but at that point it was more a way of connecting with my little girl; since I didn't see her much when I was in the hospital, it was something to hold on to. But in the following months, as I began to enter my own little circle of opioid-withdrawal hell, that video took on incredible meaning. I must have watched it a million times, usually smiling and crying at the same time. So recently, my life had been perfect; and, just months later, I was spending a good portion of the day trying to figure out whether I wanted to die. My brain chemistry had betrayed me, and I was convinced that I would never recover—never be the same—and this video was one of the last glimpses of the life I could have had.

Of course, my opioid-starved brain, receptors desperate for that molecule they had become so accustomed to, was wrong. I did get better, and I am so very, very grateful.

Which brings us back to the Mother's Days of recent years. The holiday is about Sadiye, and it's a wonderful opportunity to celebrate her not only as an amazing mother to my baby girl but as a partner of superhero standing. Given its proximity to the accident, this celebration instantly reminds me of the myriad ways in which Sadiye saved my life, over and over. And so our happiness on this day can also have a weightiness about it—a genuine appreciation for the good moments in life—as we remember the stark contrast between that happiness we had experienced on Mother's Day in 2015 and what followed so soon after.

Mother's Day 2017 was as beautiful as the one two years before, and despite knowing that it would be a challenge, we decided to walk to our local park. It's close to three miles round-trip, and how much pain I'm in by the time we get back depends a lot on contingent features of the day: how good I've been about physical therapy, how tired I am, if I step wrong at any point, and who knows what else. So we set out, and it turned out to be a particularly difficult day. It took us three hours to complete, and I was in a lot of pain by the end.

But the thing is: that's okay. Pain is part of recovery, and I spend a lot of my life that way. So enduring pain in order to experience sunshine and family is no real cost, especially for such a meaningful celebration. As more time passes and I have more experiences like this, I have come to realize that this is our new normal. It's wonderful even when it's hard, and uplifting even when it's frustrating. It's recovery. It's progress. Our day was beautiful despite the pain, as I was so acutely aware of what my life could have become.

The United States is also struggling to make progress regarding its own pain—pain caused by injury and lifestyle, as well as pain caused by addiction and a skyrocketing overdose death rate. I wish I could say I was as optimistic about the country's progress as I am about my own, but there are very real reasons to be worried.

Over the course of this book, I've pulled together several related crises: a pain crisis, an opioid crisis, and the crisis of our own making as we threaten to exacerbate each in the name of the other. In the time it took me to write this book, it's likely that more than one hundred thousand Americans died from opioid overdose. And though the specific number is a bit contentious, a 2011 National Academies report suggests that as many as one hundred *million* people live with chronic pain. Numbers like this are absolutely staggering—virtually unable to be comprehended, to be made real. What they seem to mean is that America is in serious, severe pain of different kinds, and the reader who doesn't know anyone affected by one of these crises is likely very rare.

I *want* to say that I think we're on the road to getting better. After all, I've written here about wonderful colleagues, scientists, and physicians who are doing great work. The opioid crisis is constantly in the news, and legislation is introduced at the state and federal levels practically every day. Surely this means we're moving in the right direction, right?

I really wish it did, and there are certainly bright spots. Individual states have implemented evidence-based interventions regarding opioid prescribing, addiction care, and harm reduction, with impressive outcomes. But they are the exceptions. As I write this, more than a decade after we began to hear about the prescription opioid problem—indeed, more than a decade after Purdue Pharma admitted to wrongdoing and paid $635 million in fines—we still don't know when the opioid crisis will peak. This powerful, seductive, deadly class of drugs, descended from and inspired by the poppy plant, continues to drive an unprecedented public health crisis of addiction and overdose death. Although I laid out an evidence-based set of basic interventions that would help us turn the tide, including massive investments in addiction treatment and harm reduction services, the country as a whole has passed on act-ing at the scale needed to make meaningful change.

It's tempting to think that we have made more progress on the prescription side of things. Although the broader drug overdose crisis continues to devastate the country, I've mentioned several times that prescribing peaked shortly after 2010 and has been trending down. However, even this bit of news is contaminated with pessimism.

The first reason is that prescribing still remains high—about three times the rate of the early 1990s, in fact. So while many have been quick to celebrate the decline in prescribing, we have to admit it hasn't really fallen that far. Much of the increased prescribing seen during the "decade of pain" remains.

In addition, the well-documented decrease in prescribing is a very specific measure of how many opioids are going out into the country—namely, it's a measure of the number of prescriptions writ-ten. And that does seem like an eminently sensible thing to measure. Fewer prescriptions written sounds like a good thing. However, when a team of researchers decided in 2018 to look at prescribing another way—by looking at the number of Americans who received *any* pre-scription opioids—they found that the data tells a different story. Even as the number of prescriptions has gone down, the proportion of patients receiving any opioid has not significantly decreased.

On its own, this new piece of data isn't necessarily bad. Perhaps clinicians used to write prescriptions for good reasons, but then wrote too many refills. If they have been reducing the number of inappro-priate refills, that would explain the data.

Unfortunately, I've suggested throughout these pages that cli-nicians have often, in recent decades, written prescriptions when it's not appropriate—for moderate acute pain, minor procedures, or as first-line treatment for chronic pain. Eliminating these prescrip-tions should result in a smaller population receiving any opioid pre-scriptions, which we're not seeing. That makes me worry that we're not making progress regarding some of the lowest-hanging fruit and instead must be achieving prescription reductions elsewhere. And while there are likely many other places where reduced prescribing would be appropriate, some opportunities to reduce prescribing are ethically fraught (like, recall, dramatic and nonconsensual dose reductions for legacy patients). My concern, then, is that a reduction in the number of opioid prescriptions written may not reflect an increase in *responsible* prescribing.

The bottom line is that we are not, by and large, acting decisively in an evidence-based way to tackle the myriad problems raised by opioids. Although we don't know everything about how to turn the corner on this crisis, we know a lot, and we're simply not doing it. Our healthcare system is deeply, deeply broken, and we don't seem to care enough to change the overarching way that we deal with either pain or addiction.

We have to do better. We *must* do better. Because lives are depending on it. If you can't hold in your mind the sheer scope of our problems with opioids, then bring it down to individuals. Listen to the stories your friends and family tell about mishandled pain care, iatrogenic dependence, or their struggles with addiction. Read them in the newspaper. Note just how prolific they are.

Since beginning to work in this field, the number of stories I've heard is overwhelming. I've become a collector of tragedy, and I'm haunted by it. If you don't think you know anyone who has been affected by opioids, then it's likely you just haven't been let in. Because the numbers are really that staggering. Statistically, it would be surprising if you were really so protected. I know that it wasn't until I went public with my own story that some people opened up to me about their struggles. The stigma and shame are real, leading people to keep their experience a dark little secret.

That's part of why all of us have a role to play in fixing the issues I've discussed. I've laid a lot at the feet of doctors, nurses, hospitals, and the broader healthcare system. But the rest of us have our work cut out for us too. We all need to foster a different relationship with pain and develop a different understanding of medicine—what it does and doesn't owe us, and what we should expect from our doctors.

We also need to understand addiction and expand our circle of empathy, demanding that our elected officials do the same. I hope I have sparked some new thoughts and feelings about addiction in this book, but it's only the smallest of starts. Others have written beautifully on this topic, and I urge interested readers to continue their education. Because so much of what we need to do requires abandoning that outdated, unhelpful "moral model" of addiction and replacing our instinct to judge with an instinct to help.

The set of issues and questions that arise at the nexus of pain, medicine, and the opioid crisis won't be adequately addressed without a massive shift in values. Medicine can be improved and public health interventions can be introduced, but they won't be unless we demand them.

That's why I wrote this book. I want to demand change, but I want you to also. And *demanding* isn't the kind of thing we do when we're complacent. We demand when we're angry and uncomfortable—when we feel the urgency of a situation. So I hope to have shared some of the urgency I feel about pain, medicine, and drug use—urgency that comes from intimate familiarity with suffering.

If I succeeded, that urgency has likely made you feel uncomfortable. Good. Me too. Now let's do something about it.

ACKNOWLEDGMENTS

Writing a book always requires something of a village; writing a personal book even more so. In addition to all of the people who helped me in terms of getting words on pages, making them as accurate as possible, and getting them published, there is another group of people to whom I owe a great debt: those who helped me survive the story I tell. And, unsurprisingly perhaps, some people show up in more than one group. I'll start by thanking those who exist in every group—who helped me in every way possible. This group has only one member, to whom I owe so much I can't possibly do it justice here. If you've read this book all the way through, and you're still with me, you know who it is.

Sadiye: thank you for everything.

My partner in life and in all things, Sadiye was my emotional support and my advocate during the events documented herein. She has been my rock over the years I worked on this book, taking on more than her share of family obligations while I added 'becoming an author' to my day-job at the university. And as a brilliant and insightful commenter, she has read innumerable drafts of papers, chapters, and the full book, providing feedback, serving as my external memory, and being a partner in every aspect of the endeavor. I simply could not have done this without her.

In addition to Sadiye, several other people worked to help me make it through the aftermath of my motorcycle accident. My dad drove from Indiana to Maryland the day after I landed in the hospital, and stayed with Sadiye, providing emotional support both to her and to me. After he left, my mom moved into our basement for nearly two months to keep me company and help as she could. It had been a long time since I had needed my parents to take care of me, and I'm grateful that they were willing to step into that role once again.

As I was undergoing multiple surgeries and living in hospitals, several dear friends helped with childcare, which was a godsend during a very frantic, scary time. Especially noteworthy contributions were made by Michael Holt, Amina Metidji, and Debbie Glass, without whom Sadiye may have lost her mind (she assures me this is an accurate assessment). Sinem's daycare provider at the time, Maryam Geramifar, was an incredible resource, taking Sinem into her home on the day of the accident (which happened practically outside her house) and being phenomenally understanding in the months that followed.

My colleagues at Johns Hopkins were also wonderful. I spoke on the phone with then-director of my institute, Ruth Faden, and my faculty mentor, Jeff Kahn (who took over as director shortly after) starting the day after the accident. Both assured me that my brand-new faculty job was secure, and that we would figure everything out. I didn't set foot in my office for months, and yet they managed to keep their promise, helping me to work from afar.

Crucial to that endeavor was the effort of my colleague Julia Chill, who personally drove my on-boarding paperwork out to my house so that I could begin work as faculty from my bed. As I slowly recovered, then, she also drove out of her way in order to pick me up and shuttle me to and from campus when I needed to attend a meeting. Our drives were not only necessary if I wanted to get to work, but a lovely shared commute. Indeed, thanks to our car-pool, Julia would be one of the earliest colleagues to learn of my very personal struggle with opioid dependence.

I also want to thank my sister, Elizabeth Slunaker, who became a real cheerleader from afar as I progressed through recovery. She probably has no idea (until now!) how much her uplifting texts, video chats, and Facebook posts have meant over the years.

And my Baby Girl (not so baby anymore), Sinem: you gave your dad a reason to do some of the hardest things he's ever done. I'll never forget that.

I want to close this first section by thanking the healthcare staff who took care of me over the course of many months. In particular, the nurses at every hospital were uniformly outstanding, and they helped me to understand the power that intimate care-taking has in the medical context. I wish I had written down names, as my memory of them has been wiped away by drugs and trauma; but I *do* remember their warmth and humanity.

All of my occupational and physical therapists, too, were fantastic. My surgeons have been amazed by my recovery, and I think a lot of the credit for that goes to these individuals. So for pushing me, even when I called you a sadist for it (I was joking, I promise!): thank you.

And finally: the doctors. This one is complicated, obviously. I just spent an entire book describing the failures of the medical system, which I discovered when my doctors screwed up. And I've been angry about that. But I've also noted that none of my doctors were malicious, nor were they failing to live up to the standards of their field; it's just that their fields' standards are problematic. And what's certainly true, despite the hardship I experienced, is that a large group of technically talented physicians saved my foot and treated my pain. They weren't perfect, but people are complex.

So to all of my doctors: I'm grateful for what you did for me, even when I'm mad about what you did *to* me. And if any of you read this and recognize yourselves: I'm really not trying to make you feel bad. But I do want you to do better.

The second group of people who deserve thanks comprises those who helped me turn this endeavor into a book. It was a not a fore-gone conclusion that I would publish this story, and the fact that I did is due to very many people who helped in very many ways.

For helping me to turn a fledgling first attempt at a book proposal into something that might actually catch a reader's attention, I owe truly massive thanks to two people: Michelle Jabes Corpora, who not only provided sharp edits on an early draft, but who also helped me to believe that I might be able to write this book; and Kelly Heuer, who provided incredibly detailed feedback on a full proposal, and made it immeasurably better.

Since I had no earthly idea how to go about finding an agent, this book may well still be an unread file on my computer but for the interest and kindness of my friend and colleague, Gail Geller, who introduced me to Todd Shuster of Aevitas Creative Management—and similarly, if Todd hadn't been willing to read my pages, and then pass them on to his colleague, Jane von Mehren. I am incredibly grateful to both Gail and Todd for helping to shepherd me into the publishing world.

Jane, then, became not only the best agent I could ask for, but an incredible teacher as well; over the course of several months, she helped me to find my voice and a compelling version of the story I wanted to tell. Ultimately, she helped me sell that story to Jonathan Jao at HarperCollins, who is a masterful editor. He seemed to know the best version of this book well before I did, and gave me exactly the feedback I needed in order to extract it from me. Thank you, Jane and Jonathan, for helping to make this happen.

I also want to thank my dad for championing my ambitions as a writer. He did this not only by copyediting a penultimate version of the proposal and thus saving me from many errors, but (and it truly pains me to admit this) by pushing me to write from my earliest years. Yes, dad, this means I'm officially thanking you for assigning me essays over my summer breaks in elementary school.

The final group of people I have to thank are the content experts who helped me along the way. I have tried to explain many difficult concepts in this book, and to the extent that I have succeeded at any of it, I owe a massive debt to my friends and colleagues named here.

Brendan Saloner has had an outsized influence on the way I think about many of the problems I explore, given that he is one of the first people with whom I really discussed these issues. I'm also grateful to Indre Viskontas for several important discussions in which she helped me to understand some of the neuroscience regarding pain, opioid dependence, and addiction.

Michael Erdek, Jennifer Haythornthwaite, and Marie Stratton all read chapters relevant to their expertise and provided crucially helpful feedback. Colin Hickey, Casey Humbyrd, and Yoram Unguru not only read full drafts of the book at various stages, providing insightful commentary, but they were also graciously willing to discuss the ideas in the book over the course of many months.

Pat Carroll and Marcus Hedahl, though, truly went above and beyond the call of duty. Both read full drafts of the book, offering a level of criticism and insight that must have taken just an unfathomable amount of time. Although they come from very different perspectives (psychiatry and philosophy, respectively), Pat and Marcus both influenced this book deeply, helping me to see my own story in new ways. I'm serious when I say that I hope the book lives up to the amount of thought and effort they put into it.

This book exists because of all these people and many more—those who visited me in the hospital, those who had lengthy conversations that helped me to workshop an idea, those who taught me one of a million ideas that made it into these pages, and others, I'm sure. If there is value to be found in these pages, the credit goes largely to them. And of course, if there are errors and misunderstandings, those are mine, despite the best efforts of my wonderful friends, family, and colleagues.

So to all of you, from the bottom of my heart: thank you.

NOTES

EPIGRAPH

vii Remember, effective relief: https://www.smithsonianmag.com/science-nature
/how-advertising-shaped-first-opioid-epidemic-180968444/.

CHAPTER 1: A SALVAGE SITUATION

13 the best chance of saving my foot: Although this book is not the place to
explore the issue in more depth, it's worth noting that this frame of "limb
salvage," according to which "saving the foot" is the goal and amputation
is an evil to be avoided, is seriously problematic. Much later, I would eventually come to understand that not only should I have been less afraid of
amputation, but my surgeon should have presented it to me as a treatment
option. I would likely have recovered more quickly, gained more function
with less pain, and, crucially: I likely would have avoided the challenges
with pain medicine that this book goes on to detail. In 2018, I published an
academic paper making this point with my colleague Dr. Casey Humbyrd.
For those interested, that paper is: Casey Jo Humbyrd and Travis N. Rieder,
"Ethics and Limb Salvage: Presenting Amputation as a Treatment Option
in Lower Extremity Trauma," *Journal of Bone and Joint Surgery* 100, no. 19
(October 3, 2018): e128.

18 as many as ninety-eight thousand people die each year: Institute of Medicine, *To Err Is Human: Building a Safer Health System* (Washington, DC: The
National Academies Press, 2000). The full report can be read online for
free at https://www.nap.edu/catalog/9728/to-err-is-human-building-a-safer
-health-system.

CHAPTER 2: PAIN AND DRUGS

25 deeply philosophically puzzling: The philosophical aspect of pain (apart from
the scientific aspect) is given a helpful overview by Murat Aydede in "Pain,"
The Stanford Encyclopedia of Philosophy (Spring 2013 Edition), Edward N.
Zalta (ed.), https://plato.stanford.edu/archives/spr2013/entries/pain.

26 Pain actually happens *in the brain*: Or, alternatively, our experience of pain happens in the mind. See Kurt Baier, "Pains," *Australasian Journal of Philosophy* 40, no. 1 (1962): 1–23.

27 "unpleasant sensory and emotional experience": This definition can be found at the IASP's website: http://www.iasp-pain.org/Education/Content .aspx?ItemNumber=1698#Pain.

30 relieving pain should be a national priority: Institute of Medicine, *Relieving Pain in America: A Blueprint for Transforming Prevention, Care, Education, and Research* (Washington, DC: The National Academies Press, 2011).

30 The pain scale is thus the simple solution: An example paper from the medical literature making essentially this case for the pain scale (and accompanying faces) as part of physician training is Regina Fink, "Pain Assessment: The Cornerstone to Optimal Pain Management," *Baylor University Medical Center Proceedings* 13, no. 3 (July 2000): 236–39. In the context of the coming chapter, note both that the paper was published in the year 2000, at the height of excitement about aggressive pain treatment, and that the author discloses that she was on the speakers' bureaus for multiple pharmaceutical companies, including Purdue Pharma (maker of OxyContin).

32 "It's one hundred times stronger than morphine": I fact-checked her (much) later, and her claim checks out: according to the CDC, fentanyl is fifty to one hundred times stronger than morphine: https://www.cdc.gov/drugover-dose/opioids/fentanyl.html.

34 as my anxiety level rose, the pain got sharper: It turns out that there is a well-documented relationship between pain and anxiety. In the final chapter, I discuss the value of cognitive-behavioral therapy, which is often used for chronic pain relief, and one value of this sort of mind-body training is to help prevent one's mood from worsening one's pain. This sort of strategy is used less often, however, for acute pain. My thanks to Dr. Pat Carroll for discussion on this point.

40 They are capable of treating truly severe pain: It's worth noting here that despite the "raw analgesic power" of opioids, they are not equally effective against all pains. As I've already mentioned, in the discussion with my hospital pain team, neuropathic pain, for instance, is thought to respond significantly less well to opioids.

40 What makes something an opioid: The basic history and science of opioids to follow can be found in very many sources. An excellent place to start for those wanting more detail is M. J. Brownstein, "A Brief History of Opiates, Opioid Peptides, and Opioid Receptors," *Proceedings of the National Academy of Sciences* 90, no. 12 (June 15, 1993): 5391–93.

43 cause of death in such a case is opioid poisoning: For a good survey of the mechanism of fatal opioid overdose, see J. M. White and R. J. Irvine, "Mechanisms of Fatal Opioid Overdose," *Addiction* 94, no. 7 (July 1999): 961–72.

CHAPTER 3: THE SWINGING PENDULUM

45 "start low and go slow": Clinical recommendations will be discussed at more length later; but for the language of "start low and go slow," see the CDC's fact sheet at https://www.cdc.gov/drugoverdose/pdf/guidelines_factsheet-a .pdf.

46 In the nineteenth century: The following history is a synthesis of very many sources, all of which I am indebted to. In what follows, I provide specific references for particular, or controversial, claims, but I take much of the general history to be well established, as a result of the good scholarly work and reporting done in the following sources: Sam Quinones, *Dreamland: The True Tale of America's Opiate Epidemic* (New York: Bloomsbury Press, 2015); Barry Meier, *Pain Killer: An Empire of Deceit and the Origin of America's Opioid Epidemic*, updated ed. (New York: Random House, 2018); John Temple, *American Pain: How a Young Felon and His Ring of Doctors Unleashed America's Deadliest Drug Epidemic* (Guilford, CT: Lyons Press, 2016); Martin Booth, *Opium: A History* (New York: St. Martin's Press, 1996); Keith Wailoo, *Pain: A Political History* (Baltimore: Johns Hopkins University Press, 2014); Johann Hari, *Chasing the Scream: The First and Last Days of the War on Drugs* (London: Bloomsbury Circus, 2015); Anna Lembke, *Drug Dealer, MD: How Doctors Were Duped, Patients Got Hooked, and Why It's So Hard to Stop* (Baltimore: Johns Hopkins University Press, 2016); Marcia L. Meldrum, "The Ongoing Opioid Prescription Epidemic: Historical Context," *American Journal of Public Health* 106, no. 8 (August 2016): 1365–66; Andrew Kolodny et al., "The Prescription Opioid and Heroin Crisis: A Public Health Approach to an Epidemic of Addiction," *Annual Review of Public Health* 36 (March 2015): 559–74; and I'm sure many more articles, essays, or radio stories that I've heard over the past few years and forgotten.

46 Chinese "opium dens": For discussion of opioid addiction as a "soldier's disease" after the Civil War and the role of "opium dens" operated by Chinese immigrants, see Nick Miroff, "From Teddy Roosevelt to Trump: How Drug Companies Triggered an Opioid Crisis a Century Ago," *Washington Post*, October 17, 2017, https://www.washingtonpost.com/news/retropolis /wp/2017/09/29/the-greatest-drug-fiends-in-the-world-an-american-opioid -crisis-in-1908/?utm_term=.1781a7aedd9c.

46 *this* was America's first opioid epidemic: David Courtwright, *Dark Paradise: A History of Opiate Addiction in America* (Cambridge, MA: Harvard University Press, 2001).

47 responsible for unleashing Heroin onto the world: The story of Bayer's development of Heroin can be found in many sources. A particularly good source is Richard Askwith, "How Aspirin Turned Hero," *Sunday Times* (London), September 13, 1998 (archived here: https://www.opioids.com /heroin/heroinhistory.html).

48 Roosevelt had had enough: The role of Teddy Roosevelt's administration is explored in Miroff, "From Teddy Roosevelt to Trump."

49 Harrison Act had a significant chilling effect on prescribing: For a good discussion of the Harrison Act and its effect, see Kelly K. Dineen and James M. DuBois, "Between a Rock and a Hard Place: Can Physicians Prescribe Opioids to Treat Pain Adequately While Avoiding Legal Sanction?" *American Journal of Law & Medicine* 42, no. 1 (March 2016): 7–52.

49 the term "junkie" came about: Courtwright, *Dark Paradise*, 110.

51 "it's very common for patients to say": Anastasia Toufexis, "A Conversation with Kathleen Foley: Pioneer in the Battle to Avert Needless Pain and Suffering," *New York Times*, November 6, 2001, http://www.nytimes .com/2001/11/06/health/conversation-with-kathleen-foley-pioneer-battle-avert-needless-pain-suffering.html.

51 slogan in the pain advocacy community: As reported in Judy Foreman, *A Nation in Pain: Healing Our Biggest Health Problem* (New York: Oxford University Press, 2015), 302.

52 letter to the editor: Jane Porter and Hershel Jick, "Addiction Rare in Patients Treated with Narcotics," *New England Journal of Medicine* 302, no. 2 (January 10, 1980): 123.

52 letter doesn't appear to have drawn much attention: Quinones's telling in his book *Dreamland* is, as far as I can tell, the definitive story of the role the Porter and Jick letter played.

53 we should be using these medications much more freely: Russell Portenoy and Kathleen Foley, "Chronic Use of Opioid Analgesics in Non-malignant Pain: Report of 38 Cases," *Pain* 25, no. 2 (May 1986): 171–86.

57 Purdue Pharma was owned by a family: Building on the important, early work of Barry Meier in *Pain Killer*, Patrick Radden Keefe explores the role of the Sackler family in the opioid crisis in "The Family That Built an Empire of Pain," *New Yorker*, October 30, 2017, https://www.newyorker.com/maga zine/2017/10/30/the-family-that-built-an-empire-of-pain.

57 OxyContin's label focused on low rate of addiction: The podcast *The Uncertain Hour* was able to track down an original OxyContin label—no small feat, since they were replaced with less-misleading information many years ago—and this quote was pulled from their publication of the label. See Caitlin Esch, "How One Sentence Helped Set Off the Opioid Crisis," *Marketplace*, December 13, 2017, https://www.marketplace.org/2017/12/13 /health-care/uncertain-hour/opioid.

58 told to explicitly cite the 1 percent figure: Citations of the original letter spiked after the release of OxyContin, with gross misrepresentations of its conclusions common. This is the finding of a new letter to the editor in the *New England Journal of Medicine*, which reports an analysis of citations of the original Porter and Jick letter. See Pamela Leung et al., "A 1980 Letter on

the Risk of Opioid Addiction," *New England Journal of Medicine* 376, no. 22 (June 1, 2017): 2194–95.

58 total marketing expenditures: Data on Purdue's training and marketing expenditures are taken from Art Van Zee, "The Promotion and Marketing of OxyContin: Commercial Triumph, Public Health Tragedy," *American Journal of Public Health* 99, no. 2 (February 2009): 221–27.

58 "pain as the fifth vital sign": James N. Campbell, "APS 1995 Presidential Address," *Pain Forum* 5, no. 1 (Spring 1996): 85–88.

58 an impetus to *do something about it*: In his address, Campbell says that "quality care means that pain is measured and treated."

58 appropriate response to learning about your patient's pain: This line of reasoning is made explicitly by Natalia E. Morone and Debra K. Weiner in "Pain as the Fifth Vital Sign: Exposing the Vital Need for Pain Education," *Clinical Therapeutics* 35, no. 11 (November 2013): 1728–32.

59 pain is a *symptom* rather than a sign: My thanks to Dr. Pat Carroll for making the symptom/sign distinction clear to me.

59 "Pain as the 5th Vital Sign Toolkit": The full toolkit is available online at https://www.va.gov/PAINMANAGEMENT/docs/Pain_As_the_5th_Vital _Sign_Toolkit.pdf.

59 it didn't officially endorse the language: There has been some confusion over this point, understandably. Many authors have claimed that JCAHO officially endorsed a view of pain as the fifth vital sign. However, the standards themselves did not require this idea—only that hospitals perform systematic assessments and use quantitative measures (i.e., 0–10 scores). The confusion, though, came from the fact that "fifth vital sign" language was included in JCAHO's 2001 manual, under "Examples of Implementation." Although not strictly a standard, here the manual stated that "pain is considered a 'fifth' vital sign in the hospital's care of patients." That language was sufficiently confusing so that it was modified the following year and abandoned altogether a few years later. More details on the history of JCAHO pain standards can be found in their own report: David W. Baker, *The Joint Commission's Pain Standards: Origins and Evolution* (Oakbrook Terrace, IL: Joint Commission, 2017), available online at https://www.jointcommission.org /assets/1/6/Pain_Std_History_Web_Version_05122017.pdf.

60 The company was fined $600 million: This result was reported in the *New York Times* by Barry Meier, who had, four years earlier, been one of the first to tell the story of Purdue and OxyContin in the book *Pain Killer*. See Barry Meier, "In Guilty Plea, OxyContin Maker to Pay $600 Million," *New York Times*, May 10, 2007.

61 clinicians wrote enough prescriptions: Updated statistics for the opioid epidemic will continue to be available on the CDC's website: https://www.cdc .gov/drugoverdose/epidemic/index.html.

61 INSYS Therapeutics settled: The story of INSYS is told in compelling de-
    tail in Evan Hughes, "The Pain Hustlers," *New York Times Magazine, May 2,
    2018*. The 2018 settlement is reported by Nate Raymond and Andy Thibault,
    "Insys to Pay $150 Million to Settle U.S. Opioid Kickback Probe," *Reuters*,
    August 8, 2018.

61 data from the International Narcotics Control Board: All data are available
    and can be used to run a custom report at the University of Wisconsin–
    Madison's Pain and Policy Studies Group: http://www.painpolicy.wisc.edu
    /opioid-consumption-data.

61 passing $1 billion in 2000: This data is available from the IMS National
    Sales Perspectives. Graphic representation included in Harriet Ryan, Lisa
    Girion, and Scott Glover, "'You Want a Description of Hell?' OxyContin's
    12-Hour Problem," *Los Angeles Times*, May 5, 2016.

61 fully *half* of the twelve lawsuits: Rebecca Haffajee and Michelle Mello,
    "Drug Companies' Liability for the Opioid Epidemic," *New England Journal
    of Medicine* 377, no. 24 (December 14, 2017): 2301–5.

61 the epidemic was winding up: Leonard Paulozzi et al., "Vital Signs: Over-
    doses of Prescription Opioid Pain Relievers—United States, 1999–2008,"
    Morbidity and Mortality Weekly Report 60, no. 43 (November 4, 2011): 1487–
    92. See also discussion in Andrew Kolodny et al., "The Prescription Opioid
    and Heroin Crisis: A Public Health Approach to an Epidemic of Addic-
    tion," *Annual Review of Public Health* 36 (March 2015): 559–74.

61 became the nation's leading cause: This happened for the first time in
    2009, as reported in the CDC's *National Vital Statistics Reports*. See Ken-
    neth Kochanek et al., "Deaths: Preliminary Data for 2009," *National Vital
    Statistics Report* 59, no. 4 (Hyattsville, MD: National Center for Health
    Statistics, 2011). Available at https://www.cdc.gov/nchs/data/nvsr/nvsr59
    /nvsr59_04.pdf.

62 consuming 80 percent of the total: See the consumption data in Laxmaiah
    Manchikanti et al., "Therapeutic Use, Abuse, and Nonmedical Use of Opi-
    oids: A Ten-Year Perspective," *Pain Physician* 13 (2010): 401–35.

62 "overdose epidemic is doctor-driven": In Robert Lowes, "CDC Issues Opioid
    Guidelines for 'Doctor-Driven' Epidemic," *Medscape*, March 15, 2016.

62 releasing its own guidelines for prescribing opioids: Debra Dowell, Tamara
    Haegerich, and Roger Chou, CDC *Guideline for Prescribing Opioids for
    Chronic Pain—United States, 2016, Morbidity and Mortality* Recomm Rep 65
    (No. RR-1) (2016): 1–49.

63 heroin use began to increase: There is significant debate over how many
    patients are actually making the switch from a legitimate prescription to
    heroin, but the correlation is explored in essays like Richard Dart et al.,
    "Trends in Opioid Analgesic Abuse and Mortality in the United States,"
    New England Journal of Medicine 372, no. 3 (January 15, 2015): 241–48.

63 75 percent of heroin users who began using opioids: Theodore Cicero et al., "The Changing Face of Heroin Use in the United States," *JAMA Psychiatry* 71, no. 7 (July 2014): 821–26.

64 complex views on the appropriate use: See, for instance, his interview with *Vox* writer German Lopez, "A Pain Doctor Explains How He Balances His Patients' Needs with the Opioid Epidemic's Lessons," *Vox*, May 2, 2017.

CHAPTER 4: THE OPIOID DILEMMA

67 physicians who cumulatively prescribe the most: Gery Guy Jr. and Kun Zhang, "Opioid Prescribing by Specialty and Volume in the U.S.," *American Journal of Preventative Medicine* 55, no. 5 (November 2018): e153–e155. Available at https://www.ajpmonline.org/article/S0749-3797(18)32009-9 /fulltext.

68 (non-addiction-related) pain: The parenthetical here is important, as those with opioid use disorder often are in pain when they go to a doctor looking for pills; it's just that the pain is a result of their dependence and addiction rather than an injury. Although we will explore the option of offering medication-assisted treatment later in the book, it is generally not considered appropriate to prescribe opioids to patients to alleviate withdrawal symptoms except for in specialized addiction medicine clinics.

72 a "nondefinitive condition": For discussion of how nondefinitive conditions play a role in racial disparities in the healthcare setting, see Astha Singhal, Yu-Yu Tien, and Renee Hsia, "Racial-Ethnic Disparities in Opioid Prescriptions at Emergency Department Visits for Conditions Commonly Associated with Prescription Drug Abuse," *PLOS ONE* 11, no. 8 (August 8, 2016): e0159224.

74 white and black patients are treated differently: Although, as I finish this manuscript, the first data has emerged suggesting that the racial gap in prescribing has narrowed. See Jordan Harrison et al., "Trends in Prescription Pain Medication Use by Race/Ethnicity Among US Adults with Noncancer Pain, 2000–2015," *American Journal of Public Health* 108, no. 6 (June 2018): 788–90.

74 how serious the disparities are: Salimah Meghani, Eeeseung Byun, and Rollin Gallagher, "Time to Take Stock: A Meta-Analysis and Systematic Review of Analgesic Treatment Disparities for Pain in the United States," *Pain Medicine* 13, no. 2 (February 2012): 150–74.

74 false beliefs about biological differences: Kelly Hoffman et al., "Racial Bias in Pain Assessment and Treatment Recommendations, and False Beliefs About Biological Differences Between Blacks and Whites," *Proceedings of the National Academies of Sciences* 113, no. 16 (April 19, 2016): 4296–4301.

75 white children were more than *twice as likely*: Monika Goyal et al., "Racial Disparities in Pain Management of Children with Appendicitis in Emergency Departments," *JAMA Pediatrics* 169, no. 11 (November 2015): 996–1002.

75 women are less likely to have: Diane Hoffmann and Anita Tarzian, "The Girl Who Cried Pain: A Bias Against Women in the Treatment of Pain," *Journal of Law, Medicine & Ethics* 29, no. 1 (Spring 2001): 13–27.

81 "Opioid-induced hyperalgesia": A review of the science on opioid-induced hyperalgesia can be found in Marion Lee et al., "A Comprehensive Review of Opioid-Induced Hyperalgesia," *Pain Physician* 14, no. 2 (March 2011): 145–61.

81 such as the CDC: For the CDC's Guidelines, see Debra Dowell, Tamara Haegerich, and Roger Chou, *CDC Guideline for Prescribing Opioids for Chronic Pain—United States, 2016, Morbidity and Mortality* Recomm Rep 65 (No. RR-1) (2016): 1–49.

81 National Academies of Sciences: The National Academies of Sciences, Engineering, and Medicine has issued an official report, and the National Academy of Medicine has released a special publication. See National Academies of Sciences, Engineering, and Medicine, *Pain Management and the Opioid Epidemic: Balancing Societal and Individual Benefits and Risks of Prescription Opioid Use* (Washington, DC: National Academies Press, 2017); and National Academy of Medicine, *First Do No Harm: Marshaling Clinician Leadership to Counter the Opioid Epidemic* (Washington, DC: National Academy of Medicine, 2017).

81 many others have issued guidelines: Including the Federation of State Medical Boards, available at http://www.fsmb.org/Media/Default/PDF/Advocacy /Opioid%20Guidelines%20As%20Adopted%20April%202017_FINAL .pdf; the Food and Drug Administration, available at https://www.fda.gov /downloads/drugs/drugsafety/informationbydrugclass/ucm515636.pdf; and the Departments of Veterans Affairs and Defense, available at https://www .healthquality.va.gov/guidelines/Pain/cot/VADoDOTCPGProviderSum mary022817.pdf.

CHAPTER 5: ABANDONED

87 this is false: See the recent review at Tracey Mersfelder and William Nichols, "Gabapentin: Abuse, Dependence, and Withdrawal," *Annals of Pharmacotherapy* 50, no. 3 (March 2016): 229–33.

CHAPTER 6: DEPENDENCE AND ADDICTION

117 the brain tries to adapt: The overview of the science of dependence and addiction described here is collated from many different sources, including discussion with many different experts. I want to especially thank Dr. Indre Viskontas for her patient explanations and corrections. Any inaccuracies that remain are, of course, my own and not that of Dr. Viskontas or anyone else.

117 learning machine that responds to new situations: The idea that depen-

dence and addiction are both related to the brain's learning capabilities is explained in depth in Marc Lewis's fascinating book *The Biology of Desire: Why Addiction Is Not a Disease* (New York: PublicAffairs, 2015).

119   the bible of psychiatry: More about the *DSM-5* can be found here: https://www.psychiatry.org/psychiatrists/practice/dsm.

120   scientists like Carl Hart: See, for instance, Carl Hart, *High Price: A Neuroscientist's Journey of Self-Discovery That Challenges Everything You Know About Drugs and Society* (New York: Harper, 2013).

120   Marc Lewis: See Marc Lewis, *Memoirs of an Addicted Brain: A Neuroscientist Examines His Former Life on Drugs* (New York: PublicAffairs, 2012); and Lewis, *Biology of Desire*.

120   journalist Maia Szalavitz: See Maia Szalavitz, *Unbroken Brain: A Revolutionary New Way of Understanding Addiction* (New York: St. Martin's Press, 2016).

121   study that Carl Hart describes: Hart, *High Price*, 1–8.

122   choosing to use clean needles: Although her insightful comments helped me think through much of the content of this chapter, I want to especially thank Marie Stratton for suggesting that I add these "positive choices" to the examples. We know that addiction doesn't completely rob someone of agency, because they can make a wide range of decisions, many of them good and important. Indeed, those who go on to recover on their own often do so as a result of deciding to pursue a life free from drugs.

122   addiction seems to undermine our ability: Philosopher Hanna Pickard helpfully articulates what she calls the "puzzle of addiction," which is answering precisely this challenge: Why do people with addiction pursue something that hurts them? Putting the question that way can help us see why both the moral and the brain disease models have been popular. The moral model says that someone with an addiction chooses bad behavior because they're bad, weak, or vicious; the brain disease model says it's because their brain is broken. If we reject both of these options, the challenge is how to answer this question without going to either extreme. See Hanna Pickard, "The Puzzle of Addiction," in *The Routledge Handbook of Philosophy and Science of Addiction*, ed. Hanna Pickard and Serge H. Ahmed (London: Routledge, 2018).

122   Frankfurt describes a view: See, for instance, Harry Frankfurt, "Freedom of the Will and the Concept of a Person," *Journal of Philosophy* 68, no. 1 (January 14, 1971): 5–20.

123   the general model that distinguishes: Gary Watson, for instance, holds the similar view that the desires that are more "me" are those that cohere with what I take to be valuable. See Gary Watson, "Free Agency," *Journal of Philosophy* 72 (April 1975): 205–20.

123   what the rest of us do fairly effortlessly: An interesting question here is

whether most of us really do this so effortlessly. Consider the amount of time many of us spend looking at screens, or the unhealthy food choices so many of us make, despite wishing we were more productive and healthier. These sorts of considerations suggest a view in which addictive desires, motivations, and actions aren't so different from other ones—different a bit, sure, but not as different as we might like to think. I'm indebted to several colleagues for discussion on this point, particularly Dr. Pat Carroll and Marie Stratton. As Pat put the point in conversation: perhaps we should stop focusing on how different the addicted brain is and focus instead on how intensely human it is.

124 de Kenessey puts the point: de Kenessey's essay on this topic in *Vox* is a fantastic overview of how philosophers do and should think about addiction. See Brendan de Kenessey. "People Are Dying Because We Misunderstand How Those with Addiction Think," *Vox*, March 16, 2018. Available at https://www.vox.com/the-big-idea/2018/3/5/17080470/addiction-opioids-moral-blame-choices-medication-crutches-philosophy.

126 Sessions made clear his own view: For a thorough look at how Jeff Sessions began formulating a team that would return to policies that were "tough on drugs," see Sari Horowitz, "How Jeff Sessions Wants to Bring Back the War on Drugs," *Washington Post*, April 8, 2017. A year later, Sessions's deputy attorney general wrote a scathing attack on harm reduction policies, making clear that the Justice Department intended to fight any set of policies that were not strictly prohibitionist and aggressive. See Rod Rosenstein, "Fight Drug Abuse, Don't Subsidize It," *New York Times*, August 27, 2018.

127 A junkie: This is as good a time as any to flag why, when I'm not describing other, problematic views, I avoid the use of any "essentializing" terms like this. Not only are "junkie," "druggie," "dope fiend," etc. obviously stigmatizing and harmful, but even the more neutral-sounding "addict" takes a single fact about someone (that they have an addiction) and turns it into the thing by which you define them. This is what I mean by "essentializing": it makes addiction someone's essential property. So I have tried very seriously in this book to use "person-first" language, such as "someone suffering from addiction," or "person with opioid use disorder." Although it may sound slightly clunky to those not used to it, I believe it is clearly the right choice not to replicate stigma in my own work.

127 massively underfunded: In a recent paper, those working in addiction medicine consistently identified lack of funding as one of the most significant barriers to treatment. In more rural areas, this often manifested itself in badly supported institutions that were thinly distributed geographically; whereas in the cities, the issue was most often—as it was in my experience—extensive waiting lists. See Erin Pullen and Carrie Oser, "Barriers to Substance Abuse

Treatment in Rural and Urban Communities: Counselor Perspectives," *Substance Use and Misuse* 49, no. 7 (June 2014): 891–901.

128 a quarter-billion prescriptions: To be precise: 226.8 million prescriptions were written in 2015, down from a peak of 255 million in 2012. This data is from the CDC and can be found at https://www.cdc.gov/drugoverdose/maps/rxrate-maps.html.

130 heroin sets off: The mode of delivery also matters. If the reward from some action comes far enough into the future, the brain doesn't automatically associate the reward with the behavior. This means that taking a pill is less likely to lead to addiction than crushing it and either snorting it or rubbing it on your gums. And both of those modes of delivery are less addictive still than intravenous injection. The high from injecting heroin or fentanyl is so profoundly addictive because it is both immediate and intensely powerful.

131 75 to 80 percent: Lee Robins, Darlene Davis, and David Nurco, "How Permanent Was Vietnam Drug Addiction?" *American Journal of Public Health* 64 no. 12 Suppl. (December 1974): 38–43.

132 one's environment is important in determining: Bruce Alexander, Robert Coombs, and Patricia Hardaway, "The Effect of Housing and Gender on Morphine Self-administration in Rats," *Psychopharmacology* 58, no. 2 (January 1978): 175–79.

135 "Doctors don't do pain well": Judy Foreman, *A Nation in Pain: Healing Our Biggest Health Problem* (New York: Oxford University Press, 2015), 5.

136 how many patients have gone through this: In the years since I have begun working on this topic, I have collected hundreds of emails, letters, Facebook messages, and tweets from people describing their own horror of mismanaged tapers and terrifying withdrawal. Sadly, my circumstance isn't anything like as rare as we should expect.

136 medical schools reported *no teaching* on pain: Lina Mezei, Beth Murinson, and the Johns Hopkins Pain Curriculum Development Team, "Pain Education in North American Medical Schools," *Journal of Pain* 12, no. 12 (December 2011): 1199–1208.

136 eighty-seven hours: Judy Watt-Watson et al., "An Integrated Undergraduate Pain Curriculum, Based on IASP Curricula, for Six Health Science Faculties," *Pain* 110, no. 1–2 (July 2004): 140–48.

CHAPTER 7: WHAT DOCTORS OWE PATIENTS

139 I've never used the real names of either my doctors or the hospitals: My practice in this book is to use pseudonyms for my treating physicians and hospitals, whereas I've used real names for friends, family, and colleagues (with their permission).

144 oncologists often must collaborate with other specialties: I'm indebted to both Dr. Casey Humbyrd and Dr. Yoram Unguru for thoughtful discussion

on the responsibilities of physicians to coordinate treatment of complex harms that arise from routine practice.

145 surgeons don't actually tend to do the opioid prescribing: In other hospitals, prescribing may be handled not only by nurse practitioners but also by physician assistants or residents. In general, surgeons often have a way of delegating prescribing to *someone*, though the role of that someone might be slightly different in different institutions. My thanks to Dr. Casey Humbyrd for pointing this out.

147 pursuing an even slower taper increased the likelihood of success: Beth Darnall et al., "Patient-Centered Prescription Opioid Tapering in Community Outpatients with Chronic Pain," *JAMA Internal Medicine* 178, no. 5 (May 2018): 707–8.

148 "adjust the rate and duration of the taper": The CDC pocket guide is available at https://www.cdc.gov/drugoverdose/pdf/clinical_pocket_guide_tapering-a.pdf.

148 others will need medication: Dr. Lembke's CME course has been put online as an enduring, free course. Clinicians interested to take it can find it here: https://med.stanford.edu/cme/courses/online/opioid-taper.html.

149 Such patients are sometimes said to suffer from "complex persistent dependence": See further, Ajay Manhapra, Albert Arias, and Jane Ballantyne, "The Conundrum of Opioid Tapering in Long-Term Opioid Therapy for Chronic Pain: A Commentary," *Substance Abuse*, 39:2, 152-161, DOI: 10.1080/08897077.2017.1381663.

150 an excruciatingly personal essay: William B. Weeks, "Hailey," *Journal of American Medical Association* 316, no. 19 (November 2016): 1975–76.

152 many terrible possible outcomes: The seriousness of this challenge is beginning to be recognized more widely. In November 2018, dozens of clinicians, experts, and advocates signed a letter to the journal *Pain Medicine*, challenging the practice of forced or mandated opioid tapers. See Beth Darnall et al., "International Stakeholder Community of Pain Experts and Leaders Call for an Urgent Action on Forced Opioid Tapering," *Pain Medicine* (online pub November 29, 2018), https://academic.oup.com/painmedicine/advance-article/doi/10.1093/pm/pny228/5218985.

154 Langreth's article was published in November 2017: Robert Langreth, "Millions of Patients Face Pain and Withdrawal as Opioid Prescriptions Plummet," Bloomberg, November 21, 2017.

155 the following letter: The original letter was posted in Langreth's story at Bloomberg. Rather than risk changing the letter in any way, I left typos and grammar choices intact.

157 prescribe fewer *inappropriate* pills: This is essentially the argument of a paper I wrote: Travis N. Rieder, "Opioids and Ethics: Is Opioid-Free the Only Responsible Arthroplasty?" *HSS Journal: The Musculoskeletal Journal of Hospital*

for Special Surgery (online pub December 13, 2018), https://doi.org/10.1007/s11420-018-9651-3.

CHAPTER 9: PAIN, DRUGS, AND DOING THE RIGHT THING

182 fear of addiction seemed perversely puritanical when facing death: Of course, cancer is no longer the killer it once was. Whereas a cancer diagnosis used to be a death sentence, cancer patients now often live in remission for decades. Given the severity of various cancer pains, we may still think that opioids are a perfectly appropriate treatment for these patients, but the reasoning for such a conclusion must be different. If opioid use disorder is a legitimate fear (which it certainly seems to be), and many cancer patients expect to live long enough that avoiding addiction is profoundly valuable, then cancer pain is more like other forms of severe chronic pain. Which is to say: cancer patients, like all other patients, should be cared for in a way that minimizes the risks of opioid use disorder. My thanks to Dr. Yoram Unguru for patient discussion on this point.

183 the need for nuance: This is essentially the conclusion of my upcoming paper, Travis N. Rieder, "There's Never Just One Side to the Story: Why America Must Stop Swinging the Opioid Pendulum," Narrative Inquiry in Bioethics 8, no. 3 (Winter 2018): 225–31.

183 dentists were the second-highest prescribing group: Richard Denisco et al., "Prevention of Prescription Opioid Abuse: The Role of the Dentist," *Journal of the American Dental Association* 142, no. 7 (July 2011): 800–10.

184 recommend that dentists adhere to the CDC guidelines: These recommendations were strengthened in March 2018, and the *Journal of the American Dental Association* dedicated its cover story to dentists' role in the opioid crisis the following month. That issue can be found at http://jada.ada.org/issue/S0002-8177(17)X0006-8.

184 prescribing by dentists in 2017 fell to 8.6 percent: Gery Guy Jr. and Kun Zhang, "Opioid Prescribing by Specialty and Volume in the U.S.," *American Journal of Preventative Medicine* 55, no. 5 (November 2018): e153–e155. Available at https://www.ajpmonline.org/article/S0749-3797(18)32009-9/fulltext.

184 "no statistically significant or clinically important differences in pain reduction": Andrew Chang et al., "Effect of a Single Dose of Oral Opioid and Nonopioid Analgesics on Acute Extremity Pain in the Emergency Department: A Randomized Clinical Trial," JAMA 318, no. 17 (November 7, 2017): 1661–67.

185 the Tylenol definitely helped: For the record, I took Tylenol rather than ibuprofen because I was on celecoxib for my chronic foot pain, which means that I was unable to take additional NSAIDs. For patients without any complications or contraindications, many dentists will recommend ibuprofen for its anti-inflammatory properties.

188   those on opioids had slightly *more* pain: Erin Krebs et al., "Effect of Opioid vs Nonopioid Medications on Pain-Related Function in Patients with Chronic Back Pain or Hip or Knee Osteoarthritis Pain: The SPACE Randomized Clinical Trial," *JAMA* 319, no. 9 (March 6, 2018): 872–82.

188   opioids should not be considered first-line therapy: See Debra Dowell, Tamara Haegerich, and Roger Chou, CDC *Guideline for Prescribing Opioids for Chronic Pain—United States*, 2016, *Morbidity and Mortality* Recomm Rep 65 (No. RR-1) (2016): 1–49.

190   More than 15 percent of patients prescribed opioids for ten days: Anuj Shah, Corey Hayes, and Bradley Martin, "Characteristics of Initial Prescription Episodes and Likelihood of Long-Term Opioid Use—United States, 2006–2015," *Morbidity and Mortality Weekly Report* 66, no. 10 (March 17, 2017): 265–69.

190   increased the risk of misuse by 34 percent: Gabriel Brat et al., "Postsurgical Prescriptions for Opioid Naive Patients and Association with Overdose and Misuse: Retrospective Cohort Study," *BMJ* 360 (January 17, 2018): j5790.

192   Until recently, opioids could not be prescribed remotely: It is now possible for many clinicians to electronically prescribe Schedule II drugs, which are substances that have a legitimate medical use but also carry significant risk (like prescription opioids). In light of the drug overdose crisis, there has recently been a concerted effort to mandate this form of prescribing since it is more secure than physical prescription pads, which can be stolen or edited by patients. Hopefully, this evolution will also help decrease the kind of convenience overprescribing I describe in this paragraph of the main text.

193   dropped from 250 to 75 milligrams: Ryan Howard et al., "Reduction in Opioid Prescribing Through Evidence-Based Prescribing Guidelines," *JAMA Surgery* 153, no. 3 (March 2018): 285–87.

196   OPEN maintains a set of evidence-based recommendations: That website can be found at https://opioidprescribing.info.

198   also been marketed to treat fibromyalgia pain: It's worth pointing out that these medications are also under scrutiny for having been overprescribed and marketed too aggressively. See, for instance, James Paul et al., "Randomized Controlled Trial of Gabapentin as an Adjunct to Perioperative Analgesia in Total Hip Arthroplasty Patients," *Canadian Journal of Anesthesia* 62, no. 5 (May 2015): 476–84; and Christopher Goodman and Allan Brett, "Gabapentin and Pregabalin for Pain—Is Increased Prescribing a Cause for Concern?" *New England Journal of Medicine* 377, no. 5 (August 3, 2017): 411–14.

198   other modalities can reduce the reliance on opioids: One note of caution concerning the multimodal pain strategy discussed here: prescribing lots of different drugs uncarefully is not better than prescribing a single drug uncarefully. So if multimodal pain management just means "polypharmacy,"

which can produce new, dangerous effects, then it's not to be preferred. This degree of care requires significant expertise, and so the extent to which it can be practiced widely is unclear. My thanks to Dr. Pat Carroll for discussion on this point.

200 an FDA analysis of price trends for opioids: Food and Drug Administration, "FDA Analysis of Long-Term Trends in Prescription Opioid Analgesic Products: Quantity, Sales, and Price Trends," March 1, 2018. Available at: https://www.fda.gov/downloads/AboutFDA/ReportsManualsForms/Reports /UCM598899.pdf.

201 it can be as effective as morphine: See, for instance, the several studies surveyed in Richard Bukata, "IV APAP Works, so Why Don't More EPs Use It?" *Emergency Physician Monthly*, October 15, 2015.

201 no more effective than oral APAP: See Skip Hickman et al., "Randomized Trial of Oral Versus Intravenous Acetaminophen for Postoperative Pain Control," *American Journal of Health-System Pharmacy* 75, no. 6 (March 2018): 367–75. There is even a study explicitly claiming to show that IV APAP use does not lead to significantly decreased opioid use: see Isaac Wasserman et al., "Impact of Intravenous Acetaminophen on Perioperative Opioid Utilization and Outcomes in Open Colectomies: A Claims Database Analysis," *Anesthesiology* 129 (July 2018): 77–88.

202 the conclusion of multiple recent studies: Joel R. Politi, Richard L. Davis II, and Alexis K. Matrka, "Randomized Prospective Trial Comparing the Use of Intravenous versus Oral Acetaminophen in Total Joint Arthroplasty," *Journal of Arthroplasty* 32, no. 4 (April 2017): 1125–1127; Lixin Sun et al., "Comparison of Intravenous and Oral Acetaminophen for Pain Control after Knee and Hip Arthroplasty," *Medicine* 97, no. 6 (February 2018): e9751.

205 survey scores can affect a hospital's bottom line: It's unclear whether this fear is warranted. Although some literature has shown the unsurprising conclusion that patients give opioid-prescribing doctors higher marks (see Brian Sites et al., "Prescription Opioid Use and Satisfaction with Care Among Adults with Musculoskeletal Conditions," *Annals of Family Medicine* 16, no. 1 (January 2018): 6–13), another recent study has suggested that opioid prescribing does not predict survey ratings (Jay Lee et al., "Postoperative Opioid Prescribing and the Pain Scores on Hospital Consumer Assessment of Healthcare Providers and Systems Survey," *JAMA* 317, no. 19 (May 16, 2017): 2013–15).

205 common practice: According to one study, about half of all doctors have received money from a pharmaceutical or medical device company. See Bernard Lo and Deborah Grady, "Payments to Physicians: Does the Amount of Money Make a Difference?" *JAMA* 317, no. 17 (2017): 1719–20.

206 those who prescribed more got paid more: Aaron Kessler, Elizabeth Cohen, and Katherine Grise, "CNN Exclusive: The More Opioids Doctors Prescribe, the More Money They Make," CNN.com, March 12, 2018.

207 meals costing more than $20, were then associated with even higher rates of prescribing: Colette DeJong et al., "Pharmaceutical Industry–Sponsored Meals and Physician Prescribing Patterns for Medicare Beneficiaries," *JAMA Internal Medicine* 176, no. 8 (August 2016): 1114–22.

207 CME courses about opioids are funded by a conglomerate of drugmakers: Julia Lurie, "Doctors Receive Opioid Training. Big Pharma Funds It. What Could Go Wrong?" *Mother Jones*, April 27, 2018.

CHAPTER 10: AMERICA'S *THREE* OPIOID EPIDEMICS

213 took over as the leading cause of accidental death: Between the years of 2006 and 2010, traffic fatalities dipped slightly while drug overdose deaths spiked dramatically, with the former falling below 40,000 while the latter soared past it. In 2017, drug overdose deaths were nearly *double* motor vehicle deaths. Data collected from the National Highway Traffic Safety Administration (https://www-fars.nhtsa.dot.gov/Main/index.aspx) and the National Institute on Drug Abuse (https://www.drugabuse.gov/related-top ics/trends-statistics/overdose-death-rates).

213 drug crisis would eventually become the leading cause of death: Sheila Kaplan, "C.D.C. Reports a Record Jump in Drug Overdose Deaths Last Year," *New York Times*, November 3, 2017.

213 the death rate did not slow down; it *sped up*: Holly Hedegaard, Margaret Warner, and Arialdi Miniño, *Drug Overdose Deaths in the United States, 1999–2016*, NCHS Data Brief 294 (Hyattsville, MD: National Center for Health Statistics, 2017).

213 drug overdose epidemic killed more people each: AIDS deaths peaked in 1995, when 43,000 people died from the disease. More than 58,000 U.S. soldiers died in the Vietnam War. By 2016, drug overdoses eclipsed both of these numbers, with drugs killing more than 64,000 Americans. See German Lopez, "In One Year, Drug Overdoses Killed More Americans than the Entire Vietnam War Did" *Vox*, June 8, 2017.

214 disproportionally shared by minority communities: Theodore Cicero et al., "The Changing Face of Heroin Use in the United States," *JAMA Psychiatry* 71, no. 7 (July 2014): 821–26.

217 involved in less than half: Seth Puja et al., "Overdose Deaths Involving Opioids, Cocaine, and Psychostimulants—United States, 2015–2016," *Morbidity and Mortality Weekly Report* 67, no. 12 (March 30, 2018): 349–358.

217 2.1 million by one recent estimate: Center for Behavioral Health Statistics and Quality, *2016 National Survey on Drug Use and Health: Detailed Tables* (Rockville, MD: Substance Abuse and Mental Health Services Administration, 2017).

219 treatment significantly reduces mortality risk: Luis Sordo et al., "Mortality

Risk During and After Opioid Substitution Treatment: Systematic Review and Meta-analysis of Cohort Studies," *BMJ* 357 (April 26, 2017): j1550.

219   about a thousand bucks a month: The cost can range from $700 to $1,100. See further, Stephen M. Stahl, *Prescriber's Guide: Stahl's Essential Psychopharmacology*, 5th ed. (New York: Cambridge University Press, 2014).

219   can be tens of thousands of dollars: The range is far too large to provide anything like a meaningful estimate, but a quick canvass of available options for residential rehab programs reveals that $500 to $650 per day is a common estimate, with more premium facilities often charging $25,000 or more.

219   only 10 percent of those suffering: Center for Behavioral Health Statistics and Quality, *2016 National Survey on Drug Use and Health: Detailed Tables*.

221   needle exchanges do not lead to increased drug use: See, for instance, the results of John Watters et al., "Syringe and Needle Exchange as HIV/AIDS Prevention for Injection Drug Users," *JAMA* 271, no. 2 (January 12, 1994): 115–20.

221   they do attenuate the harm: The evidence is reviewed and published by the CDC at https://www.cdc.gov/policy/hst/hi5/cleansyringes/index.html.

222   "I will tell you": Megan Twohey, "Mike Pence's Response to H.I.V. Outbreak: Prayer, then a Change of Heart," *New York Times*, August 7, 2016.

222   181 cases were confirmed: Philip Peters et al., "HIV Infection Linked to Injection Use of Oxymorphone in Indiana, 2014–2015," *New England Journal of Medicine* 375, no. 3 (July 21, 2016): 229–39.

223   According to a review of the literature by the Centers for Disease Control and Prevention: The review, as well as links to fact sheets and other resources, is available at https://www.cdc.gov/policy/hst/hi5/cleansyringes/index.html.

225   Surgeon General Jerome M. Adams: Department of Health and Human Services, "Surgeon General Releases Advisory on Naloxone, an Opioid Overdose-Reversing Drug," April 5, 2018. Available at https://www.hhs.gov/about/news/2018/04/05/surgeon-general-releases-advisory-on-naloxone-an-opioid-overdose-reversing-drug.html.

227   "safe injection site": Colleen Barry, Susan Sherman, and Emma McGinty, "Language Matters in Combatting the Opioid Epidemic: Safe Consumption Sites Versus Overdose Prevention Sites," *American Journal of Public Health* 108, no. 9 (September 2018): 1157–59.

227   three and a half million people: Statistics available from Vancouver Coastal Health, available at http://www.vch.ca/public-health/harm-reduction/supervised-consumption-sites/insite-user-statistics.

228   close to three hundred open across the country: The number of needle-exchange programs in the United States comes from the Kaiser Family Foundation, available at https://www.kff.org/hivaids/state-indicator/syringe

-exchange-programs/?currentTimeframe=0&sortModel=%7B%22colId %22:%22Location%22,%22sort%22:%22asc%22%7D.

228　more than three thousand needle-exchange programs: In Australia, Needle and Syringe Programs (NSPs) include vending machines, which are used for twenty-four-hour convenience and have been a hugely successful part of the nation's effort to combat the harms that attend IV drug use. See more in Harm Reduction International's Katie Stone, *The Global State of Harm Reduction 2016* (London: Harm Reduction International, 2016), available at https://www.hri.global/files/2016/11/14/GSHR2016_14nov.pdf.

228　one needle-exchange program for every thirty-two hundred Americans: This comparison was reported by Josh Katz of the *New York Times*, with a graph showing just how much of an outlier the United States is concerning needle-exchange programs. See Josh Katz, "Why a City at the Center of the Opioid Crisis Gave Up a Tool to Fight It," *New York Times*, April 27, 2018.

228　injection sites exist in dozens of cities: A brief overview of these facilities can be found at http://www.drugpolicy.org/issues/supervised-injection-facilities.

228　save money through decreased burdens: Mary Clare Kennedy, Mohammad Karamouzian, and Thomas Kerr, "Public Health and Public Order Outcomes Associated with Supervised Drug Consumption Facilities: A Systematic Review," *Current HIV/AIDS Reports* 14, no. 5 (October 2017): 161–83.

231　between 1998 and 2012, there was evidence of a shift away: Emma McGinty et al., "Criminal Activity or Treatable Health Condition? News Media Framing of Opioid Analgesic Abuse in the United States, 1998–2012," *Psychiatric Services* 67, no. 4 (April 2016): 405–11.

235　like a drug dealer disguised as a clinical operation: John Temple, *American Pain: How a Young Felon and His Ring of Doctors Unleashed America's Deadliest Drug Epidemic* (Guilford, CT: Lyons Press, 2016).

235　exculpating ability of youth is proven: The link between young age and risk for addiction is well established. In the case of alcohol, see Ralph Hingson, Timothy Heeren, and Michael Winter, "Age at Drinking Onset and Alcohol Dependence: Age at Onset, Duration, and Severity," *JAMA Pediatrics*, 160, no. 7 (July 2006): 739–46.

EPILOGUE: MAKING A DIFFERENCE

243　documented military pain medicine efforts: Steve Silberman, "The Painful Truth," *Wired*, February 1, 2005.

243　revealing the military's drive to control pain effectively: Susan Foremke and Matthew Heineman, dir., *Escape Fire: The Fight to Rescue American Healthcare* (Los Angeles: Roadside Attractions, 2012).

245　DVCIPM team has released a new pain scale: The DVCIPM's pain scale can be accessed at http://www.dvcipm.org/site/assets/files/1084/dvprs-front -vector.pdf.

245   to be used with a list of questions: The supplemental questions can be accessed at http://www.dvcipm.org/site/assets/files/1084/dvprs-back-vector.pdf.

250   people call it: self-care: An entire issue of the journal *Pain Medicine* was dedicated to the topic of self-care: *Pain Medicine* 15, no. S1 (April 2014). See also Institute of Medicine, *Relieving Pain in America: A Blueprint for Transforming Prevention, Care, Education, and Research* (Washington, DC: The National Academies Press, 2011).

250   common suggestions: exercise: Jill Hayden, Mauritania van Tundermann, and George Tomlinson, "Systematic Review: Strategies for Using Exercise Therapy to Improve Outcomes in Chronic Low Back Pain," *Annals of Internal Medicine* 142, no. 9 (May 2005): 776–85.

250   yoga, and massage: Wayne Jonas et al., "A Time for Massage," *Pain Medicine* 17, no. 8 (August 2016): 1389–90.

251   has been shown to be effective: Dawn Ehde, Tiara Dillworth, and Judith Turner, "Cognitive-Behavioral Therapy for Individuals with Chronic Pain: Efficacy, Innovations, and Directions for Research," *American Psychologist* 69, no. 2 (February/March 2014): 153–166.

251   "maladaptive pain": Office of the Army Surgeon General Pain Management Task Force, "Final Report: Providing a Standardized DoD and VHA Vision and Approach to Pain Management to Optimize the Care for Warriors and Their Families," May 2010. Available at https://www.dvcipm.org/site/assets/files/1070/pain-task-force-final-report-may-2010.pdf.

251   the evidence does suggest that it works: Courtney Lee et al., "The Effectiveness of Acupuncture Research Across Components of the Trauma Spectrum Response (TSR): A Systematic Review of Reviews," *Systematic Reviews*, 2012, 1(46): 1–18.

251   it can work as well as pharmacotherapy: Hugh Macpherson et al., "The Persistence of the Effects of Acupuncture After a Course of Treatment: A Meta-analysis of Patients with Chronic Pain," *Pain* 158, no. 5 (May 2017): 784–93.

251   changing one's lifestyle: Nice summary reviews can be found in National Academy of Medicine, *First Do No Harm: Marshaling Clinician Leadership to Counter the Opioid Epidemic* (Washington, DC: National Academy of Medicine, 2017); and National Academies of Sciences, Engineering, and Medicine, *Pain Management and the Opioid Epidemic: Balancing Societal and Individual Benefits and Risks of Prescription Opioid Use* (Washington, DC: National Academies Press, 2017).

255   likely that more than one hundred thousand Americans: I say "likely" because data on overdose death rates lags behind by more than a year. So while I don't know, for sure, what the death rates for the last year are, we do know that all signs point to a steady increase. So, I worked on this book from mid-2015 to late 2018. In 2015, more than 33,000 people died from overdose;

in 2016, that number jumped to 42,000; and in 2017, nearly 50,000 (at the time of writing, 2017 data is still provisionary). All indications are that the numbers continued to climb into 2018.

255 as many as one hundred *million* people live with chronic pain: Institute of Medicine, *Relieving Pain in America.*

255 states have implemented evidence-based interventions: Leading the way is Vermont, with its successful "hub and spoke" model of addiction treatment. In 2017, it was one of only seven states to record a decrease in overdose death rates. For more, see German Lopez, "2017 Was the Worst Year Ever for Drug Overdose Deaths in America," *Vox*, August 16, 2018.

255 when the opioid crisis will peak: Provisional data can always be accessed at the CDC's website: https://www.cdc.gov/nchs/nvss/vsrr/drug-overdose-data .htm.

256 three times the rate of the early 1990s: Gery P. Guy et al., "Vital Signs: Changes in Opioid Prescribing in the United States, 2006–2015," *Morbidity and Mortality Weekly Report* 66, no. 26 (2017): 697–704.

256 the data tells a different story: Molly Moore Jeffery et al., "Trends in Opioid Use in Commercially Insured and Medicare Advantage Populations in 2007–16: Retrospective Cohort Study," *BMJ* 362 (August 1, 2018): k2833.

INDEX

abandonment, 150–58, 182, 238, 216

acetaminophen (Tylenol), 39–40, 164, 173, 184–85, 188, 195, 198, 201–2, 249–50. *See also* IV acetaminophen

acupuncture, 198, 204, 241–44, 251

acute extremity pain, 184

acute pain, 51, 52, 80
  CDC guidelines and, 62
  moderate, 183, 189, 195
  severe, 189–90, 196

Adams, Jerome M., 225

addiction, 39, 239. *See also* dependence; opioid crisis; opioid use disorder; withdrawal; *and specific drugs; and treatment methods*
  accidental, 234–35
  behavior and 3 Cs model of, 118–25, 225
  brain and, 118–21, 129–32
  cancer patients and, 50–51
  as chronic disease, 220
  chronic pain patients and, 187
  circle of empathy and, 236, 258
  criminalization of, 49–50, 231
  dependence and, 116–18, 129–34, 149
  developmental model of, 120
  fear of withdrawal and, 129–30, 139
  harm reduction and, 224–25
  as health issue, 119, 231
  HIV and, 221
  investing in treatment for, 255–56
  isolation and, 131–33
  lower vs. higher-order desires and, 122–25
  military and, 244
  moral model of, 50, 118, 121–22, 234–36
  OxyContin labeling and, 55–58
  pain advocacy movement and, 52–54
  philosophical models of, 120–21
  physicians and drug-seeking patients and, 66, 68, 70–75, 137
  physicians' ethical duties and, 178
  race and, 73–75, 234–36
  reversing taper and, 148, 154
  stigma and, 119, 125–26, 137, 236

addiction treatment, 116, 125–28, 217–20
  access to, 219–20
  dependency and, 107, 125, 127–28
  evidence-based and affordable, 217–18
  keeping patient alive before, 217–18, 220

addiction treatment (*cont.*)
  MAT and, 218–20
  medication for, 125
  stigma and, 127
Advil, 39, 72
Affordable Care Act (ACA;
    Obamacare, 2010), 206
Afghanistan War, 11
akratic (weak-willed), 123
alcohol withdrawal, 128–29
Alexander, Bruce, 132
alkaloids, 40–41
American Dental Association
    (ADA) guidelines, 183–84
American Medical Association
    (AMA), 48
American Pain pill mill, 235
American Pain Society (APS), 58
amputation, 12–13, 26
anesthesiologists, 199–201
anxiety, pain level and, 34
Appalachia, 60, 235
arthritic knee or hip pain, 188
aspirin (acetylsalicylic acid; ASA),
    39–40, 47, 49, 249
auricular acupuncture, 242
Australia, 228

Baltimore, 136, 214, 225
battlefield injuries, 244
Bayer, 47–48, 54, 56
benzodiazepines, 150
  deaths and, 151
  withdrawal and, 128–29
bias, 70–75, 82
bioethics, duties of prescribing
    physicians and, 114, 139–45,
    156, 174–75, 178–79, 197
black market, 63, 153, 182, 214–15
blacks

focus on whites vs., 231–37
  medical profession bias vs., 73–75
  undertreatment of pain in, 75
blame, 139–40
bowel blockage, 79
brain
  addiction and, 118–24, 129–31
  chemical receptors in, 41–42
  methadone and MAT and, 218
  opioids and oxygen in, 42, 78
  pain location and, 26
  repeated attempts to withdraw
      and, 133–34
  short- vs. long-term response to
      opioids and, 116–17
  withdrawal and, 253–54
Buckenmaier, Chester III "Trip",
    241–43, 245
buprenorphine, 100, 128, 153
  defined, 218
  MAT and, 218
  tapering and, 148–49

Campbell, James, 58
Canada, 136, 226–31
cancer patients, 50–51, 53–54, 182
carfentanil, 63
celecoxib, 40, 250, 252
Centers for Disease Control and
    Prevention (CDC), 62–63, 81,
    184, 188, 190, 223
  guidelines on pain, 62–63
  Injury Center Tapering Pocket
      Guide, 147–49
chemical receptors
  buprenorphine and, 218–19
  methadone and, 218
  morphine and heroin and, 41
  naltrexone and, 219
  psychological hooks vs., 126

short vs. long-term opioids and, 116–17
tapering and, 133
transitioning to safer opioids and, 128
chemotherapy, 143–44
children, white vs. black, 75
chronic, noncancer pain, 51–52, 62
alternatives to medication for, 250–51
bad tapers and, 154–56
dangers vs. effectiveness of opioids for, 81–82, 186–89
difficulty rating, 38
lack of plan for, post-surgery, 80–81
military and, 243
NSAIDs and, 40
opioids not first-line treatment for, 81–82, 195
post-operative pain vs., 36
prevalence of, 255
severe, 186–89, 244
trade-offs and, 250
vulnerability of patients with, 150–51
Civil War, 46
clonidine, 148
CNN, 206
cocaine, 217
crack, 122
codeine, 41, 47
cognitive-behavioral therapy (CBT), 198, 250–51
constipation, 76, 79
continuing medical education (CME), 207
cough suppressants, 47–48
Courtwright, David, 46

criminalization, 49–50, 63, 126, 214, 225, 229, 231, 233–36
cultural change, need for, 252

Darius (hypothetical patient), 71–73
deaths. See also overdoses; suicide
addicts don't deserve, 236
legacy patients and, 156, 188
decade of pain, 65, 256
Defense and Veterans Center for Integrative Pain Medicine (DVCIPM), 242–45, 251
de Kenessey, Brendan, 124
dental pain, 67, 183–86, 190
dependence, 115, 239
addiction vs., 116–18, 125–26
avoiding, after surgery, 173–74
chronic pain patients and, 187
complex persistent, 149
defined, 117, 187
as driver of addiction, 130–34
ethical duty of prescribing physician and, 178
exit strategy and supervised tapering and, 142, 154, 197
forced tapering and, 152–53
length of time to form, 195
methadone and, 225
military and, 244
stigmatization of, 126–27
warning patient about, 147
withdrawal relapses and, 139
depression, 94–97
detox, 155, 182
diacetylmorphine. See heroin
Diagnostic and Statistical Manual of Mental Disorders (DSM-5), 119–21
diarrhea, 117
digestive depression, 78–79, 81

Dilaudid. *See* hydromorphone

dopamine, 130

"dope fiend," 49–50

Dreamland (Quinones), 215

Dreser, Heinrich, 47

Drug Dealer, MD (Lembke), 148

Drug Enforcement Agency (DEA), 61

drug-seeking behavior, 39, 43–44, 66, 71–75, 151

dysphoria, 117

Emergency Medical Services (EMS), 225

emergency room (ER), 44, 67–68, 71–74, 151, 204

empathy, expanding circle of, 234–36, 258

Endo, 207

endorphins, 41–42, 116

epidural, 198

epistemic injustice, 70–71

Erdek, Dr., 169–71

Escape Fire (documentary), 243–44

euphoria, 42

exercise therapy, 198, 204, 250–52

exit strategy, 197. *See also* tapering

family and primary care physicians, 64, 67, 146, 186, 204

federal drug rebate program, 201

fentanyl, 238

defined, 41

ER and, 67

heroin and, 63–64, 215

hospital and, 10, 19, 32

safe injection sites and, 227

sleepiness and, 42

fentanyl patches, 186

fibromyalgia, 198

flu-like symptoms, 87–88, 101

Foley, Kathleen, 50–53, 56

Food and Drug Administration (FDA), 55–57, 200

Foreman, Judy, 135, 136

Frankfurt, Harry, 122–23

free flap surgery, 17–21, 45, 70, 76–77, 79, 166, 199

Frieden, Thomas, 62

gabapentin, 86–87

dependence and, 87, 92

multimodal pain care and, 198

neuropathic pain and, 23–24

gallbladder removal, 193, 196

Georgetown University, Kennedy Institute of Ethics, xi

Germany, 46

Grunberg, Neil, 242–43

"Hailey" (Weeks), 150, 153–54, 156

Hale, Doug, 154–56

hallucinogenic state (gray world), 76–77

harm mitigation, bioethics and, 141–44, 178, 196, 227

harm reduction, 220–29

investing in, 256

needle-exchanges and, 221–26, 228–31

as philosophy, 223–28

prescription heroin and, 230–31

public discussion of, 231

safe injection sites and, 227–31

Harrison Narcotics Tax Act (1914), 49, 63

Hart, Carl, 120–22

Harvard / CNN study, 206–7

health care system

availability of pain care and, 203–4, 209–10
cost bundling and, 200
safe injection sites and, 228–29
structural problems of, xii, 115, 135–41, 146–47, 153, 155–57, 170, 196, 204, 208–11, 219, 228–29, 238, 257–58
health insurance reimbursement, 203–4, 210
hepatitis B, 223
hepatitis C, 223, 227, 236
Heroin Act (1924), 49, 63
heroin-assisted treatment, 230
heroin (diacetylmorphine)
addiction and, 48–49, 122, 130
Bayer markets, as nonaddictive, 47–48, 54, 56, 60
black market begun, 49
chemical receptors and, 41
contamination of, 63, 153, 215–16
cost of, 153, 215–16
criminalization of, 49, 63, 233–36
first epidemic of, 48–49
hallucinations and, 77
harm reduction and, 221–31
legacy patients driven to, 63, 153, 217
new epidemic of, 215
overdose deaths from, 64
prohibition and, 49, 62, 69, 125–26
race and, 214–15, 233–36
rural whites and, 215
Hickey, Colin, 246–47, 252
higher-order vs. immediate, desires, 122–23
High Price (Hart), 121–22
Hippocratic Oath, 69
hip surgery, 246–48

Hispanic patients, 75
HIV/AIDS, 213, 221–24, 227–28, 236
Hoffmann, Diane, 75
Hoffmann, Felix, 47
hospitals
cost of IV APAP vs. opioids and, 199–202
JCAHO accredited, 59
lack of coordination among, 138
patient ratings and, 205
Humbyrd, Casey, 191–92
hydrocodone, 41, 43, 45, 185–86, 186
hydromorphone (Dilaudid), 10, 20, 23–24, 34–36, 42, 77
hyperalgesia, 117, 152
hypodermic needle, invention of, 46. See also needle exchange

ibuprofen, 39, 68, 72, 164, 173, 184, 188, 195, 249–50
influenza, 47
informed consent, 196–97
Insite clinic, 227–28, 230
insomnia, 98, 100, 102, 117
Institute of Medicine (later National Academy of Medicine), 18, 30
INSYS Therapeutics, 61
intensive care unit (ICU), 20, 70
International Association for the Study of Pain (IASP), 27, 28
International Narcotics Control Board (INCB), 61
Iraq War veterans, 11
isolation, 131–34
IV acetaminophen (IV APAP; Ofirmev), 23–24
cost of, 199–203
effectiveness of, 201–3

Janssen, 207
Jick, Hershel, 52–53, 58
Johns Hopkins University, xi, 4, 136,
    208, 231
  Blaustein Pain Treatment Center,
    169
  presentation on personal
    experience at, 174–79
Joint Commission on Accreditation
    of Healthcare Organizations
    (JCAHO), 59, 62
*Journal of the American Medical
    Association (JAMA)*, 150, 184,
    207
"junkie," 49–50, 125–27
Justice Department, 61

Kahn, Jeff, 179–80
Kass, Nancy, 179
Kentucky, 60
knee replacement surgery, 191–95,
    248–49
Konowitz, Paul, 135–36, 139, 147

Langreth, Robert, 154–55
legacy patients, 181, 197–98, 238,
    257
  abandoned by medical system,
    150–58
  forced tapering and, 152–54
  multimodal treatment for, 198
  nuance in approach to, 197
legislative response, 209
Lembke, Anna, 148, 149
Lewis, Marc, 120
Lidocaine, 198
lifestyle therapies, 198, 204–5,
    250–52
limb-salvage center, 17
local anesthetics, 198

lofexidine, 148
lower-back pain, 188

Mackey, Sean, 64
maintenance treatment, 218
maladaptive pain, 251
massage, 204–5, 250–51
McKesson Corporation, 61
medical education, 136, 148–49,
    207, 209
medication-assisted treatment
    (MAT), 218–20
  availability and cost of, 219–20
  harm reduction and, 224–26
  heroin as part of, 230
meditation, 198, 251
Memorial Sloan Kettering Cancer
    Center, 50, 53
memory loss, 76, 79–80
methadone, 149
  chemical receptors and, 41
  cost of, 219
  defined, 218
  harm reduction and, 224–25
  MAT and, 218
methadone clinics, 116, 128, 155
mindfulness, 204, 251
minority communities
  heroin and, 214–15
  undertreatment of pain of, 75–76
morphine, 9–10, 31–32, 67
  defined, 40–42
  history of, 46
  oxycodone vs., 55
Mother Jones, 207
motorcycle accident and foot injury,
    xii, 3–13
  boot fitted and first steps taken,
    109–11
  cost of PT after, 203–4

first experience of pain and drugs after, 31–38
first presentations on experiences following, 174–80, 199–202
first surgeries and, 11–16
free flap surgery and pain following, 16–24
opioids during recovery and, 76–81
opioid withdrawal and lack of help from doctors, 85–109
pain complaints met suspicion after, 70–71
sense of betrayal by doctors after withdrawal, 113–17
sixth surgery, and plan for minimal opioid use after, 38, 165–72, 181
walking without boot after, 161–63
Motrin, 39, 40
MS Contin (continuous release morphine), 54–55
multimodal pain care, 204
  defined, 198
  difficulty and cost of, 207–8
  failure to use, 198–99

naloxone (Narcan), 100, 225–27, 229–30
naltrexone, 218–19
National Academies of Sciences, Engineering, and Medicine, 81, 255
Nation in Pain, A (Foreman), 135
nausea, 90, 101–3, 117
needle exchanges, 221–26, 228–31
neonatal abstinence syndrome, 130
nerve blocks, 198, 243–44, 250
neuropathic pain, 23, 198
New England Journal of Medicine, 52, 61

New York Times, 51
nondefinitive condition, 72, 74
nonprescription painkillers, 43, 183–84. See also acetaminophen; ibuprofen; nonsteroidal anti-inflammatory drugs
  effectiveness of, 184
  multimodal pain care and, 198
nonsteroidal anti-inflammatory drugs (NSAIDs), 39–40, 184, 198, 250
Norcos, 191–93
nurse practitioner, 145

Ofirmev, 200–201
oncologists, potential harms of chemotherapy and, 143–44
Opana (oxymorphone), 221, 222
opioid companies, class action settlements, 61
opioid-induced constipation (OIC), 79. See also constipation
Opioid Prescribing Engagement Network (OPEN), 196
opioids
  abrupt cut offs of, 150–58
  addictive nature of (see addiction; dependence; drug-seeking behavior; tolerance)
  addressing current epidemic, 195–96, 216, 237–38
  alternatives to, 184, 187–89, 198–205
  appropriate use of, 69
  attitudes about pain and, 45–46, 208
  benefits vs. harms of, 46, 156, 174, 182–83
  bias and, 70, 73–76
  black market and, 49–50

opioids (*cont.*)
  brain chemistry and, 41–42,
    116–17
  cancer and, 51–52
  CDC guidelines and, 62–63
  CME courses on, 207
  consumption of, in U.S., 62
  cost of, 76–80, 246
  cost of, vs. alternatives, 199–205
  cost of, vs. heroin, 153
  deadly nature of, 78, 213, 238 (*see
    also* overdose deaths)
  defined, 40–41
  dentists and, 183–84
  dilemma of, 69–70, 75–76, 82
  drug company payments to
    physicians and, 205–9
  effectiveness of, 40, 42, 46, 80–82,
    184, 187–89, 246
  ERs and, 67–69
  establishing responsible
    management of, 144–48
  euphoria and, 42
  failure to manage long-term
    therapy and, 141
  family physicians and, 67,
    186–87
  future of crisis, and need to do
    better, 140, 255–58
  geographic issues and, 192, 209
  hallucinogenic state and, 76–77
  harm reduction strategies and,
    220–31, 256
  illegality of, without prescription,
    43–44, 153
  length of exposure, and risk from,
    190
  military and, 244
  mismanagement of, 129
  nuance and, 183, 186

overuse of, despite undertreatment
    of pain, 69–70
  patient education and, 191–92,
    196–97
  patients' difficulty handling, even
    with ample resources, 179–80
  patients' need for exit strategies
    for, 82, 99–100, 115–16,
    156–57, 172–73, 181–82, 197
  physicians' ethical duty and, 114,
    139–45, 156, 175, 178–79, 197
  physicians' need for training
    in management of, 68–69,
    134–36, 148–49, 197, 209–10,
    238
  physicians' slowness to change
    and, 195–96
  Purdue and, 54–55
  race and, 73–75, 231–37
  reducing inappropriate
    prescriptions, 195
  shift from prescription, to heroin,
    215–16, 237
  side effects of, 42, 76–82, 152, 250
  stigma and, 137, 157, 165, 180,
    257
  struggle to use as little as possible
    after surgery, 172–73
  subjectivity of pain and, 39
  swing from embrace to prohibition
    of, 1908–1920s, 46–49, 69
  swing from embrace to prohibition
    of, 1999–2010, 52–61, 69
  three crises, defined, 214–16
  types of pain and, 81, 150, 187–89
  types of synthetic, 34
opioid use disorder, 66, 68, 76,
    181–82. *See also* addiction;
    dependence; withdrawal
  chronic pain patients and, 188

harm reduction and, 220–30
MAT and, 218–20
prescribing practices leading to,
    142
prevalence of, 217–18
race, sympathy, and treatment for,
    232–35
transition to heroin and, 217
treatment for, 100, 128, 149
withdrawal treatment vs., 149
opium, 40–41
opium commissioner, first U.S.,
    48–49
opium poppy, 40–41, 46
overdose deaths, 61–62, 64, 78, 81,
    154, 238, 255
chronic pain patents and, 187–88
ethical duty of prescribing
    physician and, 178
harm reduction strategies and, 226,
    236
heroin and, 215–16
illicit vs. prescription opioids and,
    239
increases in, 213, 216–17
naloxone to reverse, 225
oxycodone, 20, 34, 76–77, 86, 87,
    92, 186
brain and, 41, 130
increasing use of, 61
long-acting and short-acting, doses
    of, 23
potency of, 55
Purdue adds extended release to,
    54, 72
OxyContin, 34
cost of heroin vs., 215
drug-seeking patients and, 72–73
evasion of extended-release feature
    of, 56

follow-up during home recovery
    and, 85–86
high dosage pills and, 56
illegal access to, 235
labeling of, as nonaddictive, 55–61
marketing of, 249–50
potency of, 72
Purdue develops, 54–55
rural areas and, 60–61

pain. *See also* acute pain; chronic
    pain; traumatic pain; surgical
    pain
attitudes toward, 208
backfire effect and, 81
balancing relief and risks, 249
brain and, 26
conflicting attitudes about opioids
    and, 45–46
cost of, in U.S., 30
definition of, 27
difficulty of dealing with, 38–39
difficulty of remembering
    experience of, 37–38
elimination vs. reduction of, 244–45
endorphins and, 42
feigning, 71
as "fifth vital sign," 58–59
opioids and increased sensitivity
    to, 152
personal experience of, post-
    surgery, 16–23
pre-surgery preparation for, and
    minimal opioid use, 38,
    165–72, 181, 191–95, 248–49
subjectivity of, 25–30, 38–39,
    43–44, 58–59, 71, 72
tripartite division of, 51–52
types of, and opioids, 81, 182
Pain, 53

pain advocacy movement, 51–62,
    182
"Pain as the 5th Vital Sign Mandate
    and Toolkit," 59
pain management, 39, 211. *See also*
    motorcycle accident and foot
    injury
    acute vs. chronic postsurgical pain
        and, 189–90
    conferences on, 58
    consultation on, 23–24, 71
    dentists and, 183–86
    ethical challenges of, 29–30
    gender and, 75
    incoherence of modern, 45–46
    military and, 241–45
    multimodal care and, 198–99
    need for exit strategy and, 98–99,
        115–16
    need for medical follow-up system
        for, 145–49, 208
    need for physician training in, 64,
        136–37, 157, 209–11
    nuance and, 186
    race and, 74–75
    reducing reliance on opioids and,
        64
    undertreating severe, 69
pain medication, classes of, defined,
    39–41. *See also specific types*
pain patient
    costs of opioid alternatives for,
        204–5, 208
    drug-seeking behavior and bias vs.,
        65, 70–75
    educational guidelines for post-
        surgical, 193
    need to protect, 239
    physicians' avoidance of, 137
    preferences of, for pills, 204–5

pain scale, 30–37, 59, 72, 170
    flaws in, 39
    hitting 10 on, 35–36
    learning to estimate, 32–36
    military revision of, 245–46
    rating above 10 on, 72
pain specialist, difficulty finding,
    208–9
"Patel, Dr." (orthopedic trauma
    surgeon), 11–14, 85–86,
    109–10, 161, 166–68
patents, 54
patient education, 191–92, 196–97,
    204
patient rights, 51
Pence, Mike, 221–23, 225–26,
    228–29
Percocet, 34, 67, 168, 172–73, 181,
    183, 185, 210, 247
Percodan, 34
Pfizer, 207
phantom pain, 26
pharmaceutical industry, 39. *See also*
    Purdue Pharma
    CME courses and, 207
    physician payments and, 205–8
physical therapy (PT), 13, 111, 161,
    246, 251
    cost of, 203–4, 210
    multimodal pain care and, 198
Physician Payments Sunshine Act,
    206
physicians
    bias and, 70–71
    costs of mistakes by, 139
    drugs inappropriately cut off by,
        238
    ethical duty to mitigate harm to
        patient and, 115, 134–47, 175,
        178–79, 197

failures of, to use opioids well, 195, 238
health system structural problems and, 138
need for training in opioid management, 68–69, 147–49, 197, 209–10, 238
need for training in pain management, 64–65
opioid alternatives and, 207–8
patient ratings and, 204–5
pharmaceutical industry and, 205–8
tapering for legacy patients and, 152–53
"pill for every pain" culture, 249
pill mills, 235
pneumonia, 164–65
Portenoy, Russell, 52–53, 56
Porter, Jane, 52, 53, 58
post-surgical infection, duty to minimize risk of, 143
post-surgical pain, 26, 80, 81
exposure time on opioids and, 189–91
multimodal care and, 198
surgeon's duty to lessen, 143
post-traumatic stress disorder (PTSD), 244
Pregabalin (Lyrica), 198
prescriptions
drug company incentives and, 205–7
ER and, 67–68
ethical duty to mitigate harm from, 139–45, 175, 238–39
evidence-based approach and, 238, 247
guidelines for, 193
harm reduction and, 230–31

health system fissures and, 138, 145
length of, 193
need for responsible practices and, 210–11
number written, 128, 256
overdoses despite reduced, 216–17
reckless, 234–35
reducing, 63–64, 157, 195, 209, 256
types of doctors writing most, 67
Proceedings of the National Academies of Sciences, 74
prohibition, 49–52, 65, 125–26, 183
nuance and care vs., 209
psychostimulants, 217
Purdue Pharma, 54–61, 72, 182, 207, 249, 255
conferences sponsored by, 58
lawsuits vs., 60–61
profits of, 58

qigong, 251
Quinones, Sam, 52, 215

Rat Park, 132
regional anesthetics, 198, 243
rehabilitation clinic, 107
reimbursement structure, 208, 210
respiratory depression, 42, 76, 78, 81
restlessness, 101, 117
Rieder, Sadiye, xii, 3–4, 7–10, 12–15, 17, 19–20, 32–33, 77–79, 85–86, 89, 95–97, 99–106, 108, 110, 114, 161–63, 175, 178, 253–54
Rieder, Sinem, 3–4, 15, 95, 96–98, 103–6, 178, 253
"Roberts, Dr." (plastic surgeon), 86–87, 89–90, 98, 100–101, 137, 138, 141, 148, 167–68, 171
Roosevelt, Teddy, 48

Sackler family, 57
safe injection sites, 227–31
Saloner, Brendan, 175–79
Schoomaker, Eric, 241, 243
Scott County, Indiana, 220–22
sedative effects, 42, 81
Session, Jeff, 126
Shenandoah Valley, 3
sodium channel blocker, 198
soft tissue pain, 25
Stanford University, 64
stigma, 50–54, 71, 119, 125–27, 134,
    137, 146, 154, 157, 165, 180,
    236, 257
suboxone, 100
suicide, 139, 155–56
supervised drug-consumption facility,
    227
surgery. *See* motorcycle accident and
    foot injury; post-surgical pain;
    and specific types
suspicion, uneven distribution of,
    70–72
Switzerland, 230
Szalavitz, Maia, 120

tai chi, 251
tapering
    addiction centers' failure to help
        with, 128
    CDC Pocket Guide on, 147–50
    danger of mismanagement of, 131,
        133–36
    danger of reversing, 148
    final stage of, as most difficult, 149
    legacy patients and forced, 152–53
    physicians' lack knowledge about,
        128–29, 136–37, 154
    MAT and, 218
    need for slow, 147–49

Tarzian, Anita, 75
thebaine, 41
therapy pool, 95–96
tolerance, 80–81, 115
    chronic pain patents and, 187
    defined, 117
    long post-surgery recovery time
        and, 146
    need for supervised tapering and,
        142
traumatic injury, 11–15, 67–68
traumatic pain, 74, 80–81
    failure to manage long-term
        prescription for, 141
    multimodal pain care and, 198
    opioids and, 189–90
    subjective nature of, 26
Trump, Donald, 126
tuberculosis, 47
Tylenol. *See* acetaminophen

Uniformed Services University
    (USU), 241, 242
United Kingdom, 230
University of Michigan, 193, 196
University of Toronto, 136
urban areas, 214–15
urgent care clinicians, 204

VAC changes, 15–17, 25
Vancouver, 226–27, 230
Veterans Affairs Department (VA),
    59
Vicodin, 67, 181, 183–86
Vietnam War, 131, 213

War on Drugs, 126–27, 233
War on Pain, 181, 205
Weeks, William B., 150, 153
Wen, Leana, 136, 225

West Virginia, 60
whites
  male, vs. minorities and women,
      70–71, 75–76
  opioid deaths of, vs. blacks, 232
  rise in opioid use disorder among, 76
Wired, 243
withdrawal, 157, 239. *See also*
      tapering
  buprenorphine and, 218
  criminalization and, 126
  death from unmanaged sudden,
      151, 154, 216
  dependence and, 117
  ethical duty of prescribing doctor
      and, 178
  family as aid to, 132–34, 253–54
  fear of fatality and, 128–29
  going slow as key to mitigating, 148
  inability to manage, as driver of
      addiction, 130–31, 139

  lack of help from physicians on,
      99–101, 106–7
  legacy patients and difficult,
      152–54, 187
  medications for symptom
      management during, 148–49
  naltrexone and, 219
  need for help by tapering
      specialists, 147, 197
  negative effect of reversing taper
      and, 148
  personal experience of, 86–117,
      125
  small, short doses of opioids and
      mother's experience of, 194–95
women, treatment of pain in, 75
Wright, Hamilton, 48, 49

X-rays, 29

yoga, 198, 204, 250, 252

ABOUT THE AUTHOR

TRAVIS RIEDER, PHD, is a research scholar and the director of the Master of Bioethics degree program at the Johns Hopkins Berman Institute of Bioethics. He has published on a wide variety of topics in various academic journals, such as *Health Affairs* and the *American Journal of Bioethics*, and his work has also appeared in publications such as the *Guardian* and the *Washington Post*, and on NPR's *All Things Considered*. He now spends most of his time writing, speaking, and teaching about ethical and policy issues raised by America's opioid crisis.